Tularosa

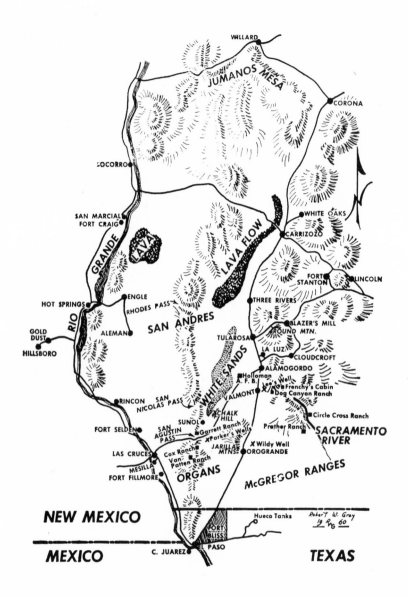

C. L. Sonnichsen

TULAROSA

Last of the
Frontier West

UNIVERSITY OF NEW MEXICO PRESS
Albuquerque

University of New Mexico Press edition
reprinted 1980 by arrangement with The Devin-Adair Co.

Libarary of Congress Catalog Card Number 80-52286.
ISBN-13 978-0-8263-0561-9 (pbk.)
ISBN-10 0-8263-0561-X (pbk.)

PRINTED IN THE UNITED STATES OF AMERICA

Library of Congress Cataloging-in-Publication Data

Sonnichsen, Charles Leland, 1901–
    Tulaosa, last of the frontier West.
Reprint of the 1960 ed. published by Devin-Adair Co., New York
    Bibliography
    Includes Index.
    1. Tularosa Valley—History.
    2. Frontier and pioneer life—New Mexico—Tularosa Valley.
    I. Title.
[F802. T8S6 1980]   978.9'65   80-52286
ISBN 0-8263-0563-6
ISBN 0-8263-0561-X (pbk.)

for Carol

Preface to the
New Edition

IN 1960, when this book was about to go to press, the Tularosa Valley, lonely and remote as it was, could not be called undiscovered country. Albert Bacon Fall, Pat Garrett and Eugene Manlove Rhodes were well known, and for fifteen years the White Sands Missile Range had been very much in the news. Three novels suggested by the Fountain murders (Florence Finch Kelly, *With Hoops of Steel*, 1900; Eugene Cunningham, *Spiderweb Trail*, 1940; Conrad Richter, *The Lady*, 1957) had been published, though none of them made any great splash. The Mescalero Apaches, the lava beds, the White Sands, the mountain summer colonies, mining activities at Orogrande—these and many other related matters occasionally caught the attention of historians and magazine writers.

After 1960, however, this modest stream of publication increased in volume and interest. In that year Richard O'Connor produced a full-length biography of Pat Garrett (New York: Doubleday), and historians like Robert N. Mullin and Philip J. Rasch, along with reminiscent old timers like Bert Judia and

James Madison Hervey, began to dig into the Garrett story. Colin Rickards in 1970, in a firmly researched little volume called *How Pat Garrett Died*, surveyed this accumulation of material and drew his own conclusions. The same year saw the publication of Glenn Shirley's *Shotgun for Hire* (Norman: University of Oklahoma Press), an account of the lethal career of "Deacon" Jim Miller, and in 1971 Robert N. Mullin produced *The Strange Story of Wayne Brazel* (El Paso: privately printed)—both dealing with reputed slayers of Garrett. Very nearly the last word was in when Leon Metz published his biography of the great frontier peace officer in 1974.

The most controversial work in the field of Tularosa history, however, has been A. M. Gibson's *The Life and Death of Colonel Albert Jennings Fountain* (University of Oklahoma Press, 1965) which paints Fountain as a frontier cavalier without fear and without reproach. At the same time Gibson openly accuses A.B.Fall and Oliver Lee of engineering the disappearance of Fountain and his eight-year-old son in 1896. The book brought cries of indignation from the families and friends of the accused men and vigorous protests from a number of reputable historians. W. H. Hutchinson, for instance, called the biography a "whitewash" of Fountain and "a conviction of murder on hearsay evidence" (*San Francisco Chronicle*, July 18, 1965). In a small book, *Another Verdict for Oliver Lee* (Clarendon, Texas, 1965) he answered Dr. Gibson at length.

Less lethal aspects of life in the Tularosa area have appealed to several writers—Dorothy Neal Jensen's *Captive Mountain Waters* (El Paso Texas Western Press, 1961), for instance, and *Cloud Climbing Railroad* (Alamogordo: privately printed, 1966) by the same author. Novelists and scenario writers have likewise been involved. Edward Abbey's *Fire on the Mountain* (New York: Dial Press, 1962) tells a story much like John Prather's, and *Scandalous John*, to which moviegoers were responding emotionally in 1971, is reminiscent of the same theme.

Time has brought changes, of course. The Apollo Program, which helped to put men on the moon, has closed down, but the scientists and technicians at White Sands Missile Range have new projects to keep them in constant motion. A new edition of this book, with some corrections and additions, may be a timely reminder that the Tularosa country is still a tremendously exciting place and will be for the foreseeable future.

C. L. SONNICHSEN

Tucson, 1980

Contents

Tularosa

Tough Country

The Tularosa country is a parched desert where everything, from cactus to cowman, carries a weapon of some sort, and the only creatures who sleep with both eyes closed are dead.

In all the sun-scorched and sand-blasted reaches of the Southwest there is no grimmer region. Only the fierce and the rugged can live here—prickly pear and mesquite; rattlesnake and tarantula. True, Texas cattlemen made the cow a native of the region seventy-five years ago, but she would have voted against the step if she had been asked.

From the beginning this lonesome valley has been a laboratory for developing endurance, a stern school specializing in just one subject: the Science of Doing Without.

Everything has been done to promote the success of the experiments. There is almost no water; no shade. High mountain walls all around keep out the tenderfeet. On the west, screening off the Rio Grande valley with its green fields and busy highways, great ridges of limestone and granite—Franklin and Organ; San Andres and Oscuro—heave and roll north-

3

ward from El Paso. Across the valley to the eastward, shut-
ting off the oases along the Pecos, the Hueco mountains
merge with the pine-cloaked Sacramentos, and these give way
to Sierra Blanca and Jicarilla, with 12,000-foot Sierra Blanca
Peak soaring in naked majesty over all.

The Tularosa country lies between the ranges, a great
pocket of sand, sun, and sparse vegetation thirty miles wide,
more or less, and over two hundred miles long. The Jumanos
Mesa, named for a long-vanished tribe of Indians, gives it a
northern boundary. To the south it merges with the Chihuahua Desert which pushes far down into Mexico.

Seen from the tops of the screening ranges, it looks like a
flat, gray-green, sun-flooded expanse of nothing, impressive
only because the eye can travel a hundred miles and more in
one leap. Near at hand it is full of surprises. The northern end
of the valley is a little less parched. Grass still grows tall on
Carrizozo Flat and bean farmers have plowed up the country
around Claunch. Nearby, two prehistoric lava flows cover
the land with an appalling jumble of volcanic rock known
locally as the *malpais*.

South of the lava flows, the vast gypsum deposits called the
White Sands spread out in a deathly, glittering world of pure
white which edges eastward a few inches every year, threatening in a few millennia to swallow up everything as far as
the Sacramentos.

Sometimes the valley floor heaves in sand dunes; sometimes
it breaks into red hummocks, each one crowned with the
delicate green leaves and lethal thorns of a mesquite bush.
There are broad swales where the yuccas grow in groves—
leprous alkali flats where even the sturdy greasewood can
barely hold its own—long inclines of tall grama grass where
the foothills rise to the knees of the mountains—and countless
acres of prickly pear and *lechuguilla* and rabbit brush.

A harsh, forbidding country, appalling to newcomers
from gentler regions. But it has its moments of intense beauty.

Sunrise and sunset are magic times. Under a full moon, that lonely, whispering waste is transformed into an austere corner of fairyland. The belated traveler catches his breath when the tender fingers of dawn pick out the tiny black shapes of the pine trees far above him on top of the Sacramentos. One does not forget the Organs blackening against the sunset, swathed in a veil of lilac shadows—the eerie gleam of the white sands at moonrise—a swarthy cloud dissolving in a column of rain, the froth of impact showing white at its foot while all around the sun shines serenely on.

The yucca is a thorny and cantankerous object, but in the spring it puts up a ten-foot stalk which explodes in a mass of creamy-white blossoms. And so it is with other sullen citizens of the desert when their time comes: the prickly pear with its rich yellow flower, the desert willow dripping with pendent pink and lavender, little pincushion cacti robing themselves in mauve petals more gorgeous than roses, the ocotillo shrouding its savage spines in tiny green leaves till its snaky arms look like wands of green fur, each one tipped with a long finger of pure scarlet.

It is big country—clean country—and if it has no tenderness, it has strength and a sort of magnificence.

To live there, has always been a risky business—a matter of long chances and short shrifts; of privation and danger. This was true of the prehistoric cave dwellers who lived only a little better than their animal neighbors in the Huecos many centuries gone by. It was true of the little pueblo communities which grew up later in the mountain canyons and wherever a wet-weather lake made existence possible on the valley floor. It was true in historic times of the peaceful Christian Indians who abandoned their unfinished church at Gran Quivira when the Apaches overwhelmed them nearly three hundred years ago.

Yes, it has always been hard country—frontier country— and for obvious reasons, the first reason being those same

Apaches. The slopes of the Sierra Blanca were their favorite haunts as far back as we have any records, and though they ranged far and wide over the desert and even moved to Mexico for decades when the Comanches descended upon them, they always came back to the mountain rivers and the tall pines. A merciless environment made them tough and almost unbeatable fighters. They kept their country to themselves as long as they were able, waging a never-ending war against hunger and thirst, Comanches and Mexicans, soldiers and settlers, until their power was broken less than a century ago.

Highways and railroads were slow in coming to a region so far removed from the gathering places of men and money. Sheer isolation did what the Apache was not able to do alone, holding off the traders and developers for years while the Rio Grande and Pecos settlements were booming.

But the most potent force of all for keeping people out was plain, old-fashioned, skin-cracking drought. The rainfall was imperceptible, and there was just enough ground water available to cause trouble. On the valley floor there was next to none at all until men got around to drilling wells. A few springs existed here and there in the Organs and the San Andres, none of them big enough to supply more than a few men and beasts. The eastern mountains were higher and better supplied. Spring-fed streams came down from the Sierra Blanca at Three Rivers, while Tularosa Creek descended the pass between Sierra Blanca and Sacramento beside the main trail from the Pecos to the Rio Grande.

Farther south, where the mile-high cliffs of the Sacramentos soar above the plain, a number of canyons drained off the water from the heights—Dog Canyon and Agua Chiquita; Sacramento and Grapevine. In Sacramento Canyon and in Dog Canyon the water was more or less permanent. But everywhere, until the skill and cupidity of man turned the liquid gold to account, it flowed out onto the flats a pitifully short distance and disappeared in the sand. Along with it, as the years passed, flowed the blood of many a man who gave up his life for a trickle of water.

Sensible men, cautious men, stayed away from such a place. But the adventurous and the hardy and the reckless kept on coming. Each one had a dream of some sort—water for his cows, solitude for his soul, gold to make him rich. For even the Tularosa country has its treasures. The ghostly ruins of Gran Quivira have been honeycombed by men obsessed with the notion that the Indians buried a hoard of gold before they left. At the northeast corner of the valley, in the Jicarilla Mountains, lies the abandoned gold camp of White Oaks, the site of rich mining properties seventy years ago. Midway between El Paso and Alamogordo, on the rocky slopes of the Jarillas, Orogrande sits solitary, remembering the days when prospectors and miners swarmed in; and a few miles away at the San Agustin Pass the abandoned shafts at Organ tell a similar tale.

But the real story of Tularosa is the story of Texas cattle-men—drifting herdsmen who began to invade the valley in the early eighties, bringing their stern folkways with them. They too ran into trouble, for their law was not the law of the Mexicans or the Indians or the Yankees who arrived during and after the Civil War. It was those proud riders who kept the Old West alive in that lonely land until yesterday. It was the clash of their ways and standards with the ways and standards of the settled citizens which caused the feuds and killings and hatreds that make up the unwritten history of the region. The Apaches and the climate and the lay of the land helped. But in the last analysis it was the Texans who made Tularosa the Last of the Frontier West.

Those times seem as remote from present-day reality as the wars of Caesar and Charlemagne, but they have left a brand on the soul of many a man and woman still living. That is why this story has never been fully told—why all of it can

never be told. For out here in the desert the West of the old
days has never quite given way to a newer America. Customs
have changed, but attitudes have held fast. To test this fact,
try asking questions about certain people and events. Old men
clam up and change the subject. Young ones who have heard
something, hesitate a long time before telling what they know
about the sins and tribulations of their grandfathers. Once it
was dangerous to talk about these things. Even now it is not
considered wise. The fears and loyalties of yesterday still
cast their shadows on us who live on the edge of the desert.
On the streets of El Paso or Las Cruces or Alamogordo you
can still hear the click of bootheels belonging to men who
played their parts in dramas which would make a Hollywood
movie look tame. Their sons and daughters still live among us
—fine people, too—and their friends still frown on loose discussion.

For these reasons this is not an easy story to tell, but it is
time someone told it. So let's go back to the beginning, before the Texas cattle crowded in, ate the grass down to the
roots, and trampled the plain into dust—back to the days
when the country was the way God made it; bunch grass
growing up to a horse's belly; miles of yellow flowers in the
wet years; little rainwater lakes at the foot of the Organs
and the San Andres, long since dried out and buried in dust;
sun and sand and sixty long miles to town.

With Plow and Rifle

THE year 1862 was hard on the Mexican farmers along the Rio Grande. The rains came in floods, and the river went on a furious rampage. It drowned the fields, invaded the streets of the little *placitas*, and gnawed at the adobe houses. The riverside hamlet of Colorado, on the west bank where Rodey now stands, was hard hit. One by one the houses crumbled and slumped into the swirling, murky water. Family after family got out with what they could carry and camped, homeless, on higher ground.

Other communities fared likewise, including a settlement near present-day Ysleta. The survivors gathered at Mesilla in a mood to take desperate measures. What could they do? How could they keep going?

"We will go and take up land on the Tularosa," said Cesario Durán, setting his firm jaw.

There was a startled silence among the men gathered in council.

"But the Indians," objected José Candelaria. "You know what happened to the men who tried it two years ago. They

9

planted a crop and left it for the Apaches, and some of the men died before they could get out. Do you think Santana would let us settle in his front yard without a fight?"

"No, we will have to fight. But what can we lose? We have nothing now. If we die, we won't have any less. Besides, the Yanqui soldiers are there and will help us. I have heard that they are raising corn for their horses in Temporal Canyon, and Santana will not want trouble with them. We must try to get together a large colony. The more men we have, the safer we will be. The land is good and there is plenty of water. We are brave men, and we can have it for ourselves. *Vamonos, pues!* Let's go!"

There were speeches pro and con—objections and answers stated with much dignity and gravity. At the end they decided that the risk was worth taking. So word went up and down the river and more homeless men gathered at Mesilla. By the first of November more than a hundred of them were ready to move.

They all knew that this was no pleasure trip. They were proposing to settle within a few miles of some of the main Indian camps. The only men who had ever been able to live in that country were the hands at the sawmill higher up on the Tularosa River—*la maquina*, the Mexicans called it—which had supplied timber for churches and other buildings up and down the Rio Grande since before the year 1800. "The Machine" was important enough then to rate a guard of Mexican soldiers, but that was long ago. When Fort Stanton was established in 1855 to control the Mescalero braves, the troops had kept the road open, but no man had been bold enough to settle along that highway. Now the Civil War had begun; the Confederates had come and gone; and the "California Column" of Union troops was in possession of the military posts. What Cesario Durán had heard about them was true—a detachment was actually encamped in Temporal Canyon eight miles north of the Tularosa, raising a crop of horse feed in the rich bottom land.[1] But it was also true that a small band of immigrants had tried to colonize the proposed townsite in 1860 and had been driven out before they could gather their crops. It was risky business, and they all knew it, but they went ahead making careful plans. They even organized their village government before they set out. Cesario Durán, as was right, was the first *alcalde*.[2] His friend José Candelaria was sheriff. It was agreed that the men would go in first, prepare the land and throw up living quarters, and bring the women and·children in the spring.

They moved out during the first week in November, Durán and Chávez, Saenz and Candelaria, Romero and Carillo, with many more whose names are still spoken in the town they made.[3] They unloaded their tools and provisions under the great cottonwoods at the edge of the marshy land where the Tularosa fanned out and lost itself among reeds and marsh grass a mile from the mouth of the canyon.

It was those *tules*—cattails—which gave the place its name: *tule*, a reed; *tular*, a reedy place; *tularosa*, adjective meaning full of reedy places.

The day was November 7, and for many years after that the men and women of Tularosa kept the anniversary with feasting and holiday.[4]

There was not much time for joy on that first November 7. The Apaches spotted them at once and the men had to be watchful every minute. They went about the job of putting up adobe huts and clearing the fields-to-be with guns strapped to their backs and guards posted on all sides. Their vigilance paid off, for the Indians never attacked in force. But there was much stealing and driving off of stock, and sometimes small skirmishes and narrow escapes.

When the women and children came in the spring, the Indians seemed to realize that the new settlement was there to stay unless they did something about it, and the tempo of the skirmishing went up. On one little raid they got away

with four oxen, and when a party of pursuers caught up with
them, they slaughtered the livestock rather than let it be recaptured. Several sheepherders were killed near Round
Mountain, a cone-shaped landmark ten miles up the valley
known in those times as Dead Man's Hill. Once the Apaches
tortured a captive in sight of his *compañeros,* who were still
putting up a fight.[5]

Sometimes they even invaded the settlement. The old men
still tell about the day in that spring of 1863 when some of
the women were frying bread in one of the adobe huts which
had a narrow window high up near the ceiling. The door was
barred, but the prowlers smelled the bread, climbed up to the
window, and started fishing for the loaves with long sticks.
When the loaves were all eaten and the terrified women had
made no move to resist, one bulky chief decided to come on
in. He had squeezed halfway through the window before one
of the *señoras* in desperation picked up a pail of hot lard
and threw the contents all over him. His screams frightened
off the rest of the band, but they took the cattle and horses
with them when they left.[6]

It was hard going, but the Durans and the Carillos and the
Candelarias and their kin had no intention of giving up. They
went on with their ditching and planting, though sometimes
half the men stood guard while the other half worked. The
first irrigation water flowed through the community *acequia*
on April 2, 1863—the feast day of Saint Francis of Paula.
The settlers thereupon agreed that Saint Francis should be
their patron saint.[7]

Other immigrants heard of the settlement and came to try
their luck. Juan García and his brothers led a caravan from
Jarales, near Socorro, and started a colony of their own at
nearby La Luz. This band lived in dugouts for some time,
because the Indians could not shoot arrows through the
earthen roofs. Later, as the village grew, they made an
adobe-walled corral where the central plaza is now, and the

stock was driven in for safety every night. It was necessary
to take these precautions, for as yet the men had only muzzle
loaders to defend themselves with. One shot and you were
finished, while an Apache could keep on shooting arrows
almost as fast as lightning.[8]

The climax of the Indian menace came in 1868. It was
April 2, Saint Francis' special day. A wagonload of supplies
was coming down the Tularosa Pass from Fort Stanton,
bound for Fort Selden on the Rio Grande. Sergeant Glass and
five troopers were riding as escort. Near the outskirts of
Tularosa they decided that all was safe and that they could
turn back. Leaving the wagon to go on alone, they started
up the canyon and had backtracked as far as Cottonwood
Springs when they encountered a band of warriors. Glass sent
a soldier back to Tularosa for help, and the Round Mountain
battle, as it came to be known, was under way.

The messenger got instant action. All Tularosa felt that
this was a showdown and that its best efforts were called for.
Twenty-six of the citizens, with Teodoro Carillo and José
Durán[9] in the lead, came charging up the pass as fast as horseflesh could carry them. Those left behind gathered to hope
and pray, and they made a vow that if there was no loss of
life in the coming battle, they would build a church in honor
of Saint Francis.

The five troopers had taken cover in an old fortification a
mile or so west of Round Mountain—Dead Man's Hill—
where the twenty-six Mexicans joined them in making their
stand.[10]

One old Indian, willing to die to set an example for his
men, leaped into the doorway of the fort and was instantly
shot to pieces. The rumor has come down through the years
that his scalp, raised on a pole, was the central object in the
celebration held in Tularosa that night.

The Apaches tell a different story about the Round Mountain skirmish. They say their warriors never had any inten-

tion of attacking the Mexicans and that they got away as fast
as they could when the two groups met accidentally. Since
the only casualty among the settlers was a man named
Nieves, who got an arrow through his wrist, the fighting
could not have been desperate. The grateful citizens carried
out their vow, however, and a year later they finished the
little church where the village still worships.[11] The names of
their twenty-six defenders can be seen enshrined under glass
near the entrance.

The years that followed were peaceful, comparatively,
though the settlers guarded their fields as late as 1884.[12] An
engineer named Bailey laid out the town for them in 1862—
possibly as a courtesy of the Yankee troops. Later the citizens
got around to acquiring title to their property through Pablo
Melendres, probate judge of Doña Ana County. He acquired
a grant of 320 acres which he divided among the families
already in residence.[13] The population grew to six hundred.
Houses and stores—great, thick-walled blocks of adobe—
rose out of the brown earth. Fruit trees and grapevines came
into bearing, making a green oasis on the edge of the desert.
Nobody bothered to dig a well or make a cistern. The mountain water was so clean and sparkling that it was brought to
the houses in buckets every morning for drinking and cooking, and nobody ever seemed to get sick.

It was not necessary, however, for anyone to drink water.
The block around the church was one great vineyard, and in
the season of harvest, tubs of grape juice sometimes used to
be placed ten feet apart all around the block. Ask for a drink
and you got fresh grape squeezings or new wine.[14]

That was all destroyed by the great flood of 1895, when the
creek made a new channel and tore up its bed so badly that
the old days of clear water were gone forever.[15]

Meanwhile Tularosa enjoyed its Golden Age. The simple
citizens had everything they wanted, without the inconven-
iences of civilization. They were not quite cut off from the

world, for the mail came in from Las Vegas and Fort Stanton by way of Mescalero three times a week—at least in theory. "Tri-weekly," according to the local wits, meant "Try to get through and try to get back in less than three weeks."

Year by year things got better, and the Indians subsided. Dr. J. H. Blazer, an Iowa dentist, came into the country after service in the Union army and in 1866 got possession of *la maquina*, the venerable sawmill. He became postmaster, innkeeper, forage agent for the army, friend of the Indians, and tower of strength for the whole region. When peace could be kept, he kept it.

Then in 1871 Vincent Colyer came down from Washington by presidential order to relocate the Indians on reservations and provide for them according to their needs. That took some of the pressure off, also. In fact, the citizens had no more serious difficulties with their Indian neighbors, even when Victorio left the Mescalero reservation in 1878 and embarked on his wild career of murder and rapine. But the men of Tularosa well knew that their salvation was in their own hands, and they carried their guns to the field until Victorio was killed in 1880 and his friends were subdued and disarmed.

It was not the Indians who brought Tularosa's Golden Age to an end. It was the invading Gringos. In 1874 several of them settled in Tularosa and bought up land. The one best remembered was Pat Coghlan, an Irish immigrant who located in Texas after serving in the Army and drifted west in the early seventies. He bought lots in town and acquired some fine ranch property at Three Rivers, north of town. The first permanent store in Tularosa was his. He had a famous saloon and wagon yard where everybody stopped and refreshed himself. Before long he was being spoken of as the king of Tularosa.

But Pat was not a refining influence. He got Billy the Kid to supply him with stolen cattle which he used to fill his beef

contract with the army at Fort Stanton, and his saloon was no
Sunday school. There were fights and murders on the streets
of Tularosa and La Luz. There was trouble at the *bailes* when
tough Gringos insisted on dancing with the Mexican girls.
The fruit trees bore bravely; the roses bloomed in the spring
and the grapes ripened in the fall; but Tularosa was no longer
what it had been. Cowmen and miners tramped the once-
peaceful streets. Colored troops of the Tenth Cavalry bathed
their tired feet in the *acequias*. The Golden Age was over.

Even so, that green haven was long remembered by weary
travelers who wrapped themselves in its cool shade in the
years before the railroad and the automobile. Gene Rhodes,
who appears later in these pages as the Bard of the Tularosa,
recalled it wistfully when he was far away in exile:

Each generation of Oasis made sorties against the desert, with con-
quest of new fields; builded new streets, and lovingly lined those
streets with cottonwoods. They arch and meet now, those old
trees, home of a million mockingbirds to thrill the dawn with un-
imaginable sweetness. Literally the town cannot be seen from the
outside. There are no towers and minarets and things. The houses
are adobe, one story high and a block long—recumbent skyscrapers.

Strangers arriving by rail condemn this prodigality of shade
trees as wasting the slender resources of water and soil; but those
who come in from the desert find no fault with the arching cottonwoods.

Indeed, Oasis has all the drawbacks you mention and some you
would never guess; civically speaking, it is "link'd with one virtue
and a thousand crimes." Yet—for all that deep and cool and generous shade, and the brave tinkling of her hundred acequias—men
in the world's showplaces think with a pang of that dim and far
old town, and name her puny river with a kindling eye, as Naaman
spake of Abana and Pharphar, rivers of Damascus.[16]

Texas Cattle

O<small>N</small> J<small>UNE</small> 10, 1877, John Good decided he would go to town. He saddled up at the corral, made sure his ancient revolver was in working order, and set out at a jog trot. It was twelve miles from his ranch to Blanco City through the cedar-studded Texas hills, and he had plenty of time—or so he thought. As a matter of fact he had just time enough to get into trouble.

Blanco City was not much more than a wide place in a cow track. Five minutes after arrival you had seen everybody in town. Good had barely hit the main street when he was accosted by a man named Robinson, who seemed indignant. Apparently he found something very familiar in Good's horse. We do not know the details, but he made some forcible remarks which Good resented. He told Robinson where to go.

"We might as well settle this right now," Robinson remarked, and went for his pistol. Unfortunately for him, his gun caught in his clothes for a moment. Good got in four center shots while the other was struggling. Robinson was able to fire only one wild slug before he died.

Good gave himself up at once, well knowing that any Texas jury would have to call it self-defense.[1]

This was the beginning of the Exodus of John Good. Quite probably his neighbors made it clear to him that though the law exonerated him, they did not. At any rate he left the country and began a series of moves which eventually brought him to a smoke-stained career in New Mexico.

John and his brother Isham had been close to trouble for some time. In the lonesome limestone hills west of Austin they were well, if not favorably, known. There they held their own with the rough characters who haunted the cedar brakes and periodically blasted each other into eternity.[2] John was the number-one man of the clan, a great big full-bearded, hell-raising fellow who ran cows for a living, raced horses and played poker for fun, and bullied his neighbors from lifelong habit. Isham was a much milder character and stayed pretty much in the background; but anywhere there was a foreground, John Good was going to be in it.

John's name sometimes came up in connection with a killing or a jail delivery,[3] and Isham was in the black books of the Rangers in 1877. That was the year Major John B. Jones and his Frontier Battalion made the great roundup of undesirable characters in the hill country. Isham had seven indictments outstanding against him, but the Rangers agreed to forgive and forget if he would turn against his outlaw friends. At the same time they hoped to find some other excuse for bringing him into court. Frank Jones reported to his commander: "Good is a notorious cow thief, and if there is any chance the authorities of this County would like very much to have him by the next term of District Court."[4]

So a migration was clearly in order. By the fall of that year, 1877, John Good was living in Coleman, 150 miles northwest, and his new neighbors were much upset about it. A report came to Austin that "the people of Coleman, Brown, and Comanche Counties have written a letter to one John H. Good accusing him of harboring the worst characters in West Texas. They state that in consequence of this fact his presence is no longer needed in the country. They give him until the first of October. Good protests and says he is innocent." [5]

Innocent or not, he took his time about moving on. He was still at Coleman in 1878 when Rufe O'Keefe spent a night at his hotel, but in 1880 he had settled on ranch property fifty miles northwest of Colorado City. Billy King, a Texas cowboy who was drifting west toward a career as a Tombstone saloonkeeper, stopped off to punch Long S cows for Lum Slaughter and went on roundups with John's tall son Walter.

King was present in 1881 when Henry Mason, a boss for Slaughter, gathered up Good's stock and trailed it to La Luz in New Mexico.[6]

Good may or may not have realized it, but he was playing his part in a great westward migration of Texas cattlemen. It started with the Civil War. Unlike the rest of the South, Texas escaped the ravages of conflict. After 1865 it became the new frontier, where land was cheap, game was plentiful, and life was supposed to be blissful. The four-dollar cow went up the beef trail to the forty-dollar market, and tales of easy money spread even to the other side of the Atlantic. The white-topped wagons swarmed across the Red River and the Sabine, bringing new settlers every day. Along with them came plows and barbed wire, to the despair of the old-time cattlemen who thought the range should be permanent and free, like the air.[7]

At the same time the Rangers and the local "minute men" were bringing the outlaws and the Indians under control, opening up the grasslands of West Texas to occupation. A vast undertow in the population began as families drifted westward—to the Panhandle, to the Big Bend. Wherever there was vacant land, they moved in, flowing across the state like a slow tidal wave. By 1880 the country was occupied as far as the Pecos.[8] The next stop was New Mexico.

Overstocking, droughts, and die-ups pushed the wave onward in 1883.[9] The hard winter of 1885-1886 gave it another shove.[10] Year after year more herds appeared in the Roswell area along the Pecos. They overflowed into the Sierra Blanca and Sacramento highlands and washed down onto the Tularosa flats. This, the Texans thought, was the country they had dreamed about.

The feeling was natural enough. Rainfall was heavy in the early eighties, and the whole area appeared to be rich with vegetation. In some places the grass grew as high as a horse's shoulder. In the swales it was thick enough to tempt men to move in and make hay. Mostly it grew in bunches and patches, however, and the bunches were pretty far apart. A horseman seemed from half a mile away to be moving through a sea of grass, but that was an optical illusion. As the herds crowded in, they cut the forage back to the roots and kept it there. Tom Fraser of Alamogordo used to say that, in the roundup of 1889, eighty-five thousand head of stock were gathered between Three Rivers and the mouth of Dog Canyon—far too heavy a burden for the range.[11] That summer a three-year drought set in. Damage to the grass cover was almost irreparable, and it never has come back to what it was.

Such ruin, of course, was hard to foresee in the early 1880s, when this was virgin country, seemingly big enough for everybody. Roswell at that time was two hundred miles from a railroad, and Tularosa was eighty miles from the tracks even after the Santa Fe went through to El Paso in 1881. The Texans were glad of it. To them it was an untamed land where they could have their old free range and their old free ways back again. They elbowed each other on the Tularosa flats and squatted in the mountain canyons where for years they did not even bother to file on the land they occupied. It was with them as it was with Abraham and Lot when they drove their cattle out of Egypt and broke up because of strife among their herdsmen.

Gene Rhodes liked to point out the similarity.

"And the herdsmen of Gerar did strive with Isaac's herdsmen, saying, the water is ours."

That was at the Well Esek. The patriarchs were always quarreling with their neighbors or with each other over wells, pasturage and other things—mavericks, maybe. Abraham, Laban, Lot, Isaac, Jacob—they led a stirring life, following the best grass. . . .

It is entirely probable that Terah went forth from Ur of the Chaldees either because the grass was short or because he had no friends on the grand jury.[12]

Rhodes saw these people as the advance guard of what he called "the Great Trek"[13] across the American continent— the fire-hardened spearhead of a world migration—and he knew, since he was one of them, that their virtues and sins were not the virtues and sins of more settled groups. It is hard to understand their history unless this fact is kept in mind: They played by a set of rules which was different from that of their Philistine neighbors.

Courage was the great virtue—no man ran from a fight or quit before he was licked. Loyalty came next—a man stood by his friends, right or wrong, win or lose. Then came steadfastness—staying by the job till it was done; forbearance toward the weak, including women and children; clannishness—a sense of responsibility to the group; an instinct for staying out of other people's business; cheerfulness under difficulties; a firm conviction that no man should expect another to right his wrongs. These were some of the chapter headings in the code by which these people lived. In Rhodes's view, such qualities were heroic virtues and made up for all crudeness, violence, and disrespect for formal codes of law. One of his conversations on this subject is well worth quoting.

"To use their own phrase," says a disgruntled character in *West Is West*, "unless a man will go through with whatever he begins 'to the last ditch and then some,' he's no good. Nothing else counts. He must be ready to fight for every reason or no reason—for a foolish cause or a bad one. . . . To be just, it is not needful that you win. They think just as well of you if you are licked or killed—just so you demonstrate that you have more pluck than brains. It is intolerable. They're savages. They make a fetish of low brute courage; they drag out a poor, second-rate virtue and make it supersede a hundred better qualities."

And Rhodes answers:

"I don't think they're savages, and I don't think they're altogether wrong. We can't afford to despise this 'brute courage,' as you call it. It may not be the highest quality, but it is the one indispensable quality." [14]

These are not empty words. Rhodes's little dialogue spotlights a rift which divided the people of southern New Mexico not many years ago and caused infinite trouble. The tenderfeet and the townspeople thought of the country people out on the cattle ranges and in the mountains as semi-savages. I once heard a retired Las Cruces merchant say of a country wife, "She was just an old ranch woman. She'd spit through a screen door."

On the other hand, the ranchers thought my friend the merchant was one of "God's frozen people," to use Rhodes's phrase.

They might have tolerated one another better had it not been for one last item in the cowman's code—murder. His elemental life, his emphasis on personal courage and self-redress, his habit of carrying deadly weapons—these things

gave him some special ideas about killing and some special reactions toward officers of the law.

It was right to shoot a man who insulted you, robbed you,
or for other reasons "needed killing." Even if it was against
the law? Yes, even if it was against the law. Your friends
stood by you if you did it, and protected you from the sheriff
as long and as well as they could.

It was justifiable also to kill an enemy who had been
warned. Once an undesirable neighbor had been notified to
leave the country, he stayed around at his own peril. If
he absorbed a bullet at any time thereafter, he was considered
to have committed suicide.

As Gene Rhodes put it, this was "the rattlesnake's code, to
warn before he strikes, no better: a queer, lopsided, topsy-
turvy, jumbled and senseless code—but a code for all that.
And it is worthy of note that no better standard has ever been
kept with such faith as this barbarous code of the fighting
man." [15]

Naturally such a system produced some hard characters.
They included wild, roistering cowboys; men who loved the
taste of their neighbors' beef; prosperous cattle barons who
wanted to run everybody else off the range—even a few
tough women like "Bronco Sue" Yonker, who once lived at
Tularosa raising fine horses, swearing expertly, and spending
pleasant moments with the cowboys in roundup camps. But
they were not the rule. And the country people were better
citizens, on the whole, than their critics allow.

There were the Coes, who came down from Missouri before 1880, bringing their relatives the Mayhills, for whom the
little town in the Sacramentos is named.[16] There was C. F. Hilton, who drove a herd of cattle up from Mexico in 1884 and
located in the high country at the head of the Sacramento
River. There was John W. Nations, who came from Nebraska in 1892 to join his Texas relatives living in Agua

Chiquita Canyon on top of the range. He kept a school in the winters and tried to teach the children manners and responsibility as well as facts and figures.[17]

The life these people lived was meager, no doubt. They had few advantages. Their pleasures were homemade. But with love and kindness and self-respect they had enough.

Outsiders misjudged them, and an occasional savage killing at a dance or roundup persuaded the strangers that the cow camps and the mountain valleys were havens for hard characters. This was not true. But when it came to a death struggle between the cattlemen and their rivals—farmers, merchants, lawyers, big landowners—the mountain people were not about to sympathize with the group that looked down upon them and gave them a bad name. They made the cattlemen's cause their own, and that made a good deal of difference later on.

John Good and his men brought in the first wave of the Texan flood which muddied the peaceful current of life in the Tularosa neighborhood. He bought five hundred irrigable acres from ten Mexican families, set up a ranch on Lost River out toward the White Sands, and began to tell the local population what to do. He completed his arrangements by forming a more or less tender friendship with "Bronco Sue" Yonker—Mrs. Charley Dawson—the handsome, unkempt scandal of Tularosa womanhood—a friendship which was broken off when Bertha Good decided her presence was needed and came out from Texas to join her husband.[18]

Rough, pugnacious, sociable, unscrupulous, and warmhearted, these first *Tejanos* were a revelation to the native population. They went their own way in spite of hell and no water. They organized Texas-style roundups, got drunk when they felt like it, and fought at the drop of a sombrero. It was noted that the wildest of them had no use for underwear or privies; that they looked down on Mexicans and Yankees;

that they considered it shameful not to shoot a man who called you a sonofabitch or spoke too freely of your wife; that they quarreled frequently about cow business as they had done back in Texas.

The Mexicans called them desperadoes and considered them about as dangerous and unreliable as the Indians. The Yankees—of whom there were a good many in the country, leftovers from the California Column and more recent invasions—observed them with special horror. And John Good was about all they could take.

He was overbearing and arrogant. As he grew rich—which he soon did—he seemed to expect other people to get out of his way. When he had a drink or two under his belt, he was apt to be quarrelsome; likewise when he got the worst of it in a monte or poker game. He thought of himself as a first-rate gambler, though earnest students of the craft, like Billy King, did not rate his abilities so high.

Still, he had his friends and supporters. He was prosperous; he was open-handed and hospitable. In the summer of 1886 he built his big house in La Luz, a ten-room adobe facing north under towering cottonwoods. Many a *baile* was held there—many an all-night poker game.[19] He even became society news in Las Cruces:

"John Good intends to christen his new adobe house on Tuesday by a big dance to which all are invited, and we opine, judging by his open-hearted, free, come one come all, eat and be merry disposition that it will be an enjoyable affair." [20]

Brother Isham came out to join him in 1886,[21] bringing his family, and the Good clan began to look like something out of the Old Testament. John was surrounded by his sons Charley, Walter, and Ivan, with at least one son-in-law. Isham fathered Lee, Ed, Bill, Milton, and four girls. Besides the blood kin there was a small army of retainers and friends who took care of John's business and fought his battles—the ones he didn't fight himself. They were all remarkably big men. John was six feet two or three. Isham not much less. Walter was six feet six.

If Pat Coghlan was the king of Tularosa, John Good was the high potentate of La Luz; but where Pat made his way by genial crookedness, Good trampled roughshod on all obstacles and opponents. It worked for a while, but Good should have known that it couldn't go on forever—not with those Texans.

The man who finally reacted was George McDonald, a young fellow who had been in the country since 1885—a stocky, red-faced, quietly courageous young man. He wanted to marry Nettie Fry and was trying to make a stake, so, having more ambition than livestock, he went to work for the Stuart brothers, who had a store in Tularosa and a ranch in the foothills seven miles northeast of town at Coyote Springs. He used to take his wages to Nettie every month, keeping out only five dollars for himself. He was doing all right until he fell foul of John Good.

They had trouble about cows and water early in their acquaintance. Good was insulting as usual and McDonald wouldn't take it. They came close to fighting several times after that. Finally, with characteristic high-handedness, Good made up his mind that the quarrel had better stop. He tried to make George shake hands, and George wouldn't do it.

"I don't have to shake hands with anybody I don't want to," he said.

Tom McDonald of Tularosa (no relation to George) was present once when trouble was mighty near. George had just gone to work for the Stuart brothers, close friends of the Goods. Next time Good saw George on the street, he stopped him.

"I understand you've gone to work for the Stuarts."

"I have," said George.

"Well, goddam it, no so-and-so like you is going to work for Stuart if I have to kill him to stop it."

With that he reached for his gun, an old six-shooter with the trigger guard broken off. The ancient weapon slipped down his pants leg. George flipped out his own pistol, pushed it into Good's stomach, and remarked grimly, "Well, by God I think I'll just kill *you*."

Tom seized his arm; somebody else grabbed Good; and no damage was done that time.[22]

But trouble was building up in the country. By now Tularosa and La Luz had become tough towns with a bad name for killings and shooting scrapes. The Las Cruces papers noted them casually almost every week:

June 19, 1886, "Murder of A. H. Howe, merchant, just outside the Mescalero reservation in Tularosa Canyon."

July 3, 1886, "Frank Rochez [Rochas], rancher in Dog Canyon, wounded by a young man named Morrison."

June 2, 1888, "Last Monday evening about five o'clock . . . W. W. Pruner, familiarly known as Jack Pruner, was shot and instantly killed by John Shears, a saloon keeper. . . . Shears had heard Pruner was making remarks about his wife. . . ."

June 16, 1888, "We have to record this week the assassination of George W. McDonald, foreman of the Stuart Brothers ranch at Coyote Canyon, about seven miles northeast from Tularosa."[23]

It was the McDonald murder that brought on the first big trouble in the valley—a feud which tore Tularosa and La Luz apart and planted seeds which ripened later on in the terrible times of the nineties. To get the straight of it, we have to drop back a bit and pick up the thread in the spring of 1884.

Blood on the Sand

I$_T$ WAS early afternoon when the two boys and Cherokee Bill came over the pass and started down the long incline toward Tularosa. They jogged along the winding cart track under the tall pines, saying little. The mountain slopes were mellow in the vivid sunlight. The sky was a tender robin's-egg blue. There had been a shower that morning, sharp enough to bring out the pungent scent of juniper and wet mold.

Perry Altman, a sandy-headed, lanky Texan in his early twenties, rode with Cherokee Bill, who was acting as guide. His half brother Oliver Lee dropped back when the road was narrow, as became an eighteen-year-old junior partner.

They had met Bill Kellam the night before when they camped on the Ruidoso. He had a place nearby, he said, in Cherokee Bill Canyon, named for him. They learned that he came from around Waco somewhere—that he had had hair-raising adventures in half a dozen Western states—that he had lived with the Indians, had some Indian blood, and had married an Indian wife. He was a hard-eyed, weather-beaten character and a real blowhard, but they liked him and he liked them.

"This is still wide-open country," he told them. "All government land and not too much competition. It's just a question of freezing onto a water hole."

"Well, we're looking for a place to settle," Perry told him. "Things were bad in Taylor County last year and we're fixin' to move out. Everything dried up. We lost some stock."

"I know just the place for you," Bill said, thoughtfully. "It's a canyon on the west side of the Sacramentos. Walls maybe a couple thousand feet high. Good water. Very little fence needed. There's an old Frenchman living there now—raising fruit trees!" Bill spat contemptuously. "It might not take much to buy him out."

Perry and Oliver exchanged glances. The look meant "This might be worth thinking over."

"I'll tell you what," Bill declared. "I'll take you to it. Have to go over that way anyhow. What time do you figure on getting out in the morning?"

"Daylight," replied Perry economically, and spread out his blankets.

There wasn't much traffic on the old road from the Pecos to the Rio Grande in the spring of 1884. In fact they had it all to themselves. But for boys who had never been very far from Little Elm Creek and the country town of Buffalo Gap, the mountains were company enough. The boys stared at the blank-faced Apaches, who gave them casual inspection as they passed the agency buildings at Mescalero, and they sniffed at the pungent odor of the wood smoke rising lazily from cooking fires on the camp ground east and west of the buildings. They stopped and looked a long time when the road climbed over a rise and gave them their first view of the vast, sun-filled trench which was to be their new home.

The sun was going down behind the black bulwark of the

San Andres when they turned into Pat Coghlan's wagon yard at Tularosa and saw the brown, friendly faces of the inhabitants for the first time.

In the days that followed, they looked the country over thoroughly, and with mixed feelings. The valley was at its best after the good years of the early eighties, but compared to the grassy plains of their home county it was wild and desolate. They yearned for running water—their old friends and neighbors—the little schoolhouse with the split-log benches where they had gone to school—the familiar faces of the family back home. When they had inspected the rocky ramparts and boulder-strewn floor of Dog Canyon, which Cherokee Bill had boasted about, Altman made a remark which has come down to posterity.

"Well, Oliver," he said, "this country is so damn sorry I think we can stay here a long time and never be bothered by anybody else." [1]

He could hardly have been more mistaken.

That winter they spent back on Little Elm Creek getting ready, and early in the spring of 1885 they returned with their cows and horses, two colored men Eph and Ed, and the whole Lee clan. The real boss of the outfit was twice-widowed Mrs. Mary Hendrick Lee, a stocky, courageous woman with snapping black eyes who knew all about sickness and took the place of a doctor wherever she lived. In Burnet County in the hills northwest of Austin she grew up and in due time became Mrs. Altman. Her husband died when their son Perry was seven. Afterward she married a New York Stater named Lee, considerably older than she was, who had been a forty-niner in California. Oliver Milton Lee was their son.[2]

After Mr. Lee died, Perry and Oliver ran the ranch. Both were good with cows and extra good with horses. Oliver in particular was a horse specialist and had already built up a fine herd when they came to New Mexico. In later years he would turn a man off quicker for abusing a horse than for any other reason.

In 1885 he was nineteen, a handsome, shy boy much admired by the girls who knew him, though he had not yet reached the stage where he preferred girls to horses. Even then he was something to look at—magnificently muscled, straight as a young pine, catlike in his coordination. He had his mother's piercing black eyes which seemed to bore into you, and a chin like the Rock of Gibraltar, but he always spoke softly.

The people who hated and feared him most in later years admitted his personal charm and confessed that he behaved like a gentleman. He did not smoke or drink. He loved good clothes. And he was careful of his language.

He had one great urge—he wanted to get ahead. He had one great talent—he was a natural shot. Those two things put together made Oliver Lee a legend in his own country before he died.

Since he was always close-mouthed, especially with strangers, we have to rely on the record for a conception of the inner forces which drove him on until he became the most powerful man in the Tularosa Valley. The country is full of stories about his wizardry with six-shooter and rifle.

Apparently marksmanship was an instinct with him. He would take an old carbine with the sights sawed off, throw a half dollar into the air, and hit it without seeming to take aim. There is one story that after a round of ordinary shooting with cowboy friends he had a pine board set up a mile away on the flat and punctured it five shots out of six.[3] He was not averse to putting on exhibitions for his friends in his young days. Later he didn't need to. They knew what he could do.

The rest of the Lee family included Perry Altman, who put up an adobe house in his arroyo eight miles west of Tularosa and soon added a frame bedroom for the bride whom he married at Buffalo Gap the following year. Perry's brother-in-law Charley Graham had a place two miles west.

Mrs. Lee had the loneliest location of all. With Oliver and her niece Nettie Fry, whom she had mothered, she moved into a two-room adobe out on the flat twenty miles from the White Sands and due west of Dog Canyon. They drilled the first well between La Luz and Ysleta there and put up a windmill which was three days on the road from El Paso. Everybody called the place Lee's Well.[4]

There was still another member of the family—Nettie's young man, George McDonald. Originally from Burnet County, as they all were, he had followed on the march to Buffalo Gap and had taken his place in the caravan when the time came to move to New Mexico. George and Oliver were closer than brothers—played together, worked together, schemed together to get ahead in the world. It was one for both and both for one.

One of their schemes brought them into collision with John Good, who controlled almost everything thereabouts and was bound to control the rest. They found a little salty spring near the foothills which they developed, digging it out and rocking it up until they had themselves a little water. Eventually they traded it to Old Man Reynolds for more cows, but they had trouble first.

Nearby, John Good owned a tank which he supplied by pipe line from the Tularosa. The boys never thought of bothering him, but he came storming up when he found what they had done and told them to move on. He was there first and he wouldn't have their cows bothering around his tank.

Peppery, hot-tempered George flushed up. "You may be God around here," he said, "but you don't scare me. You just try running us off and see how far you get."

Good glared at him. "Don't say I didn't warn you," he growled as he rode off.[5]

They had heard the snake rattle and they knew he could

strike. The country was still talking about what had happened to Charley Dawson a few months before. Dawson had quarreled with Good about cow business and they parted with a "shoot-on-sight" understanding. The meeting happened on the streets of La Luz (it was December 8, 1885) and there was a hot little gunfight. Bronco Sue, Dawson's formidable wife, came in at the end with a Winchester, but her husband had already stopped a bullet. Good wasn't hurt.[6]

George McDonald knew he was up against tough opposition, but he refused to walk softly or back down. When they met after that, Good smoldered; George looked him in the eye and said what he thought when he felt it was necessary. The legends say they were close to trouble more than once after that first run-in, but nothing really decisive happened until the roundup of 1888.

That fall the wagon was working north from Dog Canyon with Bill Earhart of the Cooper outfit as roundup boss. Earhart had fallen out with Good before the roping and branding began when he asked how many hands the 7HL expected to send.

"We're shorthanded right now," Good replied. "Can't send you any hands, but I'll have somebody come down to cut the bunch."

Earhart, who was quick-tempered and a fighter, knew this was in violation of all roundup ethics. "The hell you will," he replied. "No crew, no cut."

"The hell I won't. If you round up any 7HL cows, they belong to me and I'm coming after them."

Earhart gave ground unwillingly. "All right. You can make your cut, but you'll wait till the rest of us are through. And don't try to come in any quicker."

As the roundup got going, Earhart made sure he wouldn't be caught napping. Wat Gilmore was just a boy then, and new to the country, but he had been taken along to tend branding fires. He got a nickel apiece for starting them and had already learned to let them go out so he could make more money. Earhart called him over and told him to keep his eyes open. "You watch," he said, "and tell me if you see anybody coming."

So Wat watched, and sure enough he spotted a dust cloud off to the northeast. Half a dozen riders were coming up at a canter. Earhart looked and swore. "It's Walter Good," he said, noting the height of the leading horseman. "You boys better get a drink."

The guns were all in the wagon. Seized by a sudden and unanimous thirst, the men were able to arm themselves without anyone giving an order.

Death was just beyond the next mesquite bush for a while. Walter said he was going to cut the herd and nobody had better try to stop him. His paint horse whirled and trotted in among the cows.

Earhart hesitated only a second. Then he followed, turned in front of Walter's horse, seized the bridle and steered for the chuck wagon.

Walter could have stuck a gun in his ribs and probably had the impulse to do it. But he looked at the grim horsemen holding the herd and changed his mind.[7]

"Now stay out of there till I tell you to go in," Earhart said flatly, turning the bridle loose.

Walter changed his tactics. He saw George McDonald heating the iron for a spotted calf that two of the boys were holding. "That's a 7HL calf," he said to George. "You brand it 7HL."

"It's a maverick," George told him, "but it's been following a Cooper cow. I'm branding it for Cooper." So saying, he put the hot iron to the calf's hide and printed a neat Triangle T.[8]

Walter gave up then. But he didn't like it, and neither did his father.

This brought Jim Cooper into the mix-up, though he had

been on the edge of it for some time, and he needs a word of introduction.

The Coopers had lived near Jacksboro since before the Civil War. Ira, Clay, and Jim were tall Texas boys whose life work was cattle. Jim went to school at Denison for a few terms but soon had all he wanted. Dr. Cooper, his father, gave him a few cows and a mount of horses and he went out to the vicinity of Colorado City to build up a herd.[9]

In 1883, according to his old account books,[10] he was ranching on the Double Mountain Fork of the Brazos, and very shortly after that he caught the New Mexico fever, like his neighbors. In due time he trailed his herd to the Tularosa. With him came his brother Clay, a married man who lived quietly and made no headlines—also Billy Bean and Bill Earhart, boyhood friends from Jack County. Bean was an easygoing, middle-aged cowboy with no harm in him. Earhart was young and aggressive, had a few cattle of his own in the herd, and was spoken of as Cooper's partner.

The country took to Jim Cooper at once. He was a big man, as tall as any of the Goods and broad in proportion, with a craglike, honest face. In company he was agreeable—loved a joke and a laugh and could play the fiddle, the latter a sure key to social success. At the same time he was hard working and serious about his business. All his old friends say he was an excellent stockman who spent most of his time at his bachelor shack a few miles north of Tularosa and seldom showed up at parties or in Pat Coghlan's saloon. When he had any spare time, he rode fifteen miles up the Tularosa Canyon and went to courting Captain Brazel's pretty daughter Bonnie.

Jim brought in about three thousand head of stock, which seems to have been more than he could find grass or water for. He tried to solve his problems by running some of his cattle in partnership with John Good, who had plenty of both. About two thousand cows carried the LO partnership brand. The rest of the Cooper stock was branded JIM or Triangle T. Good's brand was 7 H L connected (**7L**).

The arrangement seems to have run on for two or three years. Then, about the beginning of 1888, it was time for an accounting, and the trouble started. John Good's cowboys had taken their beef out of the partnership herd, and the Coopers were unhappy about it. Some old ranch hands who were around at the time still argue that this was customary and ought not to have caused any argument. The Coopers couldn't see it that way.[11] They sided against John Good when the death of George McDonald set the Good party against the Lees and their friends.

Benito Montoya found George's body on the afternoon of June 13, 1888, when he was out hunting cattle. McDonald had apparently cooked his dinner, cleaned up his house, and gone back into the canyon to see about the water. A hundred yards above the troughs was the "upper spring," in the shadow of an overhanging cliff, where he probably took a drink and lay down in the shade with his head against a rock. Before he dropped off to sleep he spent a little time braiding a quirt.[12]

His eyes closed—and just at that moment somebody rose up from behind a rock twenty or thirty feet away and shot him squarely in the center of the forehead. The bullet went through his skull and flattened against the rock behind him.

As the story was told in Las Cruces, "McDonald died instantly without a struggle, not even moving his feet, which were crossed, or turning his head. His revolver being in its scabbard and his hand laying by his side showed that he never attempted to reach for it. After firing the fatal shot, the assassin got on his horse and ran up the canyon and from there to the Tularosa Canyon, where all trace of him was lost."[13]

One important fact was omitted in this account. The murderer's horse ran against a Spanish dagger growing at an angle and left a triangular piece of hide on one of the spikes. It is said that the piece was later fitted into a scar in the hide of a horse belonging to Walter Good.[14] Anyway Walter got credit for the killing.

People were ready enough to blame him, for lanky Walter had not developed into a very useful citizen. He was a good cowboy—a left-handed roper who seldom missed a throw—and he had a paint pony which was the prize cutting horse of the region.[15] Otherwise he was not much account. At this time he had been married two months or so[16] and may have begun to mend his ways. If so, he had no time or opportunity to show the world his change of heart.

When he was not working cattle, he was usually riding about the country with his "Friday," a scar-faced Mexican from Three Rivers named José Espalin.[17] And the Devil found work for their idle hands to do.

Suspicion had pointed at Espolin, and through him at Walter, when A. H. Howe, the Mescalero merchant, was murdered two years before.[18] People who have "inside information" say it was this same Mexican who did for George, but nobody really knows. It is even said and believed that the assassin was brought in from the outside, Texas fashion, and smuggled out as soon as he had done his work—and it is possible that not one but two killers ushered George McDonald into the next world, one going east and one going west to confuse possible pursuers.[19] You can hear that a detective trailed the killer to Texas, arrested him, and brought him back to Las Cruces for trial. The judge turned this man, whose name was Parker, loose when the detective did not show up to testify against him.[20]

The fertility of the pioneer mind in inventing and believing such stories is amazing. All we need to keep in view is the fact that the Lees and their friends held Walter Good responsible for the murder of George McDonald. They pointed out that he had been sent up to White Oaks that day for a small bunch of cattle and could easily have been in the neighborhood.[21] And the piece of hide was torn out of one of his best horses—if that story is true. It was a terrible, numbing blow to all of them.

It was worse for Nettie, of course. She had been planning to go with Perry to El Paso for her wedding clothes. Emma Altman had gone back to Buffalo Gap to have her first child, and Perry was preparing to meet her when the news of the murder came. He was at the station when Emma's train pulled in, and after they had had their little reunion, he took her to a bench in San Jacinto Plaza and made her sit down.

"There is some bad news," he said, "and you'd better hear it before you see Nettie. She's up in the hotel now. They killed George. Nettie was going to buy her wedding dress on this trip, but she's bought black instead."[22]

Oliver was almost as badly torn up as Nettie. George was as close to him as one man can be to another. If he had been killed in a standup fight, it wouldn't have been so bad. But to be shot from behind a rock . . . asleep . . . and just when things were beginning to break right for him! It was all wrong!

All the Lees thought sadly of the old days in Buffalo Gap. If they had only stayed there—never come to this wild country with its blood and gunsmoke. Then these thoughts gave way to sterner ones. Trouble, they knew, was just beginning and they would have to be ready.

Oliver got the flattened bullet from Tom McDonald, who had dug it out of the rock. For many years he carried it at the end of his watch chain,[23] a grim reminder of what had already happened—and what was to come.

Lead and Law

The last of his family to see Walter Good alive was his wife Roberta (Berta). He said adios to her and trotted off, coatless, on an old plug of a pony one warm Tuesday morning about the middle of August, expecting to ride out to Perry Altman's after his paint horse. Perry had come in the night before to tell him that the animal was in his pasture. Mrs. Altman was getting tired of watering it, he said, and wanted Walter to come and get his property. Walter laughed and said he would be out in the morning.

He never got there, and he never came back. Emma Altman was at home expecting him but he failed to show up. The next day, Wednesday the fifteenth, Hugh Taylor came to the Altman place looking for his brother-in-law. He said John Good was getting worried and wanted to know what had occurred.

Perry said he had no information.

Before the day was over, fifty men were scouring the country looking for the missing man. Among those who went out to search the foothills and the flatlands was Perry Altman himself. It was no use. Walter was not to be found.[1]

John Good raged like a wounded lion. He thought he knew what had happened and he had no doubt at all about who was responsible. When the story came to him that Jim Cooper, Tom Tucker, and Oliver Lee had been at Altman's house the night before Walter left, he was sure the stray-horse story was a plant and that the men had waited to do away with his son. He went to Humphrey Hill, the justice of the peace, swore out a warrant against the men for carrying weapons, and accompanied the posse which went out to make the arrests. Perry Altman was the only one they found at home. Lee and Cooper and Tucker—the last-named a seasoned warrior who had lost the top of one ear in the Graham-Tewkesbury feud in Arizona—were said to be camping out in the mountains on the Agua Chiquita.

Since they could do no better, the posse took Altman back to La Luz with them and did what they could to make him talk. Good got him into a back room and questioned him all night, storming and threatening. Toward morning he suggested that they might as well string Perry up and get it over with. Hugh Taylor said no, that wouldn't help, and they let him go.[2]

Both sides found out now what it was to be in a war. Business in the little towns was paralyzed. Everyone went armed. Fear and anxiety ate at the hearts of all. The news spread across the mountains that Good and his men were in the saddle day and night grimly determined to catch up with Lee and Cooper and wipe them out, and that the fugitives had left the mountains and departed for places unknown.

"The whole country is up in arms," said the *Rio Grande Republican*, "and such a reign of terror has not been known since the Lincoln County War."[3]

Good offered a reward of $300 for his son's return, dead or

alive, and a thousand dollars more for the arrest and conviction of the killers.

Sixty citizens of La Luz sent a petition to Las Cruces, the
county seat, asking Sheriff Ascarate to come out and disarm
the factions. Ascarate came as requested, reported that he
could find nobody to disarm, and went back where he came
from.

Charley Graham, brother-in-law of Lee and Altman, loaded
his family into his wagon and drove off for good. Charley was
a brave man but he saw no sense in getting mixed up in anything like this. He found a more peaceful haven on the slopes
of the San Mateos, far across the Rio Grande.

The fugitives sent word from the mountains that they
would not surrender to local officers but would give up to authorities from Las Cruces. And in that state matters hung
poised for a few days.

The Lees were completely unprepared for this emergency.
Mrs. Altman used to say that her husband did not own a gun
at this time and would hardly have known how to operate it if
he had—though it is hard to believe that of any Texan in the
year 1888. None of the men had enough cartridges, so Oliver
and Perry went to El Paso to buy arms and ammunition while
Good was stalking his prey up in the Sacramentos. When they
came back, they had so many cartridges they kept them in
five-gallon cans with a layer of corn meal on top and gunny
sacks over that.

Meanwhile all sorts of alarming things were happening.
Old Eph, Charley Graham's colored man, had been left alone
in the house after his master's departure. He told how he
heard someone holler "Hello" outside late one night. Instead
of answering, he took a pot shot through a window in the
general direction of the hail. In the morning he found no bodies in the front yard, but he did find that a man with very
small feet had posted himself on the roof directly above the

door, probably hoping for a shot at one of the Lee party.[4]

Such doings persuaded Perry that he ought not to leave his wife and baby alone, and when he went off to El Paso with Oliver to purchase the sinews of war, he told Emma to take the wagon and drive down to Mrs. Lee's, where she could be protected.

Emma went. But on August 26, a Sunday, she decided that it was time to get back to her own place. She made up her mind to have the colored boy drive her home by way of the Reynolds ranch in Alamo Canyon to get some fresh fruit. She was up in a tree gathering peaches when she noticed smoke rising in the direction of her house. She looked again and decided in panic that her home was really burning. With all the haste she could muster, she got down out of that tree and prepared to rush off at once. Mrs. Reynolds wouldn't let her go.

"You don't know what you'll run into over there," she advised, "and you couldn't do any good. You've got to think of that baby and yourself. Perry wouldn't want you to get into any trouble or danger. Wait here until tomorrow morning."

Early the next day Emma came home to find her house in ruins. Somebody had piled brush in the doorway and touched it off. Her little dog, who probably had objected to these proceedings, was shot and stamped into the ground by the man who did it.

The place was alive with people when she drove up. Deputy Rucker was there with his posse and all were hard at work. Some were digging under what had been the floor and some were scratching around in the corral. "What on earth for?" she demanded of them.

"We're looking for the body," Rucker replied.

Though Emma was not in a position to know it, she was already the center of the usual whirlwind of rumors. A woman who had come in while she was scrubbing the floor had spread the story that she was working furiously on blood stains that would not come out. It was said and believed—and still is—

that Walter's body had been hidden under her bed, wrapped in a sheet, until it could be disposed of. Another tale had him buried under the floor in her bedroom.

Those who could not swallow these gruesome inventions had a version of their own. They declared that Walter had been tied to a post in Altman's corral before he was shot and that shreds of his clothes (some said of his hair) were found in the bullet holes in the post.

That was why some of Rucker's men were digging in the corral and going over the planks and posts. As a matter of fact the Goods sent samples of the corral dirt to Fort Stanton for analysis to see if it was mixed with human blood. The surgeon in charge sent back word that no analysis would show whether the blood, supposing there was any, came from an animal or a man.[5]

As Mrs. Altman passed the corral, Rucker remarked in her hearing that the tracks of certain boots, very small and with a high heel, were "conspicuous" around here.

Charley Good was standing in a corner of the corral. Emma looked straight at him and said, "They were conspicuous on top of Graham's house too." Charley didn't say anything.

Which side burned Emma Altman's house? Each one accused the other. The Lees said it was an act of pure vandalism. The Goods said it was done to wipe out the evidence of crime. They pointed out that a plow and a sewing machine had been left in the adobe kitchen, which did not burn. Would the Goods have taken pains to remove these valuable objects from danger? And so on.

Two days later they found what was left of Walter Good in the White Sands. He had been dead only two weeks but the coyotes had left little but his clothes and skeleton. There was no doubt, however, that it was he. His unusual height was a giveaway. So was the jewelry he was wearing. Furthermore he had on a new pair of boots when he disappeared,

bought at the Numa Reymond store in Las Cruces. Henry
Stoes had sold them to him, and it was he who identified them.
There were two bullet holes in his left temple. His revolver
with two chambers fired lay beside him.[6]

Among the fifteen men who came on this unhappy sight
around three o'clock that August afternoon was the dead
man's father. His feelings can be imagined. Hard and tough as
he was, John Good loved his family and the iron entered deep
into his soul at that moment. It was a broken father who
started back to La Luz when the party separated, leaving
two men to guard the body while the rest scattered to their
homes. That was only the beginning of the day's troubles for
the Goods, however.

The road back lay past the Malone ranch, out west of town,
and when John Good and five of his relatives and employees
came out on a little hilltop near the place, they ran into what
looked to them like an ambush. At least it was a surprise party.
Bill Earhart, Perry Altman, Tom Tucker, Cherokee Bill, and
Oliver Lee were posted behind a ditch bank ready for action.
The two parties were perhaps 150 yards apart when the fight
commenced. Over a hundred shots were fired, most of them
completely wild. Two horses were killed and a third was
wounded, but the men all got away unscratched.[7]

The battle had its funny aspects. John and his men did a dis-
appearing act into a field of tall corn which stood beside the
road, and some of them were heard to say afterward that the
bullets cutting through the leaves sounded like the Reaper
himself. It was the first time most of the members of either
group had been in a scrape of this kind, and they were all
scared.

Perry Altman took his new six-shooter and crouched
down behind a bush to see if he could make his recent target
practice pay off. His horse, Old Black Joe, took advantage of
the moment to run away, carrying Perry's new Winchester in

the saddle scabbard. The Good men caught the horse, and he vegetated in a Las Cruces stable until the end of the legal proceedings which followed the fighting.

When the last shot was fired, the Good force rode back to La Luz, badly ruffled, and sent Deputy Sheriff Armijo after Walter's body. Another horseman was despatched to Las Cruces with an S. O. S. to Sheriff Ascarate.

The Sheriff came posthaste with twenty-five men and organized a local group of twenty-five more, placing Deputy Sheriff E. C. Rucker in charge. Since Rucker was one of Good's strong-arm men, it is easy to see why the Lee crowd were afraid to trust the officers.

They buried Walter on Friday morning, September 7, the Rev. Adolfo Cardenas of the Methodist Church at La Luz officiating.[8] His grave was dug in the shade of the giant cottonwoods in his father's yard—he always said he wanted to be buried there—and there he lies today with no mound or marker to indicate the spot.[9]

Just before the funeral a coroner's jury sat on the case and charged that Walter Good came to his death at the hands of Jim Cooper, Oliver Lee, Cherokee Bill Kellam and Tom Tucker. That laid the cards on the table.

As usual, the women got the worst of it. None of the Good women has left a record of what they went through, but the mothers and wives on the Lee side used to say that their nerves were "shattered" by the ordeal of the next few weeks. They all crowded in with Mrs. Lee—there was no place else to go. The men went off into the desert or the mountains at night, the women never knew where. Every day they expected to be attacked, and friends were always coming out from town to warn them of new plots. The same sort of thing was no doubt going on at the Good house.

Once the story was relayed to the Lee women that they would be taken to La Luz and held for questioning. Sure

enough, later that day Rucker and a big posse rode up to the
ranch. Mrs. Lee saw them coming and moved everybody out
to the windmill after locking the house.

"What is your business?" she inquired of Rucker in icy
tones.

For answer the deputy took out a paper and started to read
in Spanish. Mrs. Lee interrupted him.

"We're not Mexicans. If you want to read any papers to us,
you go back and get them done over in English. Then we'll
see."

About that time a posseman started to come through the
fence to the windmill. "Stay back," she commanded. "What
do you want?"

"A drink," he said, startled.

"Then drink out of the horse trough. It's good enough for
you."

Once, when they were expecting a raid, Mrs. Lee buried a
thousand dollars' worth of watches and money belonging to
the men. She stepped off twenty paces from the corner of the
corral, dug a hole, turned a Dutch oven over the valuables,
and covered the spot with manure. Then she got to thinking.
"Somebody's got to be left to tell the tale if they try to kill us
all," she said. "Nettie, you'd better sleep in the chicken house
where you won't be noticed."

Nettie declined. "No, I've lost George and I don't care
much what happens to me. I'll stay here with you."

Emma Altman also preferred to stay in the house.

That night they heard men whistling and other men answering. Mrs. Lee collected all the axes and knives and made
up pallets on the floor for Eph and Ed, the colored boys. Then
she gave final instructions.

"Don't do anything unless they try to break in. Then do
anything you can to them."

In the morning they found that prowlers had really been

about and that they had tied their horses behind the chicken house where Mrs. Lee had wanted the girls to sleep. They shivered for days whenever they thought of it.[10]

A few weeks of this was about all that human beings could take, and the Lee and Cooper men began trying as hard as they could to get themselves arrested peaceably—and safely. The sheriff, however, continued to be inaudible, invisible, and unresponsive, and at last they decided to make a break themselves. They wrote a letter to their friend Charles W. Moore of Tularosa, telling him that they were coming in on Saturday night, September 7, and asking him to meet them and take charge.

Moore rode out several miles to a prearranged rendezvous and led them to Coghlan's place, where everybody marveled at their heavy armament, their carefree demeanor, and the nerve they showed in coming to town at all. While they were waiting for supper, Jim Cooper found a fiddle and "regaled his friends and others present with selections." [11]

Next morning they started for Las Cruces, Moore still heading the party, hoping to make it to the county jail without further trouble. That was too much to expect, however. Jim Cooper wrote a letter to the El Paso *Times* (September 16, 1888), telling the world why:

We took supper at Tularosa and word was sent to Mr. Goode that we were starting that night for Las Cruces, and so if he had any intention of traveling the road to Cruces he could wait till the road was clear to avoid any possible chance of trouble.

We rode all Saturday night and to Lee's wells at daylight. After changing our horses and resting a couple of hours, we again went on our way. We got about twenty miles and stopped at Forrester's for dinner. We had no idea of anyone following us, but while at dinner we heard Captain Rooker [Rucker], at the head of the Goode party was coming and about the same time they came in sight. They sent us word to keep moving. We returned word not to crowd us, as we were going to Cruces. We began to think it strange, after the word sent him by his friends that they would get so close on our trail. We then saddled and were again in the road, and after traveling some ten miles were told that a man named Buchanan had left La Luz at 2 o'clock in the morning, as a runner ahead—for what reason the Lord only knows. That aroused us still more, as things looked like a trap. After taking everything into consideration, to avoid the chance of trouble and as we wanted to make a peaceable surrender to the proper authorities and not be driven like beef to a pen, we concluded to wait a few days and go in right. We then sent a man to Cruces to get papers for us, if such exist. We will then start again and this time not be turned back. This may show our friends under what difficulties we have been laboring and that we have not stayed out without a reason for we knew what to expect. Hoping our friends will remember us kindly we remain,

Jim Cooper

The moves which concluded the range war of 1888 were good training in the art of getting justice in spite of the law. Without waiting for papers to be served in due form, Cooper, Altman and Earhart came in to Las Cruces on Monday, September 17, escorted by somewhere between twenty and fifty of their friends. They engaged in their defense not one law firm but two: Waddil and Young, and Newcomb and McFie. Appearing for the prosecution were Rynerson and Wade, assisted by Colonel A. J. Fountain.

The undercurrent of bitter political feeling in the county appeared in these arrangements. Rynerson and Fountain, ex-Union soldiers and former members of the California Column, were leading Republicans. They were hand in glove with the Mexican population, had been active in organizing Republican clubs at Tularosa and elsewhere, and exuded a bad political smell to the Democratic *Tejanos*. It was almost a case of Democratic newcomers against Republican old settlers, and the rift which was visible here deepened in after years until it involved the whole of that country in a feud which made the Lee-Good trouble look like a friendly argument.

This time everything worked out well for the cowmen. They were locked up for a few days. Then, early in October, the grand jury indicted the five leaders—Cooper, Tucker, Altman, Kellam, and Lee. Judge Henderson was thus able to turn Cooper and Altman loose under a $25,000 bond. W. W. Brazel and L. S. Reynolds put up $10,000 each, and less prosperous friends made up the rest. No longer fugitives, the defendants walked out of the courtroom, free to feud or not to feud as they chose.[12]

The whole country waited breathlessly for the next round, and most people expected to hear that the six-shooters were booming again. The White Oaks *Interpreter* regretted editorially that Sheriff Ascarate was "too pusillanimous" to take the bull by the horns. The Lincoln *Independent* remarked, "unless some determined men take a hand to prevent further outrage and murders, it seems probable that the present guerrilla warfare will be continued between the Cooper and Good factions until one or both are exterminated."[13] The Tularosa correspondent of the *Republican* wrote gloomily that "business was absolutely dead."[14] Reports kept coming out of El Paso and other towns that the "gangs," armed to the teeth, were hovering on the brink of a final battle.

There was actually one meeting, and it was dramatic enough. Early in December Good and his crew had been out on a three-day roundup of their horse herd. Coming back to La Luz, they ran head-on into Jim Cooper and a number of friends. They saw each other approaching, but too late for either side to turn back without loss of face.

Several people were watching from the roadside as the meeting took place. They still tell how Fletcher Thomas, who had large mobile ears, stood alongside the road with his mouth open and his ears waggling as he waited to see what would happen.

One of the Good men pulled his Winchester from its scabbard as Jim Cooper came abreast. Cooper told him gently, "Don't do it!" and strangely enough the man didn't do it. Another got out his pistol, pointed it at Cooper, and actually fired, but Lee Good beat the barrel down and saved the situation while John Good, riding in the lead, turned and bellowed at his men, "Stop it!" [15]

Obviously Good had had enough. To prove it he made an unexpectedly generous move. Ira Cooper, Jim's brother, had come out to La Luz to try to make peace, and John Good invited him to stay at his house. Ira accepted without hesitation. The word went out and the world took note. "Ira Cooper," the news stories said, "has been since his arrival in La Luz the welcome guest of Mr. and Mrs. Good. . . . [He came here] for the express purpose of bringing about a reconciliation if possible." [16]

A little later Good threw in the towel and gave up the fight entirely. By the middle of December he had leased his five-hundred-acre place at La Luz and also his ranch land to C. P. White of Tularosa.[17] Toward the end of the month he moved to rented rooms in Las Cruces,[18] where he lived for about a year while his friends wound up his affairs. He was ruined, of course. Everything he had was sunk in the La Luz property, and there was not much use starting over at his age; but he was still alive, and that was something.

His affairs concluded, he drifted out of the country. Tom McDonald ran into him in the Deming neighborhood and again in Arizona. The last any of his old acquaintances heard, he was working for somebody else in Oklahoma, his glory departed and his purse flat.

Meanwhile Oliver Lee and Tom Tucker, taking careful note of how things had gone for Altman and Cooper, decided to give themselves up in their turn and get the preliminaries over with. They came in to Las Cruces, sued out a writ of habeas corpus, were admitted to bail in the sum of $10,000 each, and headed for home.[19] The case was argued by the same lawyers who had appeared for and against Altman and Cooper. It was the first time Colonel Fountain and Oliver Lee had taken opposite sides in a courtroom. It was not to be the last.

Some odd quirks in the testimony came out during the proceedings. According to the *Republican* (not by any means an impartial source of information), Charlie Graham's colored boy had testified before the grand jury to having seen Walter Good murdered in Altman's corral. At the habeas corpus trial, however, he denied having seen any such thing.

For all practical purposes that was all there was to it. The law's delay was put to good use in keeping the cases from coming to trial. In 1889 the venue was changed to Socorro County; the trials were postponed once; one suit was dismissed at the request of Bertha M. Good, plaintiff, and the rest were never heard of again.[20]

Thus for the first and perhaps the only time Lee, Cooper and Company had tried to make Range Law and Town Law agree, only to find that it couldn't be done. It was the first of many experiences which convinced them that there was little justice available for their kind in court procedure. The standards they lived by were too often in conflict with the other set of rules; acts which to them seemed just and right were crimes on the statute books. Nine times out of ten they came before the judge not as accusers but as accused; and they learned that survival for such as they meant circumventing the district attorney.

When it was over at last, life in Tularosa settled back into a near-normal rut. A Christmas celebration was planned with a sweepstakes race for cow ponies. The teacher of the public school left in disgust when attendance got down to one pupil, and the pupil withdrew. The first board sidewalk in town, an object of wonder and pride, was laid in front of Stokes's new store. And two drunks who tried to shoot up the town were arrested by a new and energetic constable, Cesario Durán. "With such a constable," beamed one of the citizens, much too hopefully, "our town will soon be freed of the lawlessness which has given it so bad a name." [21]

The slow leaven of time worked its changes. Jim Cooper married Bonnie Brazel early in 1890 and trailed out to a new home near Magdalena when the drought of the early nineties took a good grip on the country. Later he moved to Oklahoma, and when he died at Cheyenne in 1937 he was a prominent and respected bank president. [22]

Charlie Graham came back only to dispose of his property and returned for good to his new ranch at Cutter. Altman moved out too, first living for a while in Texas and then settling on the Crow Flats seventy-odd miles north of Van Horn and a lot farther from any place else.

Billy Earhart drifted to the Pecos country, got mixed up in another feud, and was shot in a Pecos saloon in the fall of 1896.

Nettie Fry stayed in the valley and married Bill McNew, a friend and supporter of Oliver Lee. Oliver himself took advantage of the foothold he had gained and went on to accumulate more property and prestige.

A builder and a worker, he was always in the middle of some project for improving his stock or his water supply. Sometimes these projects brought him into collision with other people; sometimes they put him crosswise with the legal authorities. He went ahead anyhow, and most of the time the authorities left him alone.

It was the McDonald murder which made a nonconformist out of him. He meant to take legal action in that case and is said to have got hold of two of Good's cowboys who could have brought the murderer or murderers to justice. Five months after it happened, he brought his witnesses in and turned them over to the district attorney. They were never called before the grand jury.[23]

His mother used to say, when his troubles and difficulties were mentioned in her hearing: "Well, we must remember that Oliver has had much to contend with." [24]

The Lives of Albert Fountain

Even before the Lee-Good business tapered off, the scene was taken over by actors in a different sort of drama. It was time for the political campaigns of 1888.

This did not signify a return of peace and harmony. In those days politics was about as lethal as pistol duels and gang fights. In fact, politics and murder could hardly be separated. The feuding would begin with speeches, parades, and persuasion—build up to bribery, vote buying, and intimidation—and end in ballot-box stuffing, miscounting, and rioting. Such tactics were normal in southern New Mexico in those days; some people think they still are.

The skirmishing in 1888 is more than ordinarily interesting, because it marks the beginning of the bitter personal rivalry between A. J. Fountain and A. B. Fall which kept the country in an uproar for years and sowed many seeds that bear fruit even to this day.

We begin with Albert Jennings Fountain, a man of many lives who gained a kind of immortality by losing the last one.

His career began in New York City on October 3, 1838.[1] His name was actually Albert Jennings, his father being Solomon Jennings, captain of a merchantman. His mother was a de la Fontaine of French Huguenot stock, originally from Paris.

Solomon had three sons—Edward, Albert, and John—and a daughter named Marguerite. John became an actor.[2] Marguerite married a Frenchman named Guion, owner of a steamship line. The Guions had two sons who later came out to New Mexico just in time to figure in the climax of Fountain's tragic drama.

Albert described his boyhood this way: "Albert J. Fountain received his education in the public schools of New York, where he made an enviable record. He won a prize that entitled him to a scholarship in Columbia College. While at Columbia he stood at the head of his classes, but on account of failing health was sent on a tour around the world with a tutor and five other students."[3]

There is no record of his matriculation at Columbia College[4]—a fact which makes one wonder how far to trust the rest of his account of his early years. One thing, however, is certain: however he accomplished it, he became a well-educated man with a fine command of ornate English.

The trip abroad must have taken place in 1857 or 1858. The six boys and their tutor saw southern Europe, the Nile country, the Holy Land. Returning to Rome, they pitched their tutor out for unspecified reasons and ran off to The Hague, where they presented themselves before the American Minister. He agreed to help them get home and sent them on to Liverpool.

Here a strange thing happened. Instead of going back to New York, the boys "slipped away" and took passage on an East Indiaman bound for Calcutta.

Tradition in the Fountain family says that this was not just a boyish whim. Albert was up to something all the time. Just before he left home, calamity had overtaken his father. We don't know what the calamity was, but it brought death to Solomon Jennings. The last letter he wrote to his wife—from somewhere in the Orient—complained that food was running out and the men were getting restless. Nothing was ever heard from him or his ship again. They disappeared from the face of the earth.

Much against the wishes of his family, Albert made up his mind to find out what had happened. He used the European tour as a means of getting away from home, and he intended all the time to try to trace his father along the China coast. In order not to give himself away, he took his mother's name and was known thenceforth as Albert Jennings Fountain.

The East Indiaman touched at Cape Town, and again the boys changed their minds. They went ashore and started to explore Africa on their own but were "recaptured" and carried to Calcutta according to plan. There they boarded a schooner bound for Hong Kong and found out too late that they were mixed up with a crew of smugglers. The Chinese officials arrested them and threw them in jail at Canton, where they stayed until the United States consul general applied enough pressure to get them out. The next stop was San Francisco, where the party broke up.

It must have been in 1859 that Albert Fountain, aged twenty, set foot on American earth again. The sky of California looked good to him. His globe-girdling and adventuring had stirred up something in him which only death could extinguish. The rest of his life was to be spent in far and perilous places, surrounded by strange people and tongues, with danger and difficulty on every side—to end in a nameless grave at last.

He liked the rowdy California town and started to build a career there. First he tried reporting, and was apparently good at it. The Sacramento *Union* sent him to Central America in 1860 to report the Walker filibustering expedition. Immediately he was in hot water again. His own version of the affair says he was arrested and condemned to be shot "for having communicated to his paper the true object of the expedition, which had been organized in the interest of slaveholders." Somehow he escaped—he merely says he "was aided" in getting away—and managed to get aboard a steamship where "he was disguised as a female by the lady passengers," so getting safely back to San Francisco.[5]

He was now ready to try something else. For some months he "read law" in the office of N. Greene Curtis and had just been admitted to the bar when the Civil War broke out. The drums began to beat. Young men everywhere signed on and marched away. In San Francisco the "California Column" of Union troops was organized, and when it left for the Rio Grande, Albert Fountain was there with a corporal's stripes on his arm. He says that his company was in the van during the long, hard march across the desert and that it defeated Cochise in a two-day battle at Apache Pass—110 soldiers against 1,200 Indians. By the time he reached New Mexico, he was a first sergeant, and on March 1, 1863, he was commissioned a second lieutenant.[6]

The Confederates had long since been driven out of the country, but the Apaches and Navajos were still to be subdued, and Fountain saw considerable skirmishing. In spite of hardship and danger, he very quickly decided to make this harsh and forbidding country his home, and as a first step to this end he married.

His wife was a fourteen-year-old girl named Mariana Pérez de Ovante whom he met when her brother, a member of his command, took him home for a visit. The wedding date was October 27, 1862. They seem to have been a devoted couple. Mariana depended on her husband absolutely, and he was both father and husband to her. What education she had, she owed to him, and he provided for her with tender solicitude. Since she was shy and retiring, he would send a wagon out to his home in later years with several dresses or other articles she was in need of so that she could make a selection without going to town. With twelve children, she had enough to do around the house without looking for activity elsewhere.

Fountain was discharged in 1865 but never thought of subsiding into peaceful pursuits. General Carleton made him a captain of cavalry and he organized a volunteer company of scouts to fight the Apaches and Navajos.[7] Wounded in Arizona, he was sent to El Paso to recuperate, and was very shortly in the middle of the turbid stream of Texas politics.

The boss of the region was W. W. Mills, collector of customs at El Paso, an intense, dynamic little man with a quick temper and a razor-sharp tongue. Before long, Fountain was made an inspector of customs and became Mills's chief assistant.

It was a hot spot to be in. Mills's group was held together in an uneasy alliance by the greed and ambition of several unscrupulous men. One was Louis Cardis, a smooth Italian who controlled the Mexican vote.[8] Another was Father Antonio Borrajo, parish priest of San Elizario, a white-haired, thin-faced, terrible-tempered old man who was absolute master in his own province. They all had their eyes on the great salt deposits at the foot of Guadalupe Peak, a hundred miles east of El Paso. These were considered public property by the Mexicans; consequently the "Salt Ring," as the group was known, did not dare make an open move to take them over. But they hoped and schemed.

For a while all went well, so well that Fountain took a leave of absence to join the forces of Benito Juarez in Mexico. He organized the *Juarista* artillery, ranking as a full colonel, and assisted at the storming of Chihuahua.[9]

Back in El Paso he found that his party had split. In 1868 A. J. Hamilton, Mills's father-in-law, was the "conservative" Republican candidate for governor. He was opposed by the "radical" E. J. Davis. Fountain supported Davis and ran for the State Senate, to the deep indignation of Mills. Davis and Fountain won. Mills was removed as collector of customs, and hell broke loose in El Paso.

Mills blamed Fountain for almost every misfortune which had come upon mankind since the Flood, attacked him in articles and pamphlets, and finally had him indicted in the United States District Court on eighteen separate counts. Fountain delayed the trial as long as possible but was finally forced into court in 1872, underwent a sensational examination, and was cleared.[10]

Meanwhile, the rift in the ring culminated in sudden death on December 7, 1870. B. F. Williams, a lawyer who belonged to the Mills faction and therefore hated Fountain, had too many drinks at Ben Dowell's saloon in El Paso and commenced abusing Fountain and District Judge Gaylord Judd Clarke. At the peak of the tirade Fountain happened to step in, and Williams opened fire on him with a derringer. Fountain defended himself with his cane as best he could, but was wounded twice. His derringer empty, Williams retreated to his room nearby and barricaded the door while Fountain stumbled home after his rifle. On the way he met Judge Clarke, who took charge at once.

First Clarke looked up Captain French of the State Police and ordered him to arrest Williams. The two went to Williams's room and told him he was under arrest. When he refused to come out, they tried to break the door down. Exasperated, he burst into the open with a shotgun and killed Clarke with a blast of buckshot. A pistol ball from French and a rifle shot at long range from Fountain finished Williams.

This could have been the beginning of feuding times in El Paso. There was much angry talk, and dire threats were aimed at Fountain. He was convinced that his life was worth very little as long as he stayed in Texas. And so, in 1875, when his term in the Legislature was up, he moved his family to Mesilla, New Mexico, and started a new life.[11]

Once established in Mesilla, Fountain carried on as usual. In a very short time he became a successful lawyer, preferring to take the side of the underdog, the defeated, and the oppressed. He talked good Spanish, befriended many an unhappy Mexican, and was known as a friend of the poor. This stood him in good stead politically, but he did not champion his *pobres* purely for political reasons. He had a deep sympathy for the race he had married into—simple and mostly gentle people who were proving no match for the rambunctious gringos who were taking their country away from them.[12] Fountain was a good fighter himself and he liked to defeat the buccaneers who had come to New Mexico to grab land or leadership or public office. Time after time he did defeat them, until he became the best-loved and most fiercely hated man in southern New Mexico. How he lived as long as he did was something of a miracle.

His best fighting, however, was done against the savages and desperadoes who plagued the country in the seventies and eighties. When Victorio began his raids in 1878, the citizens of Mesilla organized for defense and had some bloody skirmishes with the Apaches in the Kingston and Lake Valley country. Fountain's name does not appear in the accounts of these skirmishes, but when a firmer organization of militiamen seemed necessary to combat the red terror, he was considered the man to head it. He had several brushes with the redskins, two of which he later described in print,[13] but characteristically the Mescalero Apaches considered him one of their best friends. More than once he pleaded their cause as a lawyer,[14] and he had no more sincere mourners than the Mescaleros when he came to his death.

Even before Victorio's braves were over the horizon, the white desperadoes moved in. They were organized on the old Texas system. The gangs operated out of certain favorite hangouts—Socorro, Rincon, Kingston, Silver City—but they all worked together. No devilment was too low for them to

commit, but they specialized in running off horses and cattle
from the southern New Mexico counties and selling them in
Mexico. Similar gangs in Mexico brought their booty across
the line and sold it in the United States. This involved a good
deal of teamwork. And to further the depredations there were
sympathetic citizens in every town who protected the "boys"
and helped them to circumvent the law. It was expensive and
dangerous for the honest men. In the early eighties, petitions
went to the governor asking for help. Governor Sheldon responded by making Fountain a major of volunteer Cavalry
and giving him a free hand in putting down the evildoers.[15]

The militiamen, who were known as "Fountain's Greasers," first went after the Kinney Gang, which used the little
town of Rincon as a rendezvous. Rincon, in fact, was often called Kinneyville. Fountain's men killed Doroteo Saenz,
Kinney's lieutenant, captured other members of the gang, and
effectually broke up the thieves' ring.

Many a hair-raising chapter in Western history was enacted
in the course of these operations. Few details have been
handed down, but one story has survived to show how things
went.

It seems that one of Kinney's aides escaped. He was a tough
specimen—called himself "the Human Tiger" and swore that
he would kill Fountain if it was the last thing he did. Word of
these threats came to Fountain's ears; also the fact that the
Tiger was hiding in a part of El Paso then known as Concordia. Fountain, now a colonel, went after him on the morning train and had him aboard a northbound coach, safely man-
acled, by midafternoon.

George W. Baylor, the Ranger captain, was standing on the
platform as they came up to the train and noticed that Fountain's pistol was loose in its holster.

"You might get in trouble carrying your gun that way," he
advised. "Why don't you do like the Rangers—tie your gun to
your belt so you can't lose it?"

He took the cord from his own equipment, looping one end around Fountain's pistol and tying the other to Fountain's belt.

As the train carrying Fountain and the prisoner approached Fillmore station, the colonel saw a friend at the front of the coach and stepped forward to salute him. The prisoner took advantage of the opportunity to break for the rear platform and jump off. Fountain was right behind him, and they both landed rolling like tumbleweeds.

The Tiger was forty yards or so away, and when Fountain righted himself, his man was heading for the mesquite brush and liberty. Fountain reached for his gun. It had fallen out of the holster. But Baylor's cord was still attached, and the pistol was quickly brought to hand. As the prisoner cleared a little rise and was silhouetted against the darkening sky, Fountain dropped to his knees and took a two-handed aim, and that was the end of the Human Tiger.[16]

It must be confessed that this episode was described differently by men who didn't care for Fountain. Albert Fall told it to a Pinkerton operative this way:

Judge Fall . . . turned loose by first saying that he would state his position in this case; he did not like Col. Fountain any more than he did a snake; he had had dealings with him and the man was not straight and he would mould witnesses and testimony to suit his case; "he is a man who has killed several men and I will cite you one case to show you what kind of a man he was. He was conveying a prisoner for horse stealing over a line of railroad down here some years ago and at that time his son Albert was a Col. in the Militia down here; the prisoner was said to have tried to escape and was shot dead by Col. Fountain as he got off the train; Fountain said he was 90 steps from the car when he shot and killed him, but the truth of this statement was that Col. Fountain when they came in sight of the camp fires of the militia told the prisoner that the fires belonged to the militia and that it was their intention to take him from the train and hang him and he

(Fountain) advised him to drop off the train when it slowed up and get away and that he was his friend and would assist him to do this and did get the conductor of the train to slow up and the prisoner who still wore handcuffs dropped off the front platform and Col. Fountain stood on the steps of the rear platform and shot him dead as he came up to him on the road where he had dropped off; the body was powder burned so he could not have shot him at 90 steps away as he stated. Now this is only one of many cases in which this man has done dirty work." [17]

Kinney himself was captured at Lordsburg and brought back to Las Cruces by Colonel Fountain in person. He was tried and sent to Leavenworth, though he did not stay long.[18]

There was barely time for Fountain to catch his breath before his attention was claimed by a bold band of rustlers working the country near Hillsboro. Toby Johnson, Joe Askew, Tom Cooper, Joe Hubert, Charles "Tex" Hall, and others had to get out or give up. Some of the gang are alleged to have departed this life at a rope's end, but there is no real evidence to show that Fountain ever took Judge Lynch's short cut to justice. He may have, and he may not.

Then came the "Farmington Gang," which hid out at an isolated spring in the Black Range—the Kingston Gang—several independent operators. What happened to them was quick and final: John Watts, killed trying to escape; William Leland, shot down on the run; John Coleville, taken prisoner, and so on. Some escaped to Mexico, but they all ceased to function as outlaws.[19]

Governor Thornton was impressed by Fountain's success in suppressing lawlessness "effectually in two months." His fellow citizens took up a collection and gave him a magnificent silver service that is still in the possession of his descendants.[20]

Between campaigns he carried on his regular law business. He defended Billy the Kid in the famous trial at Mesilla in 1881. In February 1886 he accepted an appointment as Assistant United States District Attorney to help as special counsel in putting a stop to the land frauds which were plaguing the Territory.

Again he had to fight. One R. P. Walker sent a letter to Commissioner Sparks of the General Land office, who passed it on to Attorney General Garland, who in turn sent it to United States Attorney Thomas Smith for investigation. Smith simply mailed the letter to Fountain, withholding the author's name. It read in part as follows:

Now this man Fountain, I understand, was leader of the worst element of carpetbag society in Texas before coming here.

About nine months ago when the district court was in session, he was accused openly and in fact it was common street talk, that he had received a bribe of one thousand dollars in three separate cases, to suppress indictments against cattlemen, and land-jumpers who, if they had to receive their just deserts would most assuredly have gone to the Penitentiary.[21]

Justifiably furious, Fountain fired off a long reply dated September 10, 1887, which exemplifies his command of vigorous English and his hobnailed personality.

If it is intended to charge that any person ever "Openly accused" me in my presence of having accepted a bribe, I denounce the assertion as a wilful and malicious falsehood. It is true that during the political campaign of 1886, when I was a candidate for election to the Territorial legislature, my political opponents did fabricate and secretly circulate such a charge, and it is also true that when I was informed that such charges were being circulated, I "openly" denounced the charge as a malicious lie, and its originators and circulators as liars. I made extraordinary efforts to trace this slander to its source, and finally succeeded in trailing it into the camp of my political opponent, who heard it somewhere on the streets. . . . I was retained by the Government to assist you in certain cases, in all of those cases indictments were returned by the grand jury. Some of the indicted parties pleaded guilty, others were tried and acquitted, and the cases of a number of others are pending in court. Several of these parties sought to retain me for the defense and tendered me a retainer fee of one thousand dollars in each case. This perhaps is the foundation of the report above quoted, if it ever had foundation outside the fertile imagination of the nameless slanderer whose letter I am now answering. . . .

It is charged that at the opening of the last campaign, I was a candidate for the legislature on the Republican ticket, "and spent the very money paid him (me) by a democratic administration to defeat it &c."

It is quite true that I was a candidate for election to the Territorial legislature on the Republican ticket at the last election and had I been elected I have no doubt that I would have succeeded in making a better record than was made by the gentleman who defeated me. I have at least the gratification of knowing that I resorted to no such methods as he to secure an election. As to the expenditure of money during that election I have only to say that what money I expended was my own, and was expended for legitimate purposes, and it is an impertinence to question me on that subject. Had the government seen proper to have paid me for my services as assistant U. S. Attorney, I should have had more to have expended in that election. . . . But this malicious slanderer when he wrote the charge "that I spent the very money paid me by a democratic administration to defeat it &c" was quite ignorant of the fact that the "democratic administration" has never paid me one dollar of compensation for the services I have rendered under my appointment, as your assistant, although I have frequently written the department on the subject. . . . I cannot, consistently with my view of what is due me in my professional character, remain longer in a position that imposes upon me the humiliating necessity of answering and refuting charges based upon conjecture and "street talk" that every nameless enemy inspired by hatred or revenge may see fit to bring against me. . . . In severing my connection with the cases in which I have been associated with you, I desire to express my deep sense of gratification at your assurance that you have never been affected by the imputations upon my integrity. . . .

I remain, very respectfully,
A. J. Fountain

Shaken by such a verbal blast, United States Attorney Smith hastened to assure Fountain that he had the highest respect for his "fidelity, zeal, efficiency and ability" and begged him to reconsider. Fountain did.[22]

As if all these alarms and excursions were not enough to keep him busy, Fountain spent part of his time editing a newspaper. Early in 1877, with John S. Crouch and Thomas Casad, he founded the Mesilla *Independent*. The files of this paper for 1878-1879 have survived and much can be learned about the editor's personality from his weekly editorializing.

He loved to print an occasional column of reminiscences, usually playing himself up as the leading actor in some exciting episode of frontier days. He was violently anti-Jesuit and did not hesitate to take the hide off some members of the Catholic priesthood when he felt like it, though this distressed his wife and family. Politics, of course, was the breath of life to him, and he never failed to take a positive stand on every issue.

The figure which emerges from all this brushwork is that of a public-spirited and useful citizen who liked to have the world know about his exploits—a man who enjoyed his enmities almost as much as he loved his friendships and went forth to battle with joy—a big-hearted show-off who surprised people by turning out to be as good as he said he was.

They say that he liked to wear his militia uniform in the courtroom when he was pleading a case—that he loved to organize parades and make speeches in both Spanish and English on the Fourth of July, working up to a throbbing climax over *la bandera, nos madres,* and *la patria.* They whisper that he was a tricky lawyer and that he disposed of suspected cattle rustlers with more dispatch than legality. But you will never hear anybody say that he was lacking in sheer cold courage, that he could be bought, or that he could be intimidated. He had enemies, lots of enemies, who despised everything he did and stood for, but in New Mexico in those days it was necessary to have enemies, and it was a credit to a person to have the right ones.

In 1888 Fountain accepted the invitation of the Republicans to run for the Territorial Legislature. This was a turning point in his life, although the campaign was outwardly no different from a dozen others he had engaged in. The two parties bristled and pawed the ground and flung mud as usual. The Mesilla and Las Cruces Republicans formed a club and voted to wear uniforms.[23] The Democrats howled loudly when Fountain announced his candidacy and somebody raked up the business of his record in Texas. The old war horse accepted the challenge, defended himself in the columns of the *Republican*, and expressed the "most profound contempt" [24] for his traducers. He took note with indifference when the Democratic Club met in September to nominate a slate of candidates and put up a comparative newcomer named Albert B. Fall to run against him.

The Rise of Albert Fall

IT WAS hard times for Albert Fall in 1888. Money was short. His wife was still ailing. He was a stranger in a strange land. To make the thing complete he decided to go into politics.

He was the only one who thought he had a chance to win in that election, but the leaders of his party were happy to let him try. It did seem that Colonel Fountain, his opponent, would have to exert himself to lose. Fountain was an old hand at the game, had the Mexican vote in his pocket, and was backed by a potent political machine.

There was always a chance for a political underdog, however. Since both sides practiced every known form of skulduggery, it was possible that one or the other would be found out and exposed. Sure losers fought to the last ditch, hoping for a last-minute break.

Fall could hardly have been more than a question mark to many of the voters. The *Republican* jeeringly remarked that he had not been around long enough "to change his shirt." [1]

On the other hand, he had some notable qualifications for

68

leadership in this new country. Tall and handsome, with polished manners and complete self-assurance, he was always the Southern gentleman even in those days when poverty and illness were dogging him and his family. He had a keen mind and a talent for the intrigue and horse trading that go with politics. And he was a man of intense personal pride and ambition.

He had not yet learned to dramatize himself as he did later on, but he looked the part he had chosen to play. He wore his rich, wavy hair long and topped it with a broad-brimmed black Stetson. He wore starched and gleaming linen and set off his fine figure with a Prince Albert coat. He carried a cane and sometimes he used it on his enemies. There was self-confidence in his carriage, a quizzical gleam in his eye.

He could make speeches full of sound and fury, but he preferred to underplay his role. In the courtroom he never ranted. Quietly, humorously, he pursued a witness to confusion, glancing occasionally at the jury over the tops of his glasses with geniality. Actually he was a masterly actor with a wonderful sense of timing.

In 1888, of course, he had come only a little way down the long road which began for him in Frankfort, Kentucky, on November 26, 1861. His father was William Fall, a captain in General Forrest's regiment of Confederate cavalry who took up teaching after the war. Times were difficult; the family was poor. Albert did not get much formal schooling and had to go to work at the age of eleven in a Nashville cotton mill.[2] At first he intended to be a preacher, like his grandfather,[3] but in his late teens he began to study law instead. For two years he taught school by day and plowed through heavy tomes by night. Then his health failed and he decided to move to a milder climate in the West.[4] After taking leave of Judge William Lindsley (later United States senator from Kentucky), in whose offices he had been laboring, he drifted through Arkansas and Oklahoma to the Red River country in

Texas. At Clarksville, near Texarkana, he established a second home.

He did everything—farming, cowboying, clerking in a grocery store. For a while he is said to have functioned as a chuck-wagon cook.[5] After a year of this, when he was twenty-one, he turned up as a mucker in a mine at Nieves, Mexico.

This was his introduction to mining, a business which never ceased to fascinate him and in which he dabbled for much of his life. He graduated to the post of timberman and eventually became a foreman.[6]

He interrupted his mining, however, to attend to some unfinished business in Clarksville. He opened a small office, where he dealt in real estate and insurance, and in his spare time he courted Emma Morgan, daughter of a prominent local lawyer. Emma was a tall, stately young lady of eighteen. She was impressed by the dash and determination of her new suitor, but Albert Fall was not anybody in particular—yet; and besides she was as good as engaged to another man. She said no. Then she went to visit relatives in Tennessee to avoid further complications.

Fall was no man to be put off by such tactics. He made it to Tennessee almost as soon as Emma did, and on May 8, 1883, they were married at Woodville.[7] Fall could not have made a better choice. No man ever had a more loyal or helpful wife.

The newlyweds ran into difficulties. Fall started a grocery store to supplement his income and had bad luck with it.[8] Late in 1883 he was back in the mining business in Mexico and was apparently doing well when a rumor came to him which started his career off on a new tack.

West of the Rio Grande, in Grant and Sierra counties, New Mexico, precious metals were coming out of the ground in exciting quantities. Prospectors and hard-rock miners were swarming in. Rawhiders from other states were cluttering up the landscape. Some, at least, of the immigrants were making money, and Albert Fall decided that this might be the chance he was looking for. When the first through train reached El Paso from Mexico City early in May, he was a passenger, and as soon as horseflesh could get him there, he set up his camp at Kingston in the eastern foothills of the Black Range.

He did not get rich, but he learned plenty and made some interesting contacts. One young man who impressed him was Edward L. Doheny, in those days a tough young prospector—later a multimillionaire oil man who was crucified with Fall as a result of the scandals of the Harding administration.

The story goes that Fall first noticed Doheny when the latter was being chased by a trigger-happy drunk. Doheny ducked and dodged in and out of doors on Kingston's main street. When the time was ripe, he potted the drunk in the leg. Fall was the first man to congratulate him on his coolness and nerve, and the friendship formed at that moment lasted the rest of their lives.[9]

Back in Clarksville, Emma Fall kept the home together and waited for Albert to strike it rich. She had to carry the burden, since her husband could come home only infrequently. After three years and two babies, her health gave way. The doctors said she had the galloping consumption and advised a change of climate. Albert determined to move his family to New Mexico, where the dry, clear air sometimes worked wonders for consumptives.

It was a desperate measure. There was little money. The trip would be long and hard. And who would care for these strangers once they arrived? Emma's unmarried brother Joe Morgan solved the problem for them. He said he would come along and help—so the trek began. It ended at Las Cruces, where Emma seemed better. While she was resting for dear life, Joe Morgan took care of the children and

the house, and Albert rustled for a living. He formed a partnership in real estate with a man named Lowry and began
brushing up on his law.

A man of Fall's talents could hardly have missed success as
the country developed, but he hated to wait for distinction.
If there was a short cut, he meant to take it; and politics
looked like a possible short cut. After all, New Mexico was
new and unexploited. There were laws to be made and reg-
ulations to be set up. The Territorial Legislature was a door
to power and influence. Rashly, perhaps, but courageously he
decided to oppose Fountain in the contest for a seat in the
House.

The results were humiliating to a man as proud and sensitive as Fall. He campaigned vigorously, but he was not yet
familiar with the eye-gouging techniques of frontier politicians. Later he became a masterly infighter, but in 1888 he
was a very young Samson among some very tough Philis-
tines.

Toward the middle of October his campaign brought him
to a rally in Tularosa where, according to the opposition
press, he made a poor showing.

Fall, Beer, and Hatton, the democratic triumvirate, addressed an
audience last Tuesday at Guile's hall of about a hundred persons
of an equal proportion of democrats and republicans. The "unknown" who is entered against the talented and accomplished
Fountain in the race for the legislature, made but a poor showing
and instead of falling like a brilliant meteor in our midst he more
resembled the dark and threatening cloud which hangs o'er our
mountain tops. Who is he? and where does he come from? were
the queries heard on all sides. He displayed neither the gift of
oratory, nor a knowledge of the wants of the people whose votes
he solicited and whose interests he desired to represent. There was
a marked feeling of disappointment visible among the democratic
portion of the audience, which was demonstrated in the cold and

passive manner in which the remarks of the speakers were received.[10]

Was it such discouraging moments as these that made Fall so ruthless later on, so determined not to lose? It was certainly a bleak time for him and his party. The Democrats were struggling up the slope while the Republicans were sitting firmly and confidently on the summit, deriding the futile efforts of their adversaries.

A typical episode occurred on a certain Sunday when the Democratic Club paraded (with a band) through the streets of Las Cruces and Mesilla. The Republicans pretended to be shocked, and pointed out that this was a violation of the ordinance prohibiting Sunday meetings "except for religious purposes."

"What a disgraceful thing it is," they jeered, "to see . . . nearly all of the prominent Democratic officials openly desecrating the Sabbath and defiantly violating the law they are sworn to support. Republicans never do such things." [11]

When the ballots were counted, Fountain had won—but his plurality of forty-two votes out of more than 2,000 was much too close for comfort.[12] He knew he had been in a fight; what he did not realize was that the real battle was just beginning. Serene in victory, he entered upon his duties at Santa Fe and was promptly elected Speaker of the House.

As for Fall, the close vote was no balm to his lacerated soul. He hated defeat, and he was beginning to hate Fountain.

It was inevitable that these two men should be in opposition. They were poles apart in almost every way. Fountain was a Yankee. Fall was a Southerner. Fountain was already middle-aged and a power in the land. Fall was young and ambitious, with his spurs still to win. Fountain had married a Mexican wife and from Fall's standpoint had "gone native," identifying himself with the Spanish-speaking group, fighting their battles, talking their language, taking their point of view. Fall instinctively leaned toward the Texans and the immigrants who, like him, were trying to make a stake in the new region.

They were both proud, egocentric, fearless, but they had nothing else in common.

Fountain at first liked Fall and considered him a promising young attorney[13] but soon came to think of him as an unscrupulous opportunist who would stop at nothing. Fall, on the other hand, was convinced that Fountain was shifty and dishonest, a political trickster, a boaster, and a fourflusher.

The first round, the election of 1888, was Fountain's. About all the vanquished candidate could do at the moment was to strengthen his muscles in case the fight should be resumed, and this Fall proceeded to do. He and his partner Lowry began an advertising campaign in March 1889 describing themselves as "Real Estate, Stock and Mine Brokers." [14] A month later Fall finished his toil over the law books and was admitted to the bar.[15] But when some of the Democratic leaders suggested that he run for sheriff in the elections of 1890, he gave them a rather horrified No, declaring that "his experience in the last election has satisfied him for a lifetime." [16]

Ambition was still smoldering in him, however, and he squared off against Fountain again in the race for the State Legislature. The Republicans heaped scorn upon him: "A. B. Fall is a pigmy and a baby beside Col. Fountain and would be a nonentity in the Legislature—absolutely worthless to anybody." In retaliation, Fall put on a campaign which pushed him far ahead of all opposition. When it was over and Fountain had come in third, all the Republicans could do was to shout accusations of shame and debauchery: "free whiskey weeks before and up to the hour of election . . . over fifty illegal votes." [17]

It was a good start, but Fall was no man to be satisfied with only one iron in the fire. When his father came out from Kentucky to see him, they took Joe Morgan and went prospecting in the Organs and the Sacramentos.[18] It was the beginning of a long career in the mines of New Mexico—buying claims, staking prospectors, hoping to get rich.

During these days he first thought of starting a newspaper.[19] He needed to control public opinion. How could he do it better than through an editorial column of his own? He broached the matter to his father, and the result appeared a little later when the first issue of the Las Cruces *Independent Democrat* came off the presses with W. R. Fall's name appearing as editor.

Law business was improving too. By 1890 the mountain people and their cousins on the Tularosa flats were beginning to look to Fall for legal counsel, though most of those tough Texans habitually took counsel with a six-shooter. Mostly they were worried about water. One case during the May term of court brought W. A. Miley in from the Peñasco on the eastern slope of the Sacramentos. He was suing James Gerald and half a dozen others, charging them with taking water out of the river above his ditch. He wanted the court to rule that, since he got there first, he had priority. The defendants maintained that they had as much right to tap the stream as he did.[20]

Miley's lawyers were Rynerson and Wade, with Fountain backing up the line—all die-hard Republicans. Gerald was defended by the firm of Fall and Young. "Deacon" Young, a rather sanctimonious Democrat, was to become a useful player on the Fall team later on.

For the first time it was Fall against Fountain in the courtroom—Fountain at ease, switching from Spanish to English and back again, enjoying the sound of his big voice; Fall intense and determined, watching for every joint in his foe's armor. It was the first of many such scenes.

Mining, law, politics—Fall worked at them all as he prepared himself for bigger things. But the biggest stone that went into his foundation fell into place by itself in 1889. He was in his office one day, busy as usual, when a calm, ramrod-straight young man in dusty boots and a white Stetson stepped in. "My name is Oliver Lee," he said. "I'm looking for Mr. Fall."

"Fall is my name," Albert replied. "I've heard of you, Mr. Lee, and I'm glad to see you."

It was the beginning of a grand alliance. They had much in common, and before long they had become indispensable to each other. Fall was soon acting as the "inside man" of the team—lawyer and strategist. Lee was the "outside man"— captain of the fighting force, man of action. The troublous times that were even then just beyond the threshold drew them together "with hoops of steel." [21] It was rumored that they and their supporters were pledged to each other by oaths which it was death to break.[22] Such stories must be discounted, but one thing is sure: the friendship was closer than most blood brotherhoods, and it lasted as long as they lived.

The election of 1892 showed how effective the combination was. Fall was running again, and he was playing all the angles. His following was composed of Democrats and anybody else who would get on the band wagon. Everything that could be done to get out the vote had been done. In fact Fall had managed so well that the Republicans decided they would have to take extreme measures. They called out the militia to "guard the polls."

This was more than Fall had foreseen or bargained for. He flew about Las Cruces trumpeting that his wicked adversaries meant to intimidate honest voters and control the election, and just to make sure of an even break he sent a messenger off for Oliver Lee and his cowboys.

Lee and his fighting men rode all night, got into Las Cruces at daybreak, and were ready for business before the Republicans knew what was going on.

The polls had been set up in the old Masonic Temple. Across the street was Martin Lohman's huge, flat-roofed, one-story store building. Lohman, though nominally a Republican, was a friend of Fall's and provided scenery for the next act.

Among Lohman's employees was a rugged little Austrian immigrant named Henry Stoes who had taken to American life and politics without a hitch. He had been out on a trip the day before and knew nothing of the trouble. Early in the morning of that election day he came downtown and headed for the rear of the store where Lohman had a row of rooms for his unmarried help. He heard someone say to him, "You'd better take a look at the roof."

He looked—and saw that the adobe parapet of the store building was lined with riflemen. Every gun and cartridge in the store was up there waiting to be used. One shot and there would have been a bloody mess.[23]

The next thing anybody knew, the militiamen, under W.H.H. Llewellyn and Captain Thomas Brannigan, were marching up the street preparing to take position near the polls. They came closer, and the spectators held their breaths. Then Albert Fall stepped out into the street raising his arms and his voice. His impassioned remarks are said to have concluded: "Llewellyn, get the hell out of here with that damned militia or I will have you all killed."[24]

His arm was pointing rigidly to the rooftop where Lee and his men stood at the ready. Llewellyn and Brannigan gazed, pondered briefly, and led the militiamen back to where they had come from.

Fall got the votes that time. The Republicans immediately raised a cry of fraud. They swore that Fall had packed the polls and had even voted men from outside the United

States.[25] Their indignation got them nowhere, however. Fall went on to Santa Fe.

In the Territorial legislative councils he soon won a reputation for pugnacity spiced with a sort of formal courtesy. At the end of the session he graciously called for a vote of thanks to his Republican colleagues, moving the Santa Fe *New Mexican* to remark: "Mr. Fall is a hard and at times a bitter fighter but he has the courtesy of a brave man. His future is bright, and the old war horses of his party had best beware." [26]

Other things came his way, illustrating the old saying that "Them as has, gits." In that same year he was made judge of the Third Judicial District (Sierra, Grant, and Doña Ana Counties) and held the office till 1895, at which time he resigned—some say under pressure.

Meanwhile his friends in the Tularosa country were in the midst of terribly hard times and the whole region was moving slowly toward a little civil war with Fall and Fountain taking charge behind the opposing breastworks.

Cow Trouble

Sooner or later in desert country there is going to be a long, long drought, and when the rainless years come, everybody suffers. The nesters and hoe men go broke first. The cattlemen hang on to the last shred of endurance, and then they go broke too. A few lucky ones come through with their shirts. The rest just try to stay alive till it rains and they can start over.

The year 1888 was the last good year in the Tularosa country. In the summer of 1889 a three-year drought set in which caught people unprepared. Before this catastrophe, when grass was lush on the valley floor and plenty of water came down from the mountain slopes, many would-be farmers settled near Tularosa and La Luz, hoping to make the desert blossom. They threw up shacks and ran crazy fences around their gardens and chicken coops. The old-timers knew from the beginning that they were doomed, but nobody could tell the farmers anything.

Then came the excitement over the proposed El Paso and White Oaks railroad, and more settlers crowded in. It would

be ten long years before a locomotive whistle was heard in
that lonesome corner of creation, but the mere mention of
the word "railroad" was enough to start a boom. When it was
learned in the spring of 1888 that surveyors were actually
laying out the right-of-way, the United States Land Office in
Las Cruces was swamped with business. People from Tularosa, El Paso, Las Cruces rushed in to make entries on government land.[1]

Immediately the optimists in Tularosa began to look for
the millennium. Their little village, so far from civilization
and so torn by feuds and strife, was going to be orderly and
prosperous at last. The local boosters let it be known that this
was the garden spot of the universe. Cornstalks grew twelve
feet high, watermelons weighed forty pounds, beets weighed
twenty. Eighteen miles up the creek at Mescalero Dr. Blazer
had produced a sixty-four-pound cabbage.[2]

The population doubled in four weeks that spring,[3] and
with the immigrants came visions of a brave new world—the
Tularosa Canyon lined with smelters and factories, the plain
burgeoning with green fields, and the settlers rolling in
money.[4]

The dream was short-lived. By 1890 the cattle were "dying
by hundreds." Water holes were full of dead animals. On
Three Rivers the running water was full of maggots from the
carcasses fouling the stream above.[5] Long before this the hoe
men had begun to drift away, though many of them were reduced to eating other men's beef and breaking the law in
other ways before they gave up. They added their mite to the
tide of lawlessness that was rising higher and higher in the
nineties, though only a few old-timers now can remember
where their shanties rose out on the flats below Tularosa
and La Luz.[6]

Gene Rhodes lived through the drought, and it left a brand
on him. Years later, when he was living far away in a green
and prosperous land, that long agony was still on his mind.

Some of his stories deal with the last-ditch efforts of cow-men trying to save their herds.

"Strained, haggard and grim, August burned to a close in a dumb terror of silence. September, with days unchanging, flaming, intolerable, desperate: last and irretrievable ruin hovered visible over the forlorn and glaring levels. Twice and again clouds banked black against the hills with lightning flash and thunder, only to melt away and leave the parched land to despair." [7] That was the way he remembered it.

The panic of 1893 did not help matters at all. And hard times naturally gave an extra nudge to the lawlessness which was already tormenting the region. There were shootings over range rights and water. Rustling and brand blotting were on the increase. By 1893, the year the drought ended, a miniature war was in the making among the yuccas and creo-sote bushes. On one side were the little ranchers and farmers —mostly from Texas—and their friends. On the other were the big ranchers, the town politicians, and some of the older settlers.

The Texans said that the big cattle companies, with the lawyers and sheriffs on their side, were trying to gobble up the whole country and run the little men out of business. The company men accused the Texans of wholesale rustling, with intimidation and murder on the side.

They named Oliver Lee as the leader of the small operators. Tom Tucker and Cherokee Bill were still with him, and he had added Bill McNew and Jim Gililland to the inner circle. McNew, a tough Texan with ice-blue eyes, had come down from the mountains to work for Lee. The golf course at Cloudcroft is on the site of Grandpa McNew's potato patch. Bill had married Nettie Fry when she recovered a little from her grief over George McDonald's death, thereby estab-lishing himself as a member of the clan. Gililland, late of Brownwood and the cattle ranges of central Texas, was younger than McNew and another hard-fighting, iron-nerved Texan. He was a tall, lanky, rather good-looking boy and quite agreeable when he hadn't had one drink too many. He wanted to prove that he was not afraid of anything, however, and that makes a man dangerous.

Albert Fall was the friend and defender of these men, and it lost him the friendship of many good people in the towns. They thought he had sold out to the enemy. On the other hand the small farmers and ranchers in the Sacramentos and down on the flats, scrambling hard for survival in a rough country, were always devoted to both Fall and Lee, regarding them as leaders in the unending battle to keep the rich from increasing their wealth at the expense of the poor. Even now, says Thomas Fortune Ryan, owner of Fall's old ranch, "You'd better not say anything against Fall around here or you're liable to get shot." [8]

In trying to understand such opposite attitudes toward the same situation, we come back to the proposition that two different sets of folkways were in collision here. Each side played by a different set of rules and judged by different values. They lived in contact; they rubbed elbows and spoke the same language, but their notions about such things as property, law courts, and murder were strangely at variance. We know well enough how the townspeople felt about these things. Most of us, including the sons and grandsons of the men from Texas, feel the same way about them today. But if the troubles of Tularosa are to make any sense at all, we have to look very closely at the code which the Texans brought across the Pecos with their horses and their cows and their six-shooters. The whole system began with the cow.

Hardly anybody expected to eat his own beef. Strays and mavericks were always waiting to be butchered. And if you did not like a man or had had words with him, you felt a justification in taking the hide off one of his strays, arguing to yourself that he was probably doing the same for you—

as he undoubtedly was. It had been that way in Texas in open-range days when cattle were worth little, and nobody thought much about it. Later on, when the price of beef went up, there was bound to be trouble.

Everybody looked for unclaimed calves, figuring, as one of Gene Rhodes's characters put it, "that if there was any mavericks persecutin' and perusin' around, I might as well have 'em as anybody." [9]

In another passage Rhodes tells more about how the custom of mavericking operated:

In practice, if a bunch of us start up a maverick, the man swingin' the fastest loop puts his mark on, the rest of us setting on the yearlin's head, while the lucky one brands it. Of course, as a matter of courtesy, the man ownin' the range has the preference—if he catches the critter first.

And that's all right, all right, all right. But human nature is mighty similar. From branding a sure-enough maverick to getting a calf that has ambitions to be one as soon as his mammy weans him, is a mighty short step, if you're alone at the time. A bunch of you see a long-ear ten months old, take after him, and waste him. Seems like a short yearlin' is the hardest thing there is to put your rope on, in the brush. But the next day any one of the bunch sees the same calf, rising fifteen months old now, and he doesn't get away none whatever. Nor his mammy ain't with him either, along toward the last.[10]

Gene Rhodes was Oliver Lee's friend. He saw the problem with a cattleman's eyes. But even an outsider in that country soon came to realize that the blacks were not all black and the whites were not all white. Bill Orme-Johnson, an Englishman who came to the White Oaks region in 1904 and became a first-class deputy sheriff, put it this way:

The average cattleman was honest according to his ethical standards. He wouldn't steal your cow, but he mavericked—and they all did it. He wouldn't take from a little cattleman either, but the

big herds were legitimate prey. Of course one of these men was
plenty sore if he caught somebody working on him, but he would
turn around and do the same thing. Of course it wasn't so simple
to know whom a calf belonged to, and just because it was following a particular cow didn't always prove too much. The men were
sometimes pretty hard customers, and you had to do pretty much
as they did or you soon found yourself an outsider.[11]

Mavericking was not the only source of trouble. The Tularosa cattlemen had other customs which brought on mis-
understandings and worse. One was "accommodation branding." A man on roundup who found a calf following a
neighbor's cow was expected to brand the calf in the owner's
brand. Well, what happened if the calf was not at the moment following any cow with apparent seriousness? Or what
if the cow looked like one of yours and you suspected that her
brand had been altered? All sorts of doubtful situations arose
which led to hard feelings.[12]

Mrs. Lee, Oliver Lee's mother, had her own way of saying
it: "Nobody can ever understand the happenings in New
Mexico unless he has watched somebody trying to take his
living away from him." [13]

All this may serve as a warning to the movie fans who
think cattlemen are divided into two groups: fine, honest
citizens, and low, dirty crooks. It wasn't that simple. The
bloodshed and sorrow of the Tularosa valley should not be
presented as a Hollywood scenario where the rustlers are
hardened in sin and the good men are good to the core. In
real life the villains and the honest men seemed to get mixed
up together on both sides. The more one knows about what
went on, the more one hesitates to pass positive judgments
about who was right and who was wrong. And always one
has to remember that this was a game in which each side used
a different rule book.

A typical skirmish was fought between the "big fish" and
the "little fish" in 1894. It was a rainy year and there was a

large wet-weather lake near Cox's well at the north end of
the Jarillas. The men at the big Blue Water ranch turned loose
5,000 head of cattle to take advantage of it. They planned to
bring in 4,000 goats also, but Lee and his neighbors got wind
of it and turned the herd back at the top of the mesa. Repeatedly they notified Garst, the corporation manager, to
get his stock off their range. He paid no attention.

The men he sent periodically to check the herd, however,
noted after a while that a good many animals had disappeared. As a result, Garst got his cows out of there and
made a great fuss about the rustlers who were bleeding him
to death; he said nothing about his own contribution to the
misunderstanding.[14] The rights and wrongs of such a situation
were, to say the least, ambiguous.

Leaving all borderline cases aside, the country had more
than enough bona-fide wickedness to go around. And as
the nineties added one year to another, it got worse. There
was so much rustling and brand blotting that the big outfits
were seriously handicapped. It was particularly bad all
through the Tularosa country, but operations extended far
to the west and down into Mexico. There was big stealing and
little stealing. Small-time thieves would sell beef occasionally
to the butcher shops in the towns—beef which could be
bought for five cents a pound. Much rustled stock, particularly horses, was run into Mexico; many brands were altered
in the interest of building up somebody's herd.

Ironically, the man who got credit among the town men
for leading the small operators in the Tularosa country was
the first to have serious trouble. By 1893 Oliver Lee had extended his range past the southern point of the Sacramentos, and his stock wandered even farther. Sometimes his
cattle wandered so far they didn't get back.

One Sunday morning in February, George Gaither and
his son Carl, well known El Pasoans, were camping at Hueco
Tanks, thirty miles east of their home. Tremendous rock

formations, Indian caves, a reservoir of cool water, and plenty of game made the Tanks a favorite spot for such excursions. Carl's friend Maury Kemp had planned to come along, but for some reason didn't get to go. He had a .44-caliber rifle, however, which the Gaithers borrowed and took with them.

About midmorning Oliver Lee and Bill McNew rode into the Gaithers' camp and asked if they had seen a herd of cattle.

"No," said George; "no cattle have come near us."

"Well," Lee remarked to McNew, "I guess we'll have to go back to the mouth of the canyon and pick up the trail." Then he noticed the rifle and said to George, "I may have to do some fighting. Could I borrow that gun?"

George and Carl talked it over and decided that Maury wouldn't mind having them lend his rifle. They passed it over with all the spare cartridges they had.

The two men headed north, picked up the trail of the missing cow herd, and followed it at a steady trot. They traveled northwest, straight for the Anthony Pass and the Las Cruces country. Then, twenty miles out of El Paso, about where the little station of Newman is now, the tracks turned sharply south and headed for the Rio Grande, which was low at that time and easy to cross. It looked as if the stock was being taken into Mexico.

The men pushed their horses harder and came within sight of the herd. Two cowboys were easing them along. They stopped when the pursuers got close enough to be dangerous. It was about where the El Paso Municipal Airport is now.

No introductions were necessary. Matt Coffelt and Charley Rhodius were well known to Lee and McNew—both of them from the Crow Flats beyond the Huecos. Rhodius was a good-looking, red-headed, unattached cowboy in his early thirties who had taken up a little spring at the foot of the flat-topped mountain in the Cornudas. Coffelt's family lived nearby and his brother owned a ranch.[15] Neither of the boys had a bad reputation.

Things happened very fast for a few minutes. Lee said later that he went into the herd to cut out the stock that belonged to him and that Rhodius shot at him when his back was turned. The bullet missed. Lee turned and fired, fast and accurately as usual, and finished Rhodius. Coffelt tried to get in on the play and survived only a few seconds longer.[16]

As soon as the thing was settled, Lee rode into El Paso and reported what had happened. He telegraphed at once to Albert Fall in Las Cruces and got him to take over the case as soon as he could come. There were no indictments.

It was typical of Lee that just as soon as his telegram had gone off to Las Cruces, he returned Maury Kemp's rifle to Gaither's store and butcher shop as he had promised when he borrowed it.

The last reminder of this regrettable business is now buried in sand somewhere in an abandoned part of Concordia Cemetery in El Paso. Rhodius had a red-haired girl in El Paso—a woman with no other virtue than a capacity for honest devotion. The headstone she raised over her cowboy's grave carried this inscription:

CHARLES RHODIUS
Died Feb. 12, 1893
Age 33 Years

"She stoops and gently plants a flower of sweet
    perfume
To blossom forth in beauty upon a cowboy's
    tomb" [17]

A year went by before the guns talked again. Then came the Hilton murder.

C. F. Hilton had come up from Mexico in 1884 and settled on the headwaters of the Sacramento River high up under the pines. Years later the place became the headquarters of the great Circle Cross spread which Oliver Lee managed. Hil-

ton was a northerner—from Illinois—and was apparently a
pretty good sort. He had formed a partnership with an El
Paso druggist, W. A. Irvin, who was associated with Frank
Garst and Andrew McDonald in land and cattle enterprises. It
is said that these men had formed a corporation with the object of buying up land in the mountain country—land which
the little men from Texas were trying to turn into farms and
orchards.

Hilton was the manager for the big outfit and did his
best to develop the holdings in his charge.[18] Perhaps he was
too earnest. At any rate he got into a lawsuit with his neighbor James Smith over a piece of land, and the courts decided
against him. Hilton had a pile of fence rails cut and split which
all the old-timers say really belonged to him. Smith claimed
them, however, and told Hilton not to touch them. On February 18, 1894, ignoring the warning, Hilton went after
his rails. W. C. Babers, Jud McNash, and a man named Mc-
Neil went along to help him. In the middle of the operation
Smith appeared on the scene, accompanied by his father-in-
law Silas Chatfield, two Chatfield boys, and a member of their
faction named York.

They meant business. The Chatfields and York covered
Hilton's men, who were unarmed. Smith rode up to Hilton
and said grimly, "Hilton, I'm going to kill you." His first
shot knocked the old man off his horse. Hilton had a rifle in a
saddle scabbard but never even reached for it. Getting up
off the ground, he started to run but Smith shot him again
and put a third bullet into him as he lay writhing in the snow.[19]

W. A. Irvin went up to Las Cruces to try to get some action
out of the grand jury in bringing Smith to justice. The man
hid out for some time but eventually stood trial and got off.
Albert Fall was the defense attorney. One of the spectators
at the trial was John P. Meadows, who printed many of his
reminiscences many years later in the Alamogordo News.
"There seemed to be plenty of money around," he recol-

lected, and "character witnesses for Hilton were never called." [20]

Hilton was out of it. His body was buried in a shallow grave in frozen ground, to be dug up later and shipped back to Illinois. But this was only the beginning of difficulty between the corporation and the mountain men. And meanwhile the rising tide of lawlessness was forcing things toward a showdown. Something had to be done. And shortly after Hilton's death it was done.

The Temperature Rises

THE first move by the cattle barons was made less than a month after Hilton's body had been laid in the frozen earth. One morning about the middle of March 1894 they met in Las Cruces—twenty-one of them, all important ranch operators, grimly determined to stop the rustlers.

Before the day was over, the Southeastern New Mexico Livestock Association had been born.[1] W. C. McDonald, the energetic, bald-headed little manager of the Carrizozo Land and Cattle Company (later governor of New Mexico), accepted the presidency. James Cree of the great VV outfit near Ruidoso was secretary. Colonel A. J. Fountain was the Association lawyer. He would do the real fighting.

The men behind him wielded much of the influence of southern New Mexico. They came from as far west as Lake Valley—as far north as Socorro—from end to end of the Tularosa Valley. W. A. Irvin of El Paso was a member. So was Oliver Lee of La Luz.

Fountain went through the outlaws like a reaper through

a field of wheat. Before the year was out he had sent twenty rustlers to the penitentiary[2] and had undoubtedly made honest men—for the moment—out of a good many others.

Those first twenty victims, however, were just small fry. The big game was still afoot. On the green slopes of the Sacramentos bad blood was still circulating, and sooner or later it was bound to break out in trouble. Big operators like Irvin and McDonald and the late Mr. Hilton still had a score to settle with the men from Texas. It was just a question of time—and politics.

Much depended on who enforced the law. Eventually all serious matters passed through the hands of the sheriff and the district attorney—and the decisions hinged partly on which side had won in the last election. The game of politics meant life or death, freedom or jail to many people, and they played it with no holds barred.

By this time the Democrats held the advantage. District Judge Fall was calling the shots, and the Republicans were taking their turn in the role of underdog. Fall's party had little advantage in numbers, but he made up for that by shrewdness and fast footwork. He always had observers "staked out" to report on what the enemy was plotting— men like Albert Ellis, the colored Las Cruces barber, who saw and heard everything—and his countermoves usually worked. He approached the campaign of 1894 with calm assurance.

The Republicans were full of assurance also, but not of calm. This time they meant to win. They had to win. Everything depended on it. They went to work with such vigor that they almost defeated themselves, for the Democrats became alarmed and took heroic measures. They saw to it that a "committee" of citizens was waiting at the San Agustin Pass when the messenger bearing the Tularosa ballot box came through on his way to Las Cruces. Tularosa was expected to go Republican. The "committee," it is said, took the ballot box away from the messenger and burned it, ballots and all.[3]

Then there was wailing and gnashing of teeth. The Republicans contested the election, proved that the Tularosa box was full of votes for their side, and argued that if those votes had been counted they would have won.

The court proceedings pitted Fall against Fountain again. Both sides turned out in force, armed and belligerent. Fall defended his side with fury and passion, objecting loud and long to every bit of testimony that went against him. Fountain addressed his old friends on the jury with confidence and intimacy, switching from English to Spanish and back again. The tension was terrific, and more than once both sides were ready to shoot it out, but the fireworks never quite got started.[4]

Only the sheriff's office was being contested, but that one office was the key to everything else. If the Republicans could elect their man, the cattle cases would be pushed. If the Democrats won, there would be postponements and delays. Guadalupe Ascarate, the incumbent and apparent winner of the new election, was a reasonably efficient officer and a pretty good man. His great failing in the eyes of the Republicans was a receptiveness to suggestions from Albert Fall.

One result of his suggestibility was the creation of a whole squad of deputies who were, of course, allowed to wear guns on the street and anywhere else they chose. Joe Morgan was a deputy. Bill McNew was a deputy. Oliver Lee was a deputy. They were all deputies. It was not very likely that these men would go out and arrest themselves.

It gave these deputies pleasure to let the other side know just how matters stood. One of their favorite stunts was a semicomical persecution of the pistol toters on the other side. Ben Williams, strong man of the Fountain party, was their favorite target. He had been a precinct constable, a United States deputy marshal, and a collection agent for the Singer

Sewing Machine Company at a time when only a very firm citizen could make sure that the Singer Company got what it had coming.[5] At this time he was an inspector for the Texas and New Mexico Sanitary Association and was doing under-cover work for the newly organized stockmen's group. He was a good shot and a good fighter, but he was up against tough opposition.

Several times Oliver Lee relieved Williams of his weapons on the streets of Las Cruces, where Lee had a right to go armed and Williams didn't. Ben didn't like it at all.[6]

Such humiliations could be eliminated only by changing sheriffs, and that was why Fountain and his friends pulled every wire to prove that Numa Reymond had actually won the election and Ascarate was holding the job by fraud and force. They made progress too, and the case was placed on the District Court docket for final hearing. There, however, it stuck. By one means or another Fall avoided going to trial, and Ascarate continued to run the county law business as the Democrats wanted it run.

Even so, there was consternation in many a cow camp and corral out in the desert country. Fountain was getting arrests and convictions, and the small-timers did not know who would be next on his list. The Texans reacted pretty much as a unit in matters which affected their honor or livelihood, and they were convinced that Fountain meant them no good. The honest ranchers feared that they would be persecuted and driven out of business—perhaps framed and sent to prison. The dishonest ones knew their time was short unless they worked fast. The result was a deep-laid and far-flung plot to take Fountain's life.

This was the first great conspiracy. It has never to this day been discussed in print. The men who set it going never opened their mouths. But there is good reason to believe that cattlemen all over the country from Socorro southward on both sides of the San Andres were involved.

One of the shady characters whom Fountain sent up for a free vacation in the state prison at Santa Fe was Eli "Slick" Miller. After he was convicted, he became very cooperative, gave all the information at his command on every question asked him, and was even taken out of jail once to confront one of Fountain's enemies. When a Pinkerton operative went to see him in March 1896, he spilled the whole story of the conspiracy of 1894.

After the organization of the Southwestern Stock Association in March of 1894 [he began], many of the cattlemen [naming some] were talking among themselves, that it would be of no use to try to do business in the County as long as those fellows [meaning McDonald, Cree, and Fountain] were allowed to interfere. I know all this from the fact that I was thoroughly acquainted with all of them; slept with the men above named, and as they had no secrets before me, carried on the conversation in my presence.

He went on to tell how half a dozen big and little ranchers worked out the details of a plan to murder Fountain and W. C. McDonald. Eight of them were to be in at the finish, but the killing was to be done by a mysterious figure named Powder Bill.

Miller himself was offered $500 and two horses if he would participate. They raised the ante to $2,000 when he hung back. Later, seeing that he meant to stay out of it, the leader—a man from Socorro—took him aside and told him to get in or get out. He got out.

Their plan of proceeding [he went on] was as follows: they were to watch for a favorable opportunity and closely observe the locality selected for the execution of the deed. If the scheme . . . to take the victims on the road to Socorro should fail, then another place was selected, and from what I have heard recently, Fountain was taken at the very place in February 1896 that was selected by the above-named men in 1894. It was further arranged and agreed upon by all parties that [they] were to carry the dead bodies or body, from the place of the murder to the San Andres mountains. It was the plan to throw the body or bodies over some of the high ridges, so as to lodge them on a shelving or projecting rock, with which the country there is abundantly provided. In that part of the country there is very little stock, and being therefore very little or seldom visited by anyone, it was chosen to prevent detection of the crime and the finding of the dead bodies. After the killing the party was to disperse and leave in different directions, obliterate trails and tracks, and make pursuit and trailing a difficult matter. [Two of them] were to return by the way of Red Lake to their ranches so as to give the cattle there a chance to obliterate their tracks. The plot failed because of the untimely arrest of [the leader], the general scare created by it, and the sudden disappearance of [two others] who left the country." [7]

Meanwhile the Texas cattlemen were finding out that their forebodings were prophetic. By the end of 1894 the Association representatives were in full cry against Oliver Lee and his friends. Ben Williams was working on the case. The Texas Rangers were working on it. Fountain was working on it. It seemed to the cowmen that the object was to get Lee at all costs, whether he had done anything wrong or not.

The first move was to try to catch Lee off guard when his operations took him across the state line into Texas, as they sometimes did. Jim Fulgham, George Tucker, and Joe Sitter—Texas Rangers—went before the El Paso County grand jury and emerged with six indictments against Lee and McNew, four for theft of cattle and two for brand blotting. The stolen stock supposedly belonged to the big cattle company headed by W. A. Irvin, Frank Garst, and Andrew McDonald.

For some reason these cases were not pressed. It was a year before the accused were officially notified that the indictments had been returned.[8] But meanwhile other plans were afoot. During the fall of 1895 the Company brought Les Dow in to see what he could do.

Les was a spunky Texan who had been a deputy sheriff of Chavez County, New Mexico, and was now a deputy U. S. marshal working for the Texas–New Mexico Sanitary Association. His job was to police the cattle industry on both sides of the state line. Word came in that some "burnt" stock (with brands altered) were in the herd then being worked in the Sacramento Mountains by the Lee McNew outfit. Les went to look into it. He kept out of sight until the "cut" was made at the end of the roundup, and while the representatives of the various ranches were claiming their cattle, he rode in, took possession of the calf that had been described to him, and found the evidence he was looking for. Oliver Lee was not present, but Bill McNew was, and Dow arrested him, handcuffing him to the chuck wagon.[9] Hiram M. Dow of Roswell, Les's oldest son took time in 1960 to describe what followed.

Father and the cook skinned the steer and hung the carcass on the wagon for beef and then father motioned for one of the boys to come over. He took the boy's horse for a pack horse, putting McNew's bed and the hide of the steer on the pack horse and "lit out" for Lincoln, nearly a hundred miles away and over rough mountains. They were two days and a night on the road to Lincoln. McNew wanted to go by Lee's headquarter ranch but they didn't. Father took McNew and the hide to Lincoln where he delivered McNew to the Sheriff and took the hide in before the grand jury which was in session.[10]

The hide, spread out on the courtroom floor, was all the evidence the jury needed to bring in indictments for "larceny of cattle" and "defacing brands" against Lee and McNew.

The Bravest Man in New Mexico

In the 1880s the easiest thing to find in southern New Mexico—next to fresh air and jack rabbits—was a brave man. Mexicans and Indians, Yankees and Texans had one thing in common: complete control of the nerves.

Tom Fraser, who built the first house in Alamogordo, used to say after a lifetime of observation, "Men are not afraid to die. They just have to have something to die for."

It would seem that the men of Tularosa had less than most people to die for, but perhaps when a man has very little he will make the greatest sacrifices to keep what he has. So the New Mexican frontier a generation or two ago could boast of a good percentage of citizens who were able to look into the muzzle of a forty-five without a twitch of the handlebar mustache.

In this select company of the untamed it wasn't often the swaggering, ferocious Alkali Ikes who came out on top. It was the quiet, unassuming fellows who made no noise until somebody tried to insult or rob them. And they didn't have to be Texans or ex-soldiers or deputy sheriffs, either. Courage was where you found it, and you often found it in unexpected places. The bravest man who ever came to the Tularosa country was a cantankerous little Frenchman who lived a hermit's life in the wildest part of the Territory and died without leaving a trace.

He was fifty-one when he was murdered in 1894 just after Christmas—an ailing, aging foreigner who spoke broken English, dressed in rough clothes, and came only occasionally to Las Cruces. Many people recognized his stocky figure, bald head, and wind-reddened face, but hardly anyone was friendly with him or wanted to be friendly with him, and he was content to have it that way.

When he squatted in Dog Canyon, probably in the early eighties, his few acquaintances told him he was crazy.

"You've got no business living out there all by yourself," they told him. "Them Apaches will take your hair—they've got a regular road in that canyon; and if the Injuns don't scalp you, there's white men that will."

Frenchy laughed at them. "I don't hurt anybody, and nobody hurts me," he said.

"Well, the least you can do is to get your place surveyed and file a claim. You've got the best water in all that blasted country and you know how those Texas cattlemen are. They'll run you off or kill you, sure as shootin'."

"Maybe," said Frenchy.

"Hasn't anybody ever threatened you or told you to get off?"

"Yes, but I pay no attention."

"Well, when those fellows say 'git,' they mean 'git.' You *better* pay attention."

It never did any good. Frenchy would bring his supplies out of Theodore Rouault's store in Las Cruces, where he traded, load up his old buggy, and strike out across the San Agustin Pass and the grim Tularosa desert toward his cabin sixty-five miles away.[1] If he ever had any qualms, he kept them to himself. The chances are, he felt none. The whole manner of his living and dying indicate that he was just not afraid of anything.

His name was François Jean Rochas, but he liked to be called Frank and so signed himself when he wrote letters. He was born September 22, 1843, in the department of the Isère in southeastern France and migrated to the American Southwest when he was over forty.[2] Why he abandoned the old gray Roman towns and green mountains of his native country, we can never know for certain. He left a mother, father, brother, and two sisters behind him. He wrote them letters—which show that he had only a passable education—expressing disapproval sometimes of them and their ways of doing things. He may have been an odd one, a crooked stick, who didn't get on well with people. On the other hand he was fond of the few friends he had in the New World—Father Lassaigne, the parish priest at Las Cruces; Numa Reymond, the gentlemanly Swiss merchant; Theodore Rouault, another Frenchman who kept a store. He knew and liked Archbishop Lamy of Santa Fe.

Could he have had a tragic love affair? Maybe. But it was more likely his health that had taken him to the Southwest. He used to talk regretfully of his "catarrh in the head and also in the stomach."

The chances are he followed his destiny to the wildest spot in New Mexico because he found something there he wanted. He loved solitude and found comfort in the savage scenery around his tiny rock hut, the burning desert beyond his door, the remote menace of the pale blue sky over his head.

He was good at making things grow, and the Dog Canyon water irrigated fruit trees and a garden for him. He was undoubtedly the first man north of El Paso to raise his own salads.

He could not have chosen a more nakedly magnificent

place in which to live and die. The Spaniards called it *Cañon del Perro*—Canyon of the Dog—and knew it well. Where the mile-high west wall of the Sacramentos soars up from the valley floor, Dog Canyon slices through the solid rock to the top of the mountain, turning and twisting between tremendous, many-colored cliffs. It has been important to red men and white as far back as either race has been in the country— for the trail, a precarious thread of pathway which clings to the cliffs and winds among the rocks until it emerges on the pine-clad summit; and for the little river of water which skips and sings among the boulders, filling one rock basin after another until the desert below licks up the last drop.

The water and the trail made this canyon from the earliest times a favorite camping place for the Mescalero Apaches. Other paths could be followed to the top of the mountains, but this one had a special feature of its own: it was obviously meant to be used for ambushes. Halfway up, where the eternal ramparts tower as much as two thousand feet above the floor, the path launches out along an almost vertical precipice—the "eyebrow trail." When they were too closely pursued, the subtle Apaches liked to scramble up above this portion of the pathway, wait for their foes, and wipe them out with a shower of stones and arrows. They took great satisfaction in listening to the screams of men and horses plunging into the depths below.

The Mexicans followed the red raiders into that canyon more than once, and the United States Cavalry in later years fought at least three engagements there. The last of these encounters happened on April 18, 1880, when Captain Henry Carroll with detachments of two companies of the Ninth Cavalry was caught on the Eyebrow Trail and lost many of his men, swept off the pathway by giant boulders thundering down from above.

A year later, on July 17, 1881, Old Nana, the great Apache

war chief, may have left his mountain camp by way of Dog Canyon on his way to join Victorio. Near the mouth of the canyon he attacked a wagon outfit and escaped with the mules to begin one of the bloodiest chapters in Southwestern history.[3]

That was only two or three years before Frenchy set up his first camp beside the mountain water and began building his one-room stone house. A solitary settler might still expect to lose his stock, if not his life, when some red hunter came by thinking about what the white man had done to his people. Frenchy went calmly about his business. He would cross the Indian bridge when he came to it. His boldness paid off, for the Indians never gave him any trouble.

The Texans were something else, however. They came trooping in with their herds and their range code—their lust for grass and water. Every thin trickle was precious to them and worth fighting for. And Frenchy's water was no trickle. It was cold and pure and plentiful. In that desert country, particularly during the great dry-up of the early nineties, it was liquid gold. The wonder is that Frenchy lasted as long as he did.

For ten years or more he lived and labored in that canyon. He built long stretches of stone wall, which still stand. He finished his house and put up corrals for his growing herd of cattle. He had a garden and an orchard. Just before he died he wrote to his family in France boasting mildly about the trees he had planted—apple, peach, pear, and cherry.[4] He may have planted the huge cottonwood which shades the pool at the mouth of the canyon now. If he did, it is the last of his planting which survives.

On July 1, 1886, he was temporarily interrupted in his work by a shooting scrape. For some time he had been losing things that he needed, and he suspected a young man named Morrison, who had been working for him. Finally he went to La Luz, swore out a warrant, and had Morrison arrested on a charge of stealing one of his horses. A deputy picked Morrison up and brought him in for examination.

For some reason—possibly because the judge was not convinced that Morrison was a thief—they turned him loose. Immediately he set out for Dog Canyon to get even. Before daylight he got behind a strategically placed rock and waited.

Dawn filtered across the top of the mountain wall and a wisp of smoke rose from Frenchy's stovepipe chimney as he made his morning coffee. A little later he hurried out, unsuspecting, climbed the slope, and went to work on his latest wall-building project. Morrison waited till he bent over to pick up a heavy stone—then let him have it with a Winchester.

As the shot rattled and echoed among the crags, Frenchy covered a body wound with his hands and ran for his cabin. A second shot hit him in the arm but he made it—barred the door—got his pistol—and lay down on his bed to wait for whatever was going to happen next.

Nothing happened till ten o'clock that night. Then Morrison, who had been waiting all day for the wounded man to come out, decided to finish the job. He broke open the door while Frenchy lay there on the bed quiet and steady. As the door caved in, Frenchy threw down and put a bullet into Morrison, who took his turn at running after that.

In the morning Frenchy struggled painfully to the nearest ranch house, told his story, and watched a party of men take the trail of the would-be killer. Later some cowboys from Hilton's ranch lodged him in the Las Cruces jail.[5]

Frenchy's wounds soon healed and he went back to his business. He was beginning to be prosperous. Five hundred head of cattle carried his Scoop R brand, and he watched his property with a jealous eye. When stray cows belonging to the neighboring ranchmen came up the canyon, he ran them off with his dogs, who seem to have been as cross-grained as their master and just as fearless. During roundups he would look over the herd to see if anybody was stealing his stock.

One of his neighbors, a particularly sturdy Texan, resented the old man's high-handed flouting of roundup conventions and said so. Frenchy looked at him with a cold eye and said in his halting English, "You are stealing my cows. If I catch you, I have you arrested."

He knew well enough what that sort of talk could lead to, but he was not a bit scared. The Texan and his companions could hardly believe their ears and for a while were baffled by such cool defiance. They muttered, however, that somebody was going to get rid of that fool Frenchman if he didn't look out.

They watched him build his walls and tend his garden through those awful years when everybody's cattle but his were dying of thirst. They watched him sell his entire herd to Johnny Riley for $3,400 when the emergency was over. More than once he had warnings to get out or go under. He snarled back and said things in French which it was just as well nobody could understand.

Then, belatedly, he began to worry about something. He had never staked out a claim—never proved up on his water. He had no legal right to his place and he was getting too old to look forward to strife and maybe defeat. It was time to do something about it.

On December 23, 1894, he sat down at his rough table and started writing letters—which were never mailed. He wrote to his brother and sister in France telling them about his health, his garden, his desire to live without bad blood. Then he scratched off the following communication—in French— to a friend in Santa Fe:

Dear Friend

You will certainly be surprised when you receive this letter to see that I am thinking of you. However I assure you that I think of you sometimes. I have had news of you and of Mr. Baptiste Lamy through Mr. Reymond. I have had none from Lacassagne and I should like to have some. I am writing you also because I have a little need of you. I do not write English and my handwriting is bad. I should like to correspond with the Surveyor General, whose station is at Santa Fe. The land on which I live is not surveyed and I should like to know how to act to get it surveyed and I have been thinking that you would be able to get me the necessary information. I think he will need to know in what township and section I am situated. Surveyors have passed by here several times. The last one left me a plat of my place with the number of the township and the number of the quarter-section. But I can not find it and I must certainly have lost it. The name of the surveyor I cannot give you but it will be easy for you to find it. He lives in Santa Fe as does his father, who is also a surveyor. The young man stammers a good deal. He must have it on his books, I am certain. The name of the place is Dog Canyon. I hope that this will not give you too much trouble. I think you will not be too busy at this time. Here it is still warm. It has frozen a little but hardly enough for one to see. Almost all the trees still have their leaves. I hope you have continued in good health and that you have had plenty of work; the same for Lacassagne, of whom I hope you can give me news. As for me, it is always the same thing. I am just the same, except for a few gray hairs. I feel well except for this miserable catarrh in the head and also in the stomach. Well, some day one will die, and that will relieve us of all these maladies. Send me news also of Mr. Baptiste Lamy. I think perhaps you may know these people—I mean the surveyors. That will make the business easier. Since we are at the end of the year, I conclude by wishing you a happy New Year and remain always

your friend

                                                   Frank Rochas[6]

    The letters were lying on his table when he spent his lonely Christmas. They were still lying there on December 26 when three men rode up to his cabin and called him to the door. He came to the entrance with his rifle in his hand and looked at them. He knew what they had come for, and he was not afraid. He cursed them in fluent French and broken English until one of them reached quickly for his gun and fired three rapid shots.[7] Only one bullet took effect, but Frenchy knew he was finished. While the three horsemen rode away, he lay down on his bed to die.

Two days later a cowboy named Dan Fitchett rode in to La Luz and reported that somebody had killed the old Frenchman. Justice of the Peace Faustino Acuña assembled a coroner's jury and rode out to investigate. The men made their observations and ruled that Frank Rochas had died of a gunshot wound in the breast. They never even hinted that any human agency was responsible.[8]

Acuña sent Dave Sutherland to take charge of Frenchy's property. He made an inventory of the homely things that the old man had used in his daily living—"1 lamp, 2 ropes, 2 bottles olive oil, 4 glasses (drinking), 1 pants (worn)." When that was done they had the funeral at La Luz and the incident was closed. For a few days people talked about it casually: "The old Frenchman got killed—did you hear about it? Wonder who will get his money?" There was no mourning and no thought of going after the killers. After all, Frenchy had not gone out of his way to make anybody love him, and his relatives were far away.

His people in France were notified and they employed a firm of New York lawyers to look into the estate. The New Yorkers worked with Numa Reymond and Theodore Rouault to make proper disposition of Frenchy's possessions —$4,000 in money and property. His brothers and sisters got $2,457.77. The lawyers got most of the rest, though they had to take out $13.80 for the coffin and the plot in the La Luz cemetery.[9] In that forgotten grave rests what is left of Frank Rochas, the valiant Frenchman.

Oblivion hastened to claim him and the work of his hands. The scoop R brand disappeared. The road to his cabin went to pieces. His fruit trees died. The Pinkerton operative who came into the country in 1896 when the trouble broke out over Colonel Fountain became interested in Frenchy's case and built up a file about it. He reported the names of the killers to the governor, but the papers were filed away and forgotten. Year by year the memory of Frenchy in his old neighborhood grew dimmer, and at this moment there is probably not one person in the whole Tularosa country who can remember his name.

After he was gone, nobody had even squatter's rights in Dog Canyon for a long time. In November 1893 Oliver Lee had run a ditch a mile and a quarter long to carry the waste water to his place down on the flats,[10] but not till 1905 did he file a notice of water appropriation and lay claim to all the Dog Canyon water preparatory to making full use of the stream in his cattle operations. In the meantime he built a system of ditches and developed one of the finest ranch homes in the country. The great adobe house had many rooms and a corrugated-iron roof. It was surrounded by barns and corrals, and there was an orchard that put Frenchy's modest effort to shame.

It is all in ruins now. The property passed through several hands after the Lees moved away. In 1939 the water was acquired by the Government for use at the White Sands National Monument. Only memories are left at Lee's Dog Canyon headquarters—crumbling adobe walls—a few tree stumps where the orchard used to be—the skeleton of a barn.

Sometimes horseback parties from Alamogordo come out to Dog Canyon to look at the place where so much local history was made and to ride the eyebrow trail to the top of the range. They used to assemble at "Frenchy's cabin," built about 1900 and not Frenchy's at all (he lived at the mouth of the canyon near his orchard). It carried his name, however, and until it was dismantled as a hazard in the 1970s, it served as the only remaining monument to the bravest man in New Mexico.

A Gunfight and a Letter

THE main street of Las Cruces was not much to look at. It was a wide, sandy thoroughfare, sun soaked and treeless, and not very long. In front of the business houses were hitching racks where cow ponies and carriage horses dozed while their owners loafed in the dim interiors of stores and saloons—one-story adobe structures that would have been skyscrapers if they had been set on end. The red-brick convent of the Sisters of Loretto blocked off the southern end, and the El Paso road wheeled sharply to the right along the bank of the *acequia*. Just off the northern end, the Catholic church crouched in battered serenity in its barren courtyard. Las Cruces seemed a sleepy place, but in the fall of 1895 it was wide awake.

A. J. Fountain's Republicans and Albert Fall's Democrats divided the street between them. Each party stayed on its own side and thereby postponed trouble. The Republicans hung out at the Palmilla Club (a saloon with delusions of grandeur) and at Numa Reymond's store. The Democrats frequented Albert Ellis's barber shop and a few bars of their own. These places gradually took on the character of arsenals as men left their guns to be handy in case of an emergency.

Fall and Fountain hardly ever met. Each kept to his own side of the road when there was any danger of coming face to face.[1]

The ice was very thin, however, and it gave way with a crackle of pistol shots on September 15, 1895. About ten o'clock at night Ben Williams was walking homeward, his boot heels thumping vigorously on the boardwalk. Fall and his brother-in-law Joe Morgan were on the street also, standing just outside "Deacon" Young's law office. Morgan was leaning up against one of the awning posts. Quite suddenly Williams and Fall were face to face. The battle started with no preliminaries.

Morgan opened fire at short range, clipping Ben's skull above and behind the ear, and powder burned his face. Fall started shooting at almost the same time, hitting Williams in the left elbow and crippling him for life. Ben's right hand was undamaged, however, and he managed to get in a couple of shots, one of which punctured Morgan's left arm.

In a matter of seconds a crowd had gathered and the shooting stopped. Fall and Morgan were arrested and at once released on their own recognizance.

Then the curbstone oracles started in. Williams, they said, was trying to have Morgan arrested and sent back to Texas, where he was wanted for murder. The Fall supporters said no, that wasn't it at all. Williams had started shooting because the Fountain party had commissioned him to kill Fall.

Fall was noncommittal, not to say mysterious, about the affair. He said he didn't like Williams, and just decided suddenly to do something about it.

The grand jury of Doña Ana County was called into special session and heard many witnesses. Then, instead of pointing the finger of accusation at Fall and Morgan, they indicted Ben Williams and Albert Fountain for assault with intent to murder. District Judge Bantz refused to approve this action, but it showed where the sympathies of the grand jury lay.[2]

Ben Williams prudently made El Paso his headquarters after that,[3] but he continued working on the cattle cases, hoping to get enough on Oliver Lee and his cowboys to bring them into court in Texas or New Mexico or both. He dodged no more bullets, but he rigged up a special scabbard for carrying his sawed-off shotgun at his side and was ready in case something got started.[4]

That was the situation early in October when Fountain wrote an illuminating letter to the president of the Stockgrowers Association:

OFFICE OF SOUTHEASTERN NEW MEXICO STOCK GROWERS' ASSN.

Las Cruces, N. M., Oct. 3, 1895

Dear Mr. Cree:—

The *New Mexican* received yesterday contained a notice of your arrival at Santa Fe. Hence I assume you are now enroute to, or at the ranch and that this will reach you there.

I have to communicate to you matters of the most grave importance, seriously affecting the interest of all honest stock growers in this country, and especially in the vicinity of Tularosa. I had perhaps better begin at the beginning, and state the facts in detail chronologically.

In August I went to Grant County in search of Collins and I found him at work for Lyons on the Gila. My purpose was to have him accompany me to Las Cruces where I intended to use him in aiding Williams to ferret out the band of thieves operating in the eastern portion of this county. He declined to go to Las Cruces; he admitted he had evaded the officers we sent after him last May, and said the reason was he feared he would be killed if he went to Socorro; he at first denied but afterwards admitted the receipt of money sent him and gave me a receipt for it; he states that while at Central he had been informed by his friends that a man well armed had come there and made inquiry for him; that the man said he was an officer from Texas having a warrant for his arrest; that he believed this to be a plot to take him and kill him and for that reason he had concealed himself. I do not believe he told the truth. I think he made this excuse to avoid appearing at Socorro as a witness against the parties there indicted. . . . I made arrangements to communicate with Collins should it be necessary to do so and returned to Las Cruces, being called back by a telegram that Mrs. Fountain's mother was dying. She died the day following my return. In the meantime I had Williams, Cormack and others at work in the vicinity of Tularosa and La Luz and soon obtained positive evidence that a man named Dodd was running a butcher shop at Tularosa, and was killing all the cattle that came in his way. . . . Sufficient evidence was obtained to secure the indictment of all the parties by any unprejudiced grand jury, especially in one case of the killing of a V pitchfork V animal by Dodd, the eye witnesses being at hand to testify as to the stealing and killing. We were also able to prove, that in a small valley over one hundred animals had been killed by these parties. It being impossible to prevent these facts from obtaining publicity, the gang of criminals soon became acquainted with our intentions and became desperate, threats were made against Williams, myself and all others connected with the proposed prosecutions; this culminated in the shooting of Williams by Fall and Morgan in the streets of Las Cruces. I was anonymously notified, that if I attempted to prosecute these parties I would be killed. Of course I paid no attenttion to these threats. When the grand jury convened we found that a large majority were tools of Fall; the Hon. George W. Miles, being the foreman, we had when the grand jury met nine men in jail charged with cattle stealing. Dodd was under arrest awaiting the action of the jury; the witnesses against him were present; instead of investigating these cases, the grand jury proceeded to investigate Williams and myself. Fall went before the grand jury and swore that the stock association had paid men to assassinate him, and sixteen of his satellites on the grand jury did as he wished; there was no investigation of any of the jail cases. Williams was indicted for murder (killing a criminal he was attempting to arrest about a year ago) and some other indictments were found against him in connection with his arrest of Dick Wilson at Clayton (charged by J. H. Riley with horse stealing). I was honored by an indictment charging me with forging a private telegram to myself from Major Tell of El Paso some years ago, saying, "I will send you paper first mail." The message from Tell to me was of course genuine; was on our private business, and concerned nobody but ourselves; nevertheless, this ridiculous charge was made by the grand jury; the indictment was immediately dismissed by Judge Bantz when it came into court, and he read Mr. Miles a lecture on the subject. Failing to intimidate me in this manner, further threats were made of personal violence, but they were treated with contempt. In the meantime the grand jury had refused to hear any evidence against Dodd and returned no bill against him; Fall moved for his discharge, but I prevailed on the court to place him under recognizance to await the action of the grand jury. Williams is still in bed seriously wounded. Fall admits he shot him; the grand jury reported they could not find time to investigate this shooting. I learn from the inside that the gang we are after are making threats against many of the association members, and especially against yourself. In connection with these matters I enclose you two letters from Mr. Cormack who is a constable at La Luz; they will explain themselves. Williams being confined to himself was unable to appear before the grand jury, but it would have made no difference, as no testimony he could have given would have availed.

I shall now begin to fight this gang in earnest. I require funds and immediately upon receipt of your check for the quarter beginning September 1st I shall start in person for Tulerosa, and begin the work of corraling this entire gang. I find that they have no public sentiment to sustain them there or at La Luz. While I entertain no serious apprehension of any attempt on the part of the Tulerosa gang to execute their threats against yourself, yet I advise prudence on your part should you be compelled to visit any place where there may be danger of encountering them, and it would be advisable to always travel in company with some person on whom you can rely in an emergency. I regret to say that circumstances impel me to the belief that a prominent member of the association is not acting in good faith in the matter of the Tulerosa gang, but of this, I will confer with you personally. My family affairs have occasioned me very great anxiety and trouble; the shock of her mother's death has greatly affected Mrs. Fountain, and her illness is aggravated by mental trouble arising from her apprehension that my life is in danger. I entertain no such apprehension, yet were I to so believe, I should not be deterred thereby from performing my whole duty. Public opinion is with us, and the present condition of affairs cannot long exist, nevertheless, I anticipate a hard contest, one perhaps to the death.

I sincerely trust you found your family quite well on your return. Please convey to them my kindest regards.

Sincerely yours
A. J. Fountain[5]

It had to be war now. Both sides were committed to a death struggle.

About the beginning of 1896 the Texas authorities decided belatedly to move against Oliver Lee and his men. They dusted off their indictments, which had been handed down over a year before, following the testimony of the Texas Rangers, and sent Captain Hughes up to Las Cruces to negotiate. Hughes was a man of few words and mighty deeds whose name alone was a terror to Texas outlaws. In New Mexico, however, he was just another foreigner, as he learned when Oliver Lee came in to Las Cruces in response to his message. Both knew that Hughes was without jurisdiction outside his own state. About all he could do was to offer to accompany Lee back to El Paso if he chose to go. Lee did not choose to go.

Nearly fifty years later the old Ranger was still disgruntled over that episode. Sitting in the State Library in Austin, where he used to come every morning to read the papers, he told me about it. "Oliver was pretty full of swagger when I went after him," he said, his gray beard shaking a little. "He had everything his own way and wouldn't come." [6]

But though he wouldn't let Captain Hughes bring him in, Lee was perfectly willing to come in on his own, and on January 8, 1896, he did so. Sheriff Simmons took him into custody. He posted bond on each of the six cases and was immediately released. The reporters didn't get much out of him beyond a statement that he "expected to clear himself without difficulty," [7] but a few days later the papers got a story from Las Cruces—perhaps from Fall—making up for everything Lee didn't say.

The man responsible for all the trouble, the story said, was Ben Williams—still resentful because Lee had taken his gun away from him on the streets of Las Cruces. The indictments were of his manufacture and were based on his "information and belief." It was Williams who had arranged for the Rangers to be sent to New Mexico in the hope that they would kill somebody, "whereby he might acquire some cheap notoriety." Inspector Fowler thought that Lee was all right, and so did everybody else except Ben Williams. Fowler had passed the cattle which Williams swore were stolen and had stated that he believed Lee to be "one of the straightest stockmen in the Territory." [8]

That this fiery justification of Oliver Lee was not simply one man's view of the case was proved when Lee made bond. Samuel Freudenthal and Albert Mathias, prominent businessmen of El Paso, were his sureties, and he probably could have rounded up a dozen others.

Some of his friends were resentful enough over these matters to go to war, and bloodshed was barely averted at least once while the explaining and arranging were going forward in El Paso courtrooms and hotel lobbies. McNew and some more of Lee's cowboys were in town and they learned that Les Dow was on the streets. Being a cattle detective was a risky and unpopular business, so Dow was not unprepared for trouble, but he didn't want to die alone. When word came to him that the cowboys were planning to kill him and Ben Williams, he came into W. A. Irvin's drugstore to make plans for defense. Irvin and Scott White, his assistant, were in the store and Dow said to them, "If I come in here on the run, you fellows back me up."

Irvin took his gun and went up into the balcony, saying that if anybody came he would have a better chance at them there. White had a double-barreled shotgun, loaded, behind the prescription counter, and he stayed downstairs. After a while Irvin came down, a little reassured, and went to work on the books. About that time Oliver Lee and the city marshal entered.

"I just came in to tell you that everything will be all right," Lee said. "The boys aren't going to start anything. You don't need to worry."

For the moment they did stop worrying. But Irvin left town for a while shortly afterward.[9]

By the middle of January everything was coming to a head in the old Lincoln County courthouse. Ben Williams, C. L. Fowler, and Les Dow, all cattle inspectors for the Texas and New Mexico Sanitary Association, were there attending court and had secured indictments against Oliver Lee and William McNew for "unlawful branding and handling of cattle." Rangers Fulgham, Tucker, and Sitter were also present with more charges. McNew, it was reported, had gone to Las Cruces in custody to give bonds for indictments in Doña Ana County, "after which he will proceed to surrender himself to the El Paso authorities. Failing in this he will be taken there a prisoner by the above named rangers." [10]

The net was drawing tighter around these men and they were alarmed and resentful. To their way of thinking, this was persecution. McNew talked about it to his neighbor Charles Lusk one time. "Fountain can't convict us," he said. "He is just trying to break us up. It looks pretty hard to be choused around that way." [11]

The Shadow of Death

A DAY or two before he left for Lincoln to press charges in the cattle cases, Colonel Fountain called his son Jack and said, "Son, oil up your gun."

When it was cleaned and ready, the colonel took it out into the corral, where he fired some practice shots.

"Why are you doing that?" Jack asked.

"I think an attempt is going to be made on my life this time. I don't like the way things are going. I don't want to live in a place where I have to carry a gun all the time. It was that way when I left El Paso, and it is getting to be almost as bad here. One thing keeps me going. I know if I am killed, I have three sons who will avenge my death."

The whole family was worried. His wife was half sick with apprehension, and even the children felt the tension. The big stone-and-adobe house on Water Street in Las Cruces was full of silences and shadows.

Fountain was extremely fond of his children and it seemed that he wanted to be with them more than ever during those

last few days. The very night before he left he stood thoughtfully beside the piano while his daughter Maggie played.
Maggie was plump and pretty and a very positive character.
He could talk to her more plainly than to the others without
fear that the talk would get back to her gentle, apprehensive
mother.

He leaned an elbow on the piano and looked so sad that
Maggie asked him what was wrong.

"I am in great danger," he told her. "Great danger! If anything happens to me, you will know who is responsible."

Maggie had an idea. "Why don't you take Henry along?
They wouldn't take a chance on hurting a little boy."

Henry was the youngest, eight years old—a round-faced,
lovable little boy, the pride of his father's heart. He was Maggie's pride too, for she had always taken particular care of
him.

At first Fountain put the idea aside. "No," he said; "Henry
would just be in the way. I don't want him to be in any danger. There's no need for that."

They all urged him to take the boy along, however, and
finally he gave in. "All right, if he's here by noon tomorrow,
I'll take him."

In the morning Maggie sent a note to school and his teacher,
Miss Doughty, excused him. He was ready when they put the
horses to the colonel's buggy and stowed away the telescope
bag, the wooden dispatch case, the lap robe with the dogs'
heads printed on it, the lunch, the horse feed, and the other
paraphernalia necessary for a hundred-mile drive across that
lonely, windswept country. It was January 12, 1896, a bleak
and chilly day.

Before he stepped into the buggy, Fountain asked his wife
if she didn't have something to tie around his head—he had a
touch of neuralgia. She thought a minute and replied, "I'll
give you something I love very much. Be sure to bring it

George McDonald. *Courtesy of Mrs. Emma Altman*

Las Cruces in the 1890s

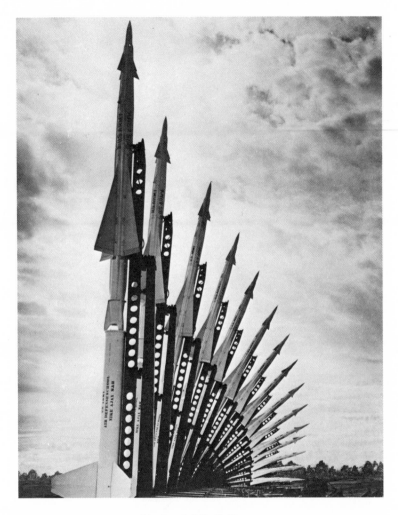

A Nike Ajax Battery. *White Sands Missile Range*

Owen and John Prather. *Courtesy of Bill Montgomery*

Albert B. Fall and Eugene Manlove Rhodes, 1930. *Courtesy of Heywood Antone*

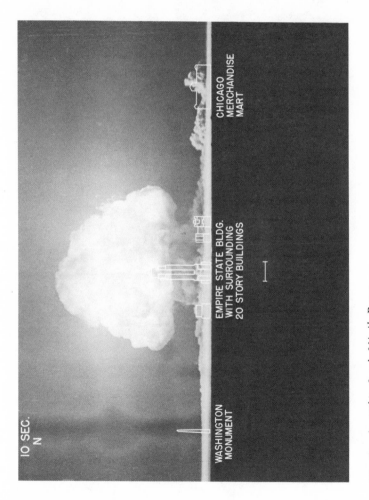

The Bomb. *White Sands Missile Range*

Lee's men butchering for the railroad crews (Jim Gilliland at right).
Courtesy of Dick Gilliland

The hanging of Jim Miller and friends. *N. H. Rose*

Pat Garrett. *Frontier Pix*

Colonel A. J. Fountain in his
militia uniform. *Historical Society of
New Mexico*

Henry Fountain at the age of five.
Courtesy of Mrs. Manuel Aguirre

Albert Fall. *Historical Society of New Mexico*

Oliver Lee. *Courtesy of S. Omar*

Bill McNew. *Courtesy of W. H. McNew*

Riders on the Dog Canyon Trail. *New Mexico State Tourist Bureau*

Malpais, "bad country," the lava flow north of White Sands. *New Mexico State Tourist Bureau*

"Frenchy's Cabin" in Dog Canyon. *New Mexico State Tourist Bureau*

Round Mountain above Tularosa Canyon. *Aultman Photo Studio*

Horsemen on the Eyebrow Trail. *New Mexico State Tourist Bureau*

back." She handed him a *rebozo* that the family had brought from Mexico many years before.[1]

With heavy forebodings they watched the colonel slap the horses with the lines and disappear at the end of the street.

The trip was ominous from the start. That night, when the man and the little boy camped beyond the San Agustin Pass, somebody or something ran off the horses. Fountain knew they would go home and that somebody would come to see about him, so he sat and waited that day and the next night. Then Albert, the oldest son, appeared with the animals and a tale about how frightened everybody had been when they trailed into the home corral late at night.[2] When they parted, Fountain tried to get Albert to take Henry back with him, but the boys talked him out of it.[3]

They jogged on past the familiar landmarks—Chalk Hill at the point of the White Sands—Pellman's Well, La Luz, Tularosa, Blazer's Mill, and finally Lincoln.

Then the familiar courtroom. The impassive jury. Les Dow and his calf skin spread out on the floor to display the reverse of the brand. Scene by scene it went on, and on the last day thirty-two indictments had been handed down against the men whom the Association called rustlers. Fountain had a lot of papers to put into his wooden box when he left the courtroom.

At the door somebody handed him a piece of paper. If he saw who it was, he never told. The paper said, "If you drop this we will be your friends. If you go on with it you will never reach home alive."[4]

They began the long, cold ride back.

Fountain and his son left Lincoln the afternoon of Thursday, January 30, drove eighteen miles, and stopped for the night with Dr. Blazer just outside Mescalero. Blazer was postmaster, Indian trader, and peacemaker in his part of that turbulent country. A former Union soldier, he had much in common with Fountain, and they enjoyed their evening together until they got on the subject of the cattle cases in Lincoln.

"We have evidence enough to convict," Fountain said, "if they don't make away with me or my witnesses." [5]

The more they talked, the more Blazer worried about what might happen. He begged Fountain to be careful and urged him to listen to a couple of Indian friends who wanted to come along as guards.

"No," the colonel said. "I think I can take care of any emergency that may arise."

In the morning they said goodbye, and the wheels turned again.

Down the road a piece, an old Apache was waiting, holding a pinto pony by a rope around its neck. He had a debt of gratitude to discharge and the horse was part of the payment. Fountain told him he had no use for the animal. "Well," said the Indian, "take it home for the children." To save argument, Fountain tied the beast behind the buggy and went his way.

He did not go on alone. Two men rode behind him, a considerable distance back, red-faced men with beards. One of them had only one eye. It is supposed they lingered behind the buggy until Fountain drove into Tularosa and tied up in front of Adam Dieter's store. Then they rode out of town.

Dieter invited the pilgrims in to eat, but Fountain said they had already had lunch (he usually carried a snack). He did need some horse feed, he said, and Dieter gave him forty pounds of oats to take along. Then he went over to La Luz, nine miles away, to spend the night with his old friend Dave Sutherland, merchant and politician.

On Saturday morning, the first day of February, they harnessed up, packed away a lunch for noontime, and began the last lap of their journey. They just missed having a passenger who might have changed things considerably. Miss Fannie Stevenson asked for a ride to Las Cruces and Fountain agreed to take her. Saturday was a wintry day, however, with a chill wind blowing. Miss Fannie, who had weak lungs, decided against making the trip.[6]

They struck out across the great empty valley toward the point of the White Sands. The lap robe, the Indian blanket, and the quilt kept out most of the cold, but the wind raked them with frigid fingers and the sun made little headway in thawing out the frozen desert world. The little boy cuddled close to his father, thinking about the warm house in Las Cruces where they would be that night.

Somewhere along the way the colonel noticed that he was being accompanied afar off by three horsemen—two on one side of the road, one on the other. They kept just ahead of him and far enough away to make identification impossible. One wore a black hat, and the other two wore light ones. There was one gray horse and two of darker color. That was all anybody was ever able to tell about them.

The colonel was worried. He was armed with a Winchester and felt able to take care of himself, but he wished Henry were safe at home. When he met Humphrey Hill on the road, bound for La Luz, he stopped briefly and told Humphrey how he felt.[7]

At noon they came to Pellman's Well on the edge of the White Sands. Fred Pellman was related to some of the colonel's enemies and was naturally no friend of his, but there was no reason why a prominent lawyer should not stop there to eat his lunch. Fountain, however, just pulled into the corral, fed his horses, and ate his snack in the buggy.

A couple of hours later, again on the road, he met mail carrier Santos Alvarado of Tularosa, just returning from depositing his bags at Luna's Well. Alvarado had seen the horsemen but noted that they turned off the road when they saw him and headed back toward the Sacramentos at a gallop.[8] He told the colonel about it when they paused to greet each other and exchange news.

Passing Luna's Well without stopping, the buggy headed into the foothills of the San Andres, where the road begins to rise toward the San Agustin Pass. Just ahead was the mile-long depression which cuts through a spur of Black Mountain. A bank eight or ten feet high rose on either side of the track, making it impossible for a traveler to see what was on the other side. At one place near the end of the cut a chalky out-cropping gave the place a name—Chalk Hill. It was a good location for an ambush. In 1894 the makers of the first plot had picked it as their second choice for the murder spot.

Two or three miles east of this place Fountain met another friend, the mail carrier from Las Cruces, Saturnino Barela. Barela was an odd figure, a wild-looking individual with a long beard mingled with a mass of unkempt hair, and a pair of inhuman eyes staring out from this thicket.[9] He considered Fountain one of his special friends.

Usually Barela was a solitary man, but this time he had company. As he passed Chalk Hill a small party was just hitching up after stopping for lunch. An old man and two women rode in the wagon; a seventeen-year-old boy named Fajardo was on horseback and he fell in beside the mail car-rier.

Just before they came abreast of Colonel Fountain, Fajardo noticed the three horsemen following the road a mile or so ahead of the buggy. He called Barela's attention to them, and they watched as the men turned aside from the road and kept their distance.

"I wonder who those fellows are," Fajardo said.

"Cowboys," Barela told him.

Fountain pulled up beside them to pass the time of day. Barela noted that he carried a rifle across his knees. They talked about the whereabouts of Tom and Jack Fountain, the colonel's grown sons. Then the colonel, seeming very uneasy, said, "Those three men ahead—do you know who they are?"

"No, I didn't get near enough to recognize them. They turned out when they saw us."

"They've been traveling in front of us for miles. I am afraid they are going to attack us." [10]

"Then why don't you turn back and spend the night at Luna's? We can go to Las Cruces together in the morning."

Fountain thought about it for some time. Finally he shook his head. "No, I have to be in Las Cruces tonight. I'll push along and take my chances."

He shook the lines and departed at a quick trot for his last rendezvous at Chalk Hill, three miles away.[11]

As soon as Henry and his father had left home, Maggie Fountain decided to go out to Captain Eugene Van Patten's ranch. Captain Van Patten, a particular friend of Colonel Fountain's, was developing a place on the western slope of the Organs at what is now called Dripping Springs. He had put up a large wooden building which he intended to use as a resort hotel. Young Howard Guion of New York had gone in with him. Maggie and Howard were practically engaged.

It turned out to be a desperately unhappy trip. At night Maggie had bad dreams in which she saw her father, very pale, out in the sand hills. Then she saw her little brother Henry, whom she loved so much. She dreamed that she tried to hold him in her arms, but each time she embraced him he slipped away from her and disappeared.

An old Mexican woman had come along so that Maggie would be properly chaperoned and have somebody to sleep with. She was very much concerned when she heard about these dreams. "I will give you a novena for the Child Jesus," she promised, and went off to look for the book.

Maggie said the novena, and came to the ninth night—the night of Friday, February 1. Again she dreamed about Henry. She tried once more to put her arms around him and

she heard him say, "Don't touch me. I'm dead. I slept between three *Tejanos* and toward morning one of them said,
'Let's get rid of the kid.' The one who did it has this picture in
his pocket. Take a good look at it because he is the one who
killed me."

He showed her a picture of a little girl with long, straight
black hair. She was wearing a white dress and sitting on one
foot with her right arm resting on a little table.

"What about Father?" Maggie asked him.

"They killed him too," answered the child.[12]

Vanished Without Trace

Barela, the mail carrier, had a warm heart in spite of his bearlike shagginess and solitary habits. Colonel Fountain was his friend and he worried about him as he covered the lonesome miles from Chalk Hill to Luna's Well where he put up for the night. The harried lawyer and the little boy were still on his mind as he hitched up in the morning and waited for Santos Alvarado to come in with the mailbag from Tularosa. On the road back to Las Cruces he kept his eyes peeled for any clue to what might have happened the day before.

With mounting disquiet he noted that the Fountain buggy had turned out of the road just beyond Chalk Hill. Stopping his team, he got out and followed on foot for thirty or forty yards—until he saw the tracks of other horses. Convinced that the worst had happened, he stumbled back to his rig and headed for home with all the speed he could muster. By six o'clock that evening he had told his story and Las Cruces was in an uproar.[1]

The Fountain family was distracted. A man went out to Van Patten's ranch to tell Maggie. Blurting out his news with no preliminaries whatever, he shocked the girl so thoroughly that she had one fainting spell after another as Howard Guion brought her back to town.[2] Albert Fountain, the oldest son, seemed about to lose his reason. With his brother Jack, his father-in-law Antonio García, and several of their Mexican friends, he saddled up in frantic haste and started out at a long lope for the San Agustin Pass, though it was already dark and a freezing wind was blowing up under an overcast sky.

Behind him, other friends of the family took time to organize a better equipped expedition, and an hour or so later half a dozen calmer men sallied out into the night. Major W. H. H. Llewellyn was in command, and with him were his nephew Lew Gans, Captain Van Patten, Henry Stoes, John Casey (a deputy sheriff), James Baird, Fred Bascom, and Robert Ellwood—the last three in a buckboard carrying provisions. Some members of both posses left in such haste that they failed to provide food for themselves, horse feed, or even blankets.

Both parties camped out on the far side of the San Agustin Pass. Shortly after daylight in the morning (it was Monday, February 3) Albert and his father-in-law pulled up at Luna's Well and learned what they already knew—that the colonel had been by on Saturday.[3] They turned back to join the second party, which had camped at Parker's Well near the Cox ranch, and then they all rode off to Chalk Hill to pick up the trail where Barela had left it.

More alarming discoveries awaited them. They found that a man had squatted behind a green bush commanding the mouth of the cut and had left two empty cartridges behind him. The track of a pony was plainly visible on the north side of the road, where Fountain could not have seen the rider till he emerged from the cut. Where the buggy turned off the road to the south, the led horse behind the vehicle had shied across the tracks as if frightened.

The possemen deduced that the man behind the green bush had held Fountain up while the horseman rode up to take charge. Then the three mysterious riders had closed in and encircled the buggy. The entire group moved a hundred yards off the road, where the buggy stopped again and the led horse swung around once more. The stop here had lasted some time. The horses had stamped their feet restlessly and a number of cigarette papers were scattered about.[4]

It was here that they found the blood. The long grass and the sleet concealed it from the first searchers, but a week or ten days after the murder it was discovered.[5] There was a patch a few inches wide where the sand was soaked to a depth of more than a foot, and blood was spattered over an area six feet across.[6]

John Meadows, a good frontiersman who spent a lot of time on the case, figured that Fountain had been shot where the buggy first stopped; that the blood had collected in his overcoat; and that the stain had been made when the horses veered off the road at a run, throwing Fountain out on the right side of the buggy. There were signs that a blanket had been laid out beside the stain, and that something heavy had been placed on it.

Meadows also found a nickel and a dime—the nickel blackened on one side as if powder burned—the change that Henry had picked up in La Luz after paying for some candy at Myers's store with a quarter his father had given him.[7]

The posse struck off, following the traces of the buggy, over rough ground and through high grass nearly straight east. On and on they went, mile after mile. It was well into the afternoon when they came across the buggy abandoned on the edge of the red sand dunes twelve miles or so from Chalk Hill.

The abductors had done a thorough job of sorting over everything Colonel Fountain had. Most of his possessions had been taken away—his rifle and dagger—his lap robe and Indian blanket—all ropes and straps—every paper in the wooden dispatch case.[8]

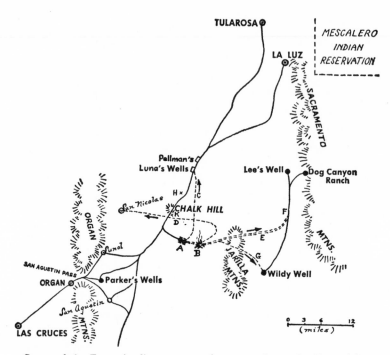

Scene of the Fountain disappearance, from map drawn by Fountain's son-in-law, Carl Clausen, and used in the courtroom. A—where buckboard was found. B—dry camp, where fire was built. C—route of big horse led by Fountain. D—route of white horse driven by Fountain. E—route taken by mounted men leading black mare driven by Fountain. F—where trail ran into road leading from Dog Canyon to Wildy Well, and where cattle were met by posse. G—single horseman going through second pass to Wildy Well. H—where mail carrier met Fountain, Feb. 1, 1896. K—where blood was found on edge of road.

A few pitiful relics were left. Henry's little hat was still in the telescope suitcase. The colonel's tie was hanging on a wheel spoke. Under the seat, neatly folded, was the *rebozo* his wife had given him when he left. Tucked away in the buggy also was the note handed to him in the courtroom at Lincoln, telling him to lay off if he wanted to see his home again.

From the abandoned buggy the trail still led eastward. Five miles more. Then, in a clump of bushes, they found there had been a camp. Three men had spent the night there—fed their horses oats, made a fire, cooked bacon on sticks, cowboy fashion. Again there was evidence that a blanket had been stretched out on the ground and something heavy placed on it.

And there were tracks. Brannigan, ex-head of the Mescalero police, noted that one of the mysterious men wore a boot with a much-run-over heel. He and Llewellyn measured the tracks and cut sticks to the exact dimensions. Llewellyn took the sticks home and mislaid them.

Among these tracks, plain as day, were the footprints of a child running off six or eight feet from the campfire. Several witnesses agreed that the tracks were made by *only one shoe*, the right one.[9] They figured that little Henry was already dead at this point and that the kidnappers had made the tracks with one of his shoes to mislead the pursuers. A particularly gruesome rumor went round that one of the murderers had taken the boy by the heels and beaten his brains out against a buggy wheel before the gang left Chalk Hill.[10]

Having learned what they could at the camp site, the posse picked up the trail again. They continued eastward toward the Jarillas—a rugged mass of granite and limestone which rises some three hundred feet above the valley floor halfway between the Organs and the Sacramentos. Nine or ten miles long and four or five miles wide, this lonesome range of hills is broken into several sections, with defiles or passes between. Oliver Lee's country lay just beyond. A few miles eastward was one of his ranches, called (from the man who originally owned it) the Wildy Well. Twelve miles farther to the northeast, at the foot of the great ramp of the Sacramentos, lay his Dog Canyon headquarters.

Just before it reached the hills, the trail divided. One horseman turned off and went through the second pass toward the Wildy Well. The other two riders, with one of Fountain's horses, took the first or northernmost pass and appeared to be heading for the mountains—possibly, the men thought, for Dog Canyon.

By now, however, it was too dark to go on, and it was beginning to snow. They camped on the eastern slope of the range, as miserable a crew as ever left a warm fireside for a winter bivouac. Those who had blankets rolled up in them and tried to sleep. The rest kept fires going lest they freeze to death and drank hot coffee as long as they had any. The horses turned their rumps to the wind and snow and stood shivering as the night wore on. There was food for only a few horses, and not one had drunk any water since they left Las Cruces. At the previous night's camp the water was bad and they had unanimously refused to drink.

In the morning the men held a gloomy council of war and it was decided that all but five of them should accompany the buckboard back to town. The five who pushed on were W. H. H. Llewellyn, the leader; Lew Gans, an experienced trailer; Deputy Sheriff John Casey; Captain Thomas Brannigan; and Henry Stoes.

Shortly after the take-off Brannigan killed an antelope and the men had something to eat, but the horses were still unrefreshed when they set off again. Stoes and Gans had the best mounts in the crowd and had remembered to bring feed. Gradually they pulled ahead of the rest as much as two or three miles. They were only a few miles from the Dog Canyon ranch when Llewellyn signaled them to return.

A big argument followed. Stoes said that they were only a short distance from the ranch and ought to go on—the horses had to have water. He added that he was a friend of Lee's and not afraid to talk to him. Why not ask Lee for information— perhaps find out who was at the house and what had been going on?

While they argued, a herd of cattle came by in charge of Lee's cowboys Dan Fitchett and W. T. White, heading for the Wildy Well. Whatever trail there may have been was obliterated under those sharp hooves, and Fountain's friends thought it was deliberately done.

Henry Stoes never believed it. The trail was already gone

in the stony, much-trampled soil. Because he refused to sign a paper supporting the majority opinion, Stoes was not called to testify at the trial three years later.

Llewellyn was determined not to go on to the Dog Canyon ranch. Instead he led the posse around the herd of cattle and headed for water at the Wildy Well. Henry Stoes' horse was so far gone when they arrived that he lay down on his side to drink out of the tank—a trough dug in the ground.

It was about four o'clock. The men camped at the well till near midnight and then set off on the long ride back to Las Cruces. The cold was so intense that they had to dismount every few miles, build fires, and exercise to bring back a little painful circulation. They reached Cox's ranch on the eastern slope of the Organs about four o'clock in the morning, more dead than alive and no closer to a solution of the mystery than when they had set out.[11]

Meanwhile Fountain's son-in-law Carl Clausen, a house painter and former Indian fighter, had been doing a little investigating on his own. While the rest of the posse headed toward Dog Canyon, Clausen and Luis Herrera followed the track of the solitary horseman making toward the Wildy Well. They had it in mind to go to the well for drinking water for the posse—and to see what they could see. Clausen noted, and later testified, that the horse seemed to have been ridden at night, for it ran into mesquite bushes once or twice and had to back off before going around the obstacle.

According to Clausen's account, five men were loafing outside. They did not see him until he was close upon them. Then, startled, they scrambled for cover. The yard was empty when he entered, except for a horse standing under saddle.

One by one, as he waited, the men emerged from the house. First came Old Ed, the colored hand, stepping sideways, pistol in hand; then another and another. Finally Oliver Lee appeared and walked toward the horse. Clausen addressed him.

"Can we fill our water kegs?"

"Yes," Lee answered curtly. "What are you fellows after?"

"We are looking for Colonel Fountain and his boy—or their bodies. Could you come out and help us?"

"No, I haven't time. And that———is nothing to us."

So saying, Lee got on his horse and rode north toward the point of the Jarillas.[12]

Back in Las Cruces the posse members told their story and added their deductions. They thought the two bodies had been tied on the backs of Fountain's horses and carried toward the Sacramentos. The townspeople, who had hoped for better news, were hysterically excited. Fountain's fellow Masons posted a ten-thousand-dollar reward for the recovery of his body. A. J. Papen, editor of the *Republican*, hit the street with an extra which reflected the stern anger of the colonel's friends:

JUSTICE IS WANTED
RETRIBUTION IS AT HAND
WANTED—ONE JUDGE LYNCH

Cheney's murderers are still at large; a murdered woman fills an unknown grave at Chamberino and her murderer still roams at liberty; Margarito Ballegos was murdered at Colorado two weeks ago and his assassins have never been captured. Cattle thieves pilfer and murder but the officers are silent. And now criminals, emboldened by official incompetence and neglect, have undoubtedly murdered an honored and respected citizen and an innocent child. . . .

THE HOUR AT HAND

A devoted wife and loving family await longingly and hopefully the coming of a kind husband and father and a dutiful son and brother upon whose living faces they may never look again. Many friends hope against fate for the return of an honored friend while many others search the plains for his living or dead body. If dead there can be no question as to at whose door the blame lies. . . .[13]

Footprints on the Desert

SEVEN miles as the crow flies from Chalk Hill, Albert Fall had a gold mine. He owned several claims at a place called Sunol, or Black Mountain Camp, northward from the Tularosa road on a broad bench at the foot of the San Andres. "Gold Camp" began to edge into all sorts of official and unofficial conversations after the Fountains disappeared. The word got round that, when the colonel and his boy were done away with, Fall was only a few miles distant. His enemies were not slow in jumping to an obvious conclusion.

Not that there was anything unusual in Fall's presence at this or any other time! The slow fever which had got into his bones during those early days in Mexico was still working, and since 1894[1] he had been hoping that this was the place where he was going to strike it rich.

He was not the only one. For two years the district had been booming in a minor way. The Amador Transfer Company of Las Cruces was carrying passengers back and forth three times a week at $2.50 a head.[2] The Black Mountain Gold

Mining Company had issued 150,000 shares of stock at a dollar a share.[3] Cagy investors who came out to look at the place almost invariably got interested when they saw the "hundreds of gold-bearing quartz veins" exposed on the surface.[4]

Fall owned one of the rough board houses at the mine, kept a few men at work all the time, and spent many happy hours there dickering, supervising, and dreaming. In 1896 he was still convinced that Sunol was "the most wonderful formation in New Mexico" and backed up his conviction by installing an expensive stamp mill at his mine.[5]

Sunol never made Fall or anyone else rich. One miner is said to have taken $12,000 worth of ore out of his prospect,[6] but no big vein was ever found. The workings were eventually abandoned, and nothing is left of Sunol now but a few battered ruins and some holes in the ground.

On the last day of January 1896, Sunol seems to have been a rather popular place. Fall and his mine manager left Las Cruces at noon and arrived at the mine in the evening. Fall's brother-in-law Joe Morgan, who had been at Tularosa on some law-enforcement business that same day, came in after dark. R. F. ("Deacon") Young, who was supposed to be Fall's man, was already there, as were Frank Hill, Charles Jones, and Hiram Yost—all cowboys.

Young and Pedro Serna arrived from White Oaks early in the evening. Young was quoted (at third hand) later on as follows: He and Serna "had stopped at Fall's place at Sunol on their way back on Friday afternoon or evening, but that there was no one at home, but about 10 o'clock that night [Friday, January 31] a rap came on the door and Young jumped up and grabbing his gun told Pedro to open the door when he told him to; Young stood back from the door and called to ask who was there, and Fall replied that it was him, so the door was opened and Fall and Joe Morgan, his brother-in-law, came in." [7]

Fall's enemies, of course, did their level best to pin something on him.[8] Every minute of his time on February 1 was accounted for and every move he made was checked. He spent the day in camp, mostly in his house, but about four o'clock he hitched up his team and started for Las Cruces. Before he was well started, one of the horses balked and would not respond to treatment. He swapped his team for a pair of mules and got in about eight-thirty that night. One rumor had him coming over the San Augustin Pass, white-faced and driving like a demon, at the time he said he reached home.[9] When all the conjectures were in, however, there was no scrap of evidence to place him at Chalk Hill at the time of the murder or afterward. About all the other side could establish was the possibility that Fall could have seen the murder from Gold Camp with a field glass—if he had a field glass—and if he happened to be looking.

It was the same with the rest of the people who chanced to leave their footprints on the desert at that particular point in time.

William F. Gililland, father of Lee's cowboy Jim Gililland, was camped with D. F. Baze and Emmett Huss at one of the little lakes near Chalk Hill. If they saw anything of what went on they never made their observations public.[10]

H. D. Parker and C. R. Scott left Tularosa the afternoon of the murder with a load of oats for the railroad surveying outfits. They said they camped at Lost River only ten miles from town, since they had a supply of liquor along and wanted to enjoy it. Mrs. Parker thought they might have gone on past Chalk Hill. If they did, and if they saw anything, they kept it to themselves.[11]

One of the Coes from Ruidoso was in the vicinity when Fountain passed, but he was some distance off the highway shooting. He had camped east of Chalk Hill with two "invalids" whom he was taking up to his place in the mountains. He insisted that he "heard no shooting nor did he see anything of the horsemen mentioned so often." [12]

It was thought for a while that the passengers in the wagon which followed Saturnino Barela, the mail carrier, from Chalk Hill just before the murder might be helpful, but their stories were never officially recorded—perhaps because there was nothing to record.

Finally there was Mrs. Eva Taylor. She had plenty to say, and said it, but her story was never used. A week after Fountain was waylaid, she made an affidavit in Lincoln to certain facts which she claimed to know. Judge S. B. Newcomb showed a copy of her statement to a detective who was working on the case.

She declared that on the night of Fountain's death she was riding toward La Luz on the stage with Alvino Guerra, the mail carrier. About two A.M. she saw a bright fire, perhaps fifteen miles away toward the White Sands. Two hours later, as the hack approached La Luz, "I saw three horsemen coming from the direction of the White Sands towards the road on which we were traveling; these horsemen crossed the road in front of us about one hundred yards and then they rode along the road on our right passing us about forty steps from [us] and coming into the stage road about three hundred yards behind us. . . ." [13]

She then made positive identification of three men, two of whom were prominent suspects later on, declaring that she had known them all for five or six years and could not be mistaken.

Mrs. Taylor's statement was never made public and Mrs. Taylor was never produced in any court. Pat Garrett hinted that she was not the sort of person whose testimony could be believed. A detective who inquired about her at Tularosa could not even find out where she was, and Alvino Guerra, who could have verified or denied her story, was never called in either.

The colonel's friends surmised in later years that Mrs. Taylor was somehow got out of the way, but it is quite possible that her character was such that it seemed best not to use her.

Who else was prowling around in the desert at this time can only be guessed at, but there were undoubtedly others. A cowboy named Jack Maxwell told several people that he had spent Saturday and Sunday, February 1 and 2, at Lee's ranch, and that Lee, McNew, and Gililland had ridden in on fagged horses after dark Saturday. They seemed very nervous and ill at ease. Lee and Gililland slept out in the brush that night, he said, and Maxwell slept with McNew.[14]

Then there was Ed Brown of Socorro. He and Emil James rode into San Marcial on February 3 on worn-out horses. William Steen signed an affidavit that Brown had cut the heels off his boots and bought a new pair before leaving town.[15] A number of investigators, including Governor Thornton, were convinced that Brown knew something and that he had probably ridden across the San Andres.

It might appear after this recital that the White Sands area, instead of being one of the loneliest spots in the United States, was fairly teeming with life on February 1, 1896. It was big country, however, and the campers and travelers were human dots on the face of the land. The dots increased and multiplied, of course, when the search parties swarmed out of Las Cruces after news of the disappearance was brought in. And that brings us back to Carl Clausen, who rode up to the Wildy Well on February 4 to get water and a short answer from Oliver Lee.

It seems that when Lee untied his horse and rode off toward the Jarillas, he was making up his mind to go to Las Cruces. He did not take the shortest route, however. That would have meant going through the second pass in the Jarillas and running the gauntlet of the men camping on the cold trail of Fountain's buggy and horses. He did not choose to do this. Instead, he rode all the way around the Jarillas and stopped at

Fall's Gold Camp before finishing his trip. Later on, his accusers hinted that this stop meant something, but they did not say just what.[16]

Lee undoubtedly did some heavy thinking during that long ride. In spite of his rough answer to Clausen's plea for aid, he must have been much disturbed by what had happened. He was fond of children and was always kind and indulgent to his own when they came along later. When he learned what had happened to Henry Fountain, he must have been greatly upset. Then there was the prospect of arrest and trial and possibly death for his friends, and even for himself. The searchers had come directly to his door. He knew what they were thinking. Even if he was not implicated—and he had plenty of witnesses to swear that he was not—it was a nasty spot to be in. Albert Fall might defend him successfully, but he could still be hurt and disgraced. It was like this man that he should ride directly to the stronghold of his enemies and ask for a showdown.

The next morning—the day after the appearance of Editor Papen's extra suggesting that he should be lynched—he was on the streets of Las Cruces trying to get himself arrested.[17]

He ran into Phil Fall, Albert's brother, who had arrived the day before from Silver City (he was deputy district clerk there), and Phil had news for him. "You're wanted," he said. "I hear they have got out warrants for you, McNew, Gililland, Jack Tucker—maybe more."

"Who has them?"

"I don't know. But we can sure find out."

They stopped first at the office of Justice of the Peace Valdez, who did not seem to be feeling well.

"I hear there are warrants out for me and some of my friends," Lee said. "Where are they?"

"I am too sick to talk about it now," Valdez replied. "Come back tomorrow."

District Attorney Young had no information either and could offer no advice about what to do.

Joe Morgan and Sheriff Ascarate were on the street. About all they could suggest was that Lee should get off the powder keg as soon as possible. They admired his nerve in coming, but there was no sense in asking for trouble. Why not go back to the ranch and get the other boys who were wanted? They were all deputy sheriffs and had a right to make arrests. Since nobody could suggest anything better to do, Lee and Morgan took off on the fifty-five-mile ride back to the Wildy Well. A messenger from Young followed them there to announce that the indictments had been dismissed. The other side had decided to bide its time a little longer.[18]

While Lee was in town, the search parties were still out combing the desert. Indian trackers had been brought from Mescalero to see what could be picked up on the now well-trampled trail of Colonel Fountain's buggy. They found the missing horses at widely separated places in the valley, and that was all they found. It was observed that the left side of Fountain's white horse was reddened with what might have been blood. Governor William T. Thornton, who came in person to Las Cruces on February 5, had samples taken of the matted hair.

Violence was always ready to break out. Major Llewellyn's men were camped near Print Rhode's house on the east side of the San Andres, and Rhode testified under oath that they tried to ambush Lee on his return from Las Cruces. A runner was to bring them word when Lee was ready to leave town, and they intended to catch him as he passed through the mining camp at Organ just west of the San Agustin Pass. "They were to lay there in them walls and kill Lee when he came out," Rhode declared. The ambushers spent the best part of a day waiting and then learned that Lee and Morgan had gone back to the ranch by another route. Rhode even accused Llewellyn of threatening to dynamite Lee's ranch house.[19] It was the contention of Fall and Lee all along that men had been hired to kill them.[20]

Much of this talk must have been close to pure imagination. Both sides were so worked up that small scraps of fact or rumor ballooned into fantastic and blood-curdling histories of plot and counterplot. Any man who knew something, or thought he knew something, was quoted extensively. Each new detail fanned the embers of all the old suspicions and grudges and enmities. Friends were friends no longer. Neighbors ceased to be neighborly. And men who had never carried guns before began to pack them now.

Pat Garrett Plays It Cautious

In the Southwest all roads led to El Paso. Dusty and tough, it was still the Big Town of the region and the logical place to go for business or pleasure. Touring stock companies performed almost every night at the Myar Opera House. Some very high-class brothels operated on Utah Street. Gambling houses flourished. And if these diversions palled, there were bull fights and other attractions across the river in Juarez, Mexico.

In the spring of 1896 practically everybody, including the principals in the Fountain affair, found it necessary to visit this rugged metropolis, which was in the throes of a new kind of excitement. Dan Stuart, the promoter, was trying to run off a world's heavyweight championship boxing match and was finding the going extraordinarily rough. Champion Bob Fitzsimmons was in town ready to defend his title. Peter Maher, champion of Ireland, was eager to take it away from him. All Stuart needed was a place to put up the ring, but where could he go? He was threatened with arrest in Arizona —in New Mexico—in Texas—in Chihuahua. A detachment of Texas Rangers had gone into camp, ready to pounce on him if he made an illegal move. While Stuart struggled to find a way out, gamblers, tinhorns, and sports of all varieties descended on El Paso, and respectable citizens from the neighboring towns mingled happily with them.

Las Cruces, only an hour away by train, was always well represented. Ben Williams had been practically a resident since his gun fight with Fall. Lee was a frequent visitor. Meetings were inevitable on this neutral ground, and more than once a lethal encounter was avoided by the skin of somebody's teeth. Jack Fountain was one who just missed a shooting scrape.

The colonel's three sons, Albert, Jack, and Tom, had been torn with grief and worry. With their mother prostrated, their sisters distracted, and their neighbors expectantly waiting for them to do something, those boys had much to think about. They all felt that they should go after the murderers, but so far there was no way of knowing positively who they were. Besides, if one of them got killed, the shock would probably finish their mother. So they ground their teeth and marked time.

Fall seized the opportunity to get Albert, the oldest and most emotional of the sons, off in a room by himself and talked to him until he had convinced the boy that whoever planned the murder, it was not Fall.[1]

Since Tom was not very dependable, that left Jack to do the job alone—and he was well able to do it. Jack was a cowboy himself, a muscular fellow with plenty of nerve and determination. He would have done something if only he had known what to do.

Ben Williams stayed with him a good deal and stood ready to back him up if more trouble should break out. Two weeks after Colonel Fountain's disappearance, they were carrying rifles about the streets of Las Cruces and refusing to be disarmed. The same day they left town: "Williams and Fountain took the train for El Paso tonight and Fall has been warned to look out for them." [2]

Two days later Lee and Tom Tucker got off the Las Cruces train and went to the English Kitchen in El Paso for dinner. Jack Fountain and Ben Williams were standing in front of the Palace Drug Store nearby.

The word spread quickly that there was going to be a fight—that Jack Fountain was waiting for Oliver Lee to come out of the restaurant and this would be it. A crowd of hopeful hangers-on collected, each one ready to take cover if anything broke loose, but to their intense disappointment neither side seemed anxious to get into a street fight.

Hope continued to flourish, however, and there was so much talk that both Fountain and Williams thought it necessary to deny the report that they had come in to do murder. "I did not come to El Paso to kill Judge Fall, Mr. Lee, or any other man," Jack stated. "Kelly of Las Cruces[3] is responsible for all this talk about my being influenced to kill somebody. . . . I have had more than enough of it." [4]

The very day that Jack's statement was published, bloodshed was averted again by a hair's breadth. Dan Stuart solved his problem at last by accepting an invitation from Judge Roy Bean, "Law West of the Pecos," to stage his match at the hamlet of Langtry, 400 miles away. On February 20 a special train carried the fans eastward. Extra officers were needed to police the crowd of sports, and the United States marshal in El Paso deputized Lee, Gililland, and McNew. Fifty years later Jack Fountain remembered how that came out.

Les Dow was in town—the same Les Dow who had secured the evidence against McNew during the roundup of 1895— and he was furious at what the marshal had done. He came down to the station platform, walking very fast, and joined the crowd of men waiting to get aboard.

"Boys, gather round," Dow said. "I have something on my chest and I want to get it off." Looking straight at the marshal, he went on: "What on earth do you mean by making deputies out of these men? Don't you know who they are?" In copious and exact terms he told what he thought of the new officers, finishing by inviting any one of them, "or any two," to step out into the road with him and have it out. His challenge was not accepted for the simple reason that none of the three was there to hear him.

A week or two later Lee and Dow finally had their meeting. It happened in Santa Fe. Dow came up to Lee in a bar and said, "Oliver, this thing has gone as far as it can and I'm ready to settle it. I'm willing to do it peacefully or otherwise, but there has to be an end to it."

Lee put out his hand. "All right, Les," he said. "Let's shake on it." [5]

While such episodes were providing the barroom and poolhall oracles with material for conversation, some high-level horse trading was going on in El Paso hotel rooms. The leaders of both parties were in town, as was Governor Thornton himself, and they were debating one issue—should they or should they not call Pat Garrett in to take charge of the investigation?

It would have to be a bipartisan decision, since the district judge had not yet made up his mind who was legally sheriff of Doña Ana County. The group which met in Governor Thornton's room included Major Llewellyn, District Clerk George Curry, Sheriff Ascarate, Fall, and several prominent Republicans from Las Cruces—top men from both sides.

At first the negotiations got nowhere, thanks to Albert Fall. He broke up the first meeting—said it was all a farce; just politics.[6] Many of the men thought the idea was too good to give up, however, and Thornton was one of them. Eventually a wire went off to Uvalde, where Garrett was raising horses and resting on his laurels. The famous frontiersman lost no time in reaching a decision. He got on a train and came back to his old stomping grounds at once.

The council was waiting for him in El Paso. Within the week Pat was a deputy sheriff in Las Cruces on a salary of three hundred dollars a month.[7] It was understood that he was to take full charge of the Sheriff's office as soon as arrangements could be made. Pat had to travel a long and weary road, however, before the job he wanted was his.

First it was necessary to throw Guadalupe Ascarate out, and this could be done only by getting the election contest before the district court. Thornton helped out by putting pressure on Judge Bantz to call the case, and Judge Bantz obliged. Within a very few days the hearing was held and the Republicans got the decision.[8] Numa Reymond was now sheriff of Doña Ana County. It was expected that he would make Garrett chief deputy—then resign in order to give Pat the big job. But an unexpected hitch arose.

Reymond was willing to make Garrett a deputy but balked at giving him complete charge. He wanted Oscar Lohman, a brother of his business partner, to go in as chief deputy, and of course Garrett would not listen to that. It became necessary for the businessmen of Las Cruces to make an arrangement with Lohman—and there is a story still around that they paid Oscar a thousand dollars to step aside. Garrett was kept on the hot seat for several weeks at a critical stage of the Fountain investigation, unable and unwilling to move decisively until his own status was cleared up.

When it was all signed and sealed, Numa Reymond had endured as much pressure as Garrett. He packed up and went back to Switzerland for a long visit, thereby missing considerable excitement in his home county.

By this time something new had been added to the explosive mixture in Doña Ana County. Governor Thornton had called in the Pinkertons. Operative J. C. Fraser of the famous detective agency left Denver on March 2, called on the governor in Santa Fe two days later, got a thorough briefing, and arrived at Las Cruces on the fifth.

Fraser knew his business. He made himself known to only a few men at first and moved about quietly, posing as a salesman of mining machinery. Llewellyn and the other Republicans told him all they knew or imagined about Fall, Lee, and company, and he tried to join forces with Garrett. There, however, he struck a snag. Every lead he suggested Pat had already looked into and "there was nothing to it." When he talked of making an on-the-spot investigation, Garrett discouraged him with the comment that everybody had been interviewed already and they were all "scared to death of this gang." It was obvious that Pat was playing his cards close to his chest and did not want help from anybody. He told Fraser plaintively that "if he could be made sheriff in place of the present incumbent he would have things where he could start right in." [9] While he was waiting, he said as little as possible about anything, and since Pat was not talkative, this extra restraint made him about as communicative as a clam. Fraser reported, in a remarkable understatement, that Garrett was "a man who says very little, so anything I learn from him is through questions." [10]

Eventually Fraser decided to see Fall and lay his cards on the table. Garrett had already introduced him without revealing his business. On March 18 a meeting with Fall and Lee was arranged. Fraser had hoped to interview them separately, but Garrett paid no attention to his wishes. He had only a few minutes alone with Fall, who was friendly and seemed anxious to be of assistance. Quite frankly he admitted that he didn't like Fountain "any more than he did a snake" and acknowledged that Jack Fountain was accusing him publicly of having planned the murder in the very room where they were sitting.

By this time Oliver Lee had come in, and they both laughed when Fraser asked Fall to account for his time on the afternoon of the murder. Fall told a straight story, indicating that he had arrived at Las Cruces at 8 P.M. "I know the time because I went home and ate my supper, and we have a clock."

Fraser then turned to Lee and began to question him, but Fall interrupted. "I want to explain Mr. Lee's position in this case," he said gravely. "As you know, Mr. Lee has been accused of being connected with the disappearance of Colonel Fountain. The warrants issued for Mr. Lee are proof enough of that in themselves, and I, as Mr. Lee's attorney and friend, have advised him not to talk to anyone as to where he was on that day or any other day. When the time comes, I have the papers and witnesses to prove where Oliver Lee was." He extended his hand, looking at Lee, and added, "I have papers you know nothing about."

Lee said nothing.

"I have told you what I would not tell another damn man in this town," Fall added, "about where I spent my time on that Saturday."

At the end of the conversation Fraser invited the two men to the corner saloon for refreshments, and they went, but he observed that Oliver Lee did not smoke or drink.[11]

On March 20 Fraser set out on a tour of the White Sands —Tularosa country on his own, with Morgan Llewellyn as driver. He dredged up a great deal of gossip and some interesting facts, but there were limits on his time and expense money and he had to pass over several promising leads— notably an interview with Mrs. Taylor and Alvino Guerra. Back in Las Cruces, he spent a couple of unprofitable days, during which he got pretty much of a brush-off from Garrett, and left for Denver on March 25.

The Pinkertons were not through yet, however. On his way out, Fraser learned that Colonel Mothersill of the Detroit Ranch of the Jornada was afraid a couple of his cowboys—Hiram Yost and Frank Hill—knew something about the Fountain business, and from that time on the detectives concentrated their efforts on the country west of the San Andres.[12]

W. B. Sayers, replacing Detective Fraser, was in Santa Fe on April 15 to report to the governor and take up the investigation once more. He had an interview with Slick Miller, the cooperative convict in the state penitentiary who knew all about the first conspiracy to kill Fountain, and with the governor's encouragement Sayers took up a new line of action. He went after Ed Brown of Socorro. Brown was the one who had aroused suspicion when he rode into San Marcial three days after the murder, his boots in tatters and his horse played out.

Sayers got Brown to come into San Marcial from his ranch forty miles out and then wired Governor Thornton to come down to Socorro. At Socorro the two of them talked the situation over with Sheriff H. O. Bursum and worked out a scheme for making Brown tell what he knew. Bursum would arrest him on a charge of shipping out misbranded cattle. That way they could keep him in jail and apply all the pressure at their command. Brown was only a week away from trial on several other counts. By offering him a way out of these troubles, Sayers and Thornton hoped to break him down.

On May 2 Brown was in jail according to plan. The most serious and concentrated effort was made to get something out of him. Thornton even authorized a pass from the penitentiary for Slick Miller, who was brought face to face with Brown in his cell at Socorro. It was all to no purpose. Brown insisted steadily that he knew nothing about the Fountain business, though he was willing to go along with the officers and help hunt for the bodies.[13] When it was impossible to hold him any longer, he was released on bond, and that was the end of what the officers had considered their best chance to learn something. On May 13 Sayers left Socorro, and the Pinkerton Agency appeared no further in the Fountain case. The game of blind man's buff was continued thenceforward by local talent, with Pat Garrett in complete charge.

It might be worth noting that a spiritualist named Dr.

Meyer was holding forth in El Paso at this time, and his séances were causing more than a little interest. On April 24, who should come into the meeting but the spirit of Colonel Fountain! Meyer asked him to tell how it happened, and he replied:

"I was killed three miles east of the White Sands and within fifteen minutes' ride of Chalk Cliffs. Two Americans and two Mexicans were my murderers. They threw a rope over my head and dragged me some distance." [14]

We have to admit that Dr. Meyer had more answers than Garrett's cautious researches had produced up to that time.

New Days—Old Ways

In April 1897 Gabriel blew his horn over Tularosa. The little community came suddenly, explosively, to life. Events were unfolding before the citizens so stupendous as to make all previous human struggles seem petty. Now at last they were to be allowed to join the human race. Finally they could hope to see their country opened up to something like civilization.

The railroad was really coming.

For years it had been a dream that optimists liked to cherish and pessimists liked to laugh at. Ever since the early eighties it had been agitated, and in 1889 a man named Morris R. Locke had laid a few miles of track northward out of El Paso before going broke. Jay Gould had bought this deceased El Paso and White Oaks Railroad at a receiver's sale and had given it up in his turn.

From time to time thereafter rumors came to El Paso that the project had been revived, and eager reporters would assure the world that "hope lives again." [1]

The man who repeatedly whipped up these gusts of joyful anticipation was Charles B. Eddy, a promoter who had had a large share in building the railroad which was turning the Pecos Valley into a Western Paradise. Since 1895 he had been examining the resources which might make a railroad through the Tularosa basin profitable—the gold, the coal, the timber, the cattle, the industries that might add support or come into being if his plans materialized. Satisfied at last, he got Jay Gould to turn over the El Paso and White Oaks assets, such as they were, and at the same time interested the Rock Island directors in an extension of their own line from Liberal, Kansas, to connect with the road of his dreams.

Two weeks after Colonel Fountain's disappearance he made a public announcement that he was going to begin moving dirt. "Eddy says one gang is coming over the mountains from the north and a new gang will start twenty miles north of El Paso tomorrow. Eddy will go slow to hold his franchise and give El Paso time to raise its subsidy." [2]

In April 1897 Eddy made his big play. He brought a party of Eastern capitalists in a private car as far as San Antonio, New Mexico, a few miles down the Santa Fe from Socorro, and took them cross-country on a glorified camping trip to White Oaks and the adjacent mountain country—thence south along the proposed railroad to El Paso.

It was an expedition calculated to make the eyes of an old-time Westerner pop out of his head. Though the visitors slept in bed rolls and took their meals at a special chuck wagon, they traveled in luxurious four-horse coaches and hacks and had everything their pampered hearts could desire.[3]

Among those who met the invading capitalists at San Antonio and conducted them into the wilds was Oliver Lee. Perhaps he did not know it, and perhaps he did not care, but these men had come to put an end to the sort of life Oliver Lee knew, and the rules by which he lived. When the caravan

left for White Oaks and Tularosa, the Old West began to fade
in this nook of the wild country, as it was fading elsewhere,
though it was harder to kill in that neighborhood than almost
anywhere else.

Albert Fall was at San Antonio, too, and turned on all his
charm for the assembled magnates. He managed to detour
them to his gold camp at Sunol, but apparently no one offered
to buy him out. The party went on to El Paso, where they
astonished the natives by coming down to dinner at the Ven-
dome in full evening dress.[4] Then they disappeared to consider whether there was a possibility of making two dollars
grow where one had grown before in the Tularosa Valley.

In October they agreed to back Charles B. Eddy in his
project, and before the month was over he had incorporated
the El Paso and Northeastern Railroad.

Then the dirt began to fly as fast as Charles B. Eddy could
arrange it. Meanwhile, work went forward on other details
that had to be attended to. Water was one of them. Test wells
along the right of way produced nothing that was usable in
a locomotive boiler. Heavily mineralized, the water foamed
and ate out the pipes and ruined the machinery. Unless the
company could get hold of rights to enough mountain water
to supply the need, the whole enterprise would fold up.

A lot of money changed hands during the next few months
as a result. It was reported in March 1898 that "within the
next thirty days the El Paso and Northeastern will pay out
more than $25,000 in the Sacramento mountains for ranches
upon which they have already secured options. This does not
include any of the La Luz options, which are now being paid
off, and which will amount to over $50,000." [5]

The whole country was turned upside down. The railroad
planned to bring in a large colony of Pennsylvania Dutchmen
to settle the newly acquired mountain lands. Farms and
ranches that were formerly worth a few ponies now sud-

denly began to sell for $700—$1,000—$2,000.[6] Axemen in-
vaded the forests to cut ties. Well drillers labored (mostly in
vain) to find water enough for the construction crews. The
track layers reached the New Mexico line by the end of
January 1898 and built on—past the Jarillas and within three
miles of Oliver Lee's Wildy Well.

In April, Lee sold Charles B. Eddy his Alamo Canyon
ranch, with its water rights, for $5,000. The surveyors moved
in and laid out the town of Alamogordo before the tracks
arrived on June 15.

Onward toward La Luz the great beast crawled, and the
hoe men and homesteaders were there ahead of it. It was
worse than the invasion of 1888, when the nesters had assumed that there would always be rain. Four thousand acres
of public land were preempted within a few days after the
tracks reached the vicinity of La Luz.[7]

At the new townsite of Alamogordo the activity was tremendous. Lawyer W. A. Hawkins, following the wishes of
Eddy, drew up airtight conditions which provided that no
liquor could be sold on any lot in the new town except in
Block 50—a provision that still stands. To add beauty to decency, Eddy shipped in 44,000 pounds of cottonwood trees
and there was an orgy of planting.

Years later a Sunday-school teacher asked her class if they
knew who made the earth. One boy, who had seen these doings in his infancy, replied that he didn't know who made the
earth, but his father had helped Mr. Eddy put in the trees.

Since then Alamogordo has gone marching on. Most of
Eddy's cottonwoods have long since been replaced by Chinese
elms. Likewise the farmers and orchard men disappeared when
the next dry spell came. Early in the 1900s they found out the
hard way, as their predecessors of 1888 had found out before
them, that this country was no place for hoe men. Uncle
Billy Mauldin told me one time that they all went to Cali-

fornia. Only a few of the immigrants hung on and left descendants who have made a place for themselves in the community.[8]

The birth of Alamogordo appeared to use up all Eddy's strength for a while. The tracks crept forward very slowly after that and did not reach their objective at White Oaks Junction for more than a year. The new day had dawned, however, and many a resident of Tularosa and La Luz got fearfully aboard a passenger coach for the first time in his life, only half believing that in three hours he could make a journey which formerly had taken him two days by horse and wagon.

These were marvels indeed, but the Tularosa country was a rugged and resistant place, where a revolution was not going to be accomplished overnight. The old ways and the old personalities kept right on functioning as if Gabriel had not blown his horn over Tularosa at all.

Politics, for instance, went on as usual. In the fall of 1896 the elections passed off almost sedately. W. H. H. Llewellyn went to the Territorial House of Representatives and became speaker. Albert Fall went to the Council, or upper house, along with George Curry, a friend of Fall and Lee who was not considered a partisan for either side. Garrett got the sheriff's post, running as an Independent Democrat.[9]

In Santa Fe, Fall kept things pretty well stirred up. Once he walked across to the Republican side of the Council Chamber and slapped the face of Charley Spiess, former law partner of Republican boss Tom Catron.[10] It was not the first or the last time Fall applied the back of his hand or the length of his cane to a political or personal rival, and now as always he got away with it.

Only occasionally he ran up against a man who was as determined as himself. One of the few was Governor Miguel Otero. In 1897 he wished to replace Fall in the office of solicitor general. When Fall boggled at handing in his resignation, Otero immediately appointed E. L. Bartlett to the office, "vice Albert B. Fall, removed." Fall fussed and fumed but he "stayed removed" and even became friendly with Otero when he saw that there was no point in doing otherwise.

Otero began to press the Fountain case again. The game of blind man's buff slowed down after the first few months of frantic searching and speculating. The Republicans had done about all they could for the moment, and the Democrats didn't figure there was anything they needed to do. No more posses went out in search of the bodies. No peace officers embarrassed Oliver Lee during the visit of the railroad magnates by approaching him with papers to be served. There was still some talk, but it was beginning to take strange new directions.

Rumors began to go around that Fountain was not dead at all. He had merely slipped away for his own reasons—boredom, domestic troubles, an irrational urge to do something sensational. Nobody knew who started these rumors, but Fountain's friends felt sure they had been planted with malicious intent. You could hear that the colonel had been seen in Mexico. In Cuba. In Texas. In Hawaii.[11] Isidoro Armijo, a devoted friend of Fountain's, was so exercised by these reports that he spent a year and a half south of the border going from village to village and from rancho to rancho in a fruitless attempt to find the vanished pair.[12]

Otero let it be known that he expected action from the Doña Ana County officials, and the word went round that something was going to happen. A story still extant shows how tense the situation was.

It seems there was a poker game in Tobe Tipton's saloon at Tularosa a few days before matters came to a head. The players were Oliver Lee, A. B. Fall, George Curry, Tipton, and Jeff Sanders. Play suddenly ceased when Pat Garrett's lanky form appeared in the doorway, and there was a tingling silence as Tipton got up, welcomed the unexpected guest, and invited him to join the game. Pat acknowledged Tobe's introductions and said he would sit in.

It was stud poker, and Garrett's luck was bad. About the time he called for a new deck, hoping to change his luck, George Curry dropped a small conversational bombshell into the game.

"I've been hearing," he remarked, "that the Doña Ana County grand jury is going to indict somebody in this crowd for doing away with the Fountains. My guess is that somebody in this bunch may want to hire a lawyer before long, and I have an idea that the lawyer he is going to hire might be sitting in this here game."

Tipton used to say, "There was more dynamite gathered around that poker table than could be found in any other room in New Mexico. There we were, sitting on a powder keg, and Curry deliberately struck a match."

Nobody said anything for a minute. Then Lee looked at Garrett and said in his quiet voice, "Mr. Sheriff, if you wish to serve any papers on me at any time, I will be here or out to the ranch."

Garrett was equally suave. "All right, Mr. Lee. If any papers are to be served on you, I will mail them to you or send them to George Curry here to serve on you."

Excusing himself, he got his horse out of Tipton's corral and headed for Las Cruces, keeping a weather eye to the rear.[13]

When anybody was thinking of doing something to him, Oliver Lee usually made it a point to be on hand so as not to delay the proceedings. In this case a hint was enough. He went immediately to Las Cruces to see what the grand jury was going to do about him. He stayed around for a couple of days, making his headquarters at Henry Stoes' store, where there were bathing facilities.

Nothing happened. The grand jury met, considered, and

adjourned without mentioning Lee's name. Much puzzled, Lee decided to go away and forget about it. He left a package of clothes with Stoes, saying that he was going to run down to El Paso for a few days. This was April 2.

No sooner had he boarded the train than Garrett appeared before Judge Parker and presented affidavits to support a request for bench warrants against Lee, McNew, Gililland and Bill Carr. Garrett's deposition concluded with a promise to show that "Oliver M. Lee, William McNew, and James Gililland are the parties who murdered Colonel Albert J. Fountain and his son, Henry Fountain." [14]

A second affidavit, signed by Thomas Brannigan and W. H. H. Llewellyn, told about the search party which went out on February 2 and found tracks pointing to "one Oliver Lee, William McNew, one Carr and one Gililland. . . ." [15]

Parker issued the warrants. It was a rather odd procedure, since the grand jury had been assembled for the handling of just such matters. Garrett explained two years later why he went about his job this way.

"Why," Pat was asked as he sat in the witness chair, "were bench warrants issued for the defendants?"

"Because their attorneys had access to the grand jury room and had they been indicted, I'm satisfied the prisoners would have known it before the officers." [16]

The game of blind man's buff began all over again, with Lee and Garrett taking the leading parts.

Whether by accident or design, no immediate attempt was made to serve the warrants on Lee. When he returned from his jaunt to El Paso, he went directly to Henry Stoes' place and got his clothes. "Henry," he said, "Pat Garrett will shoot me in the back if he ever arrests me, and will claim it was self-defense. I won't let them take me that way." And he rode off to his own country without opposition.

The people who didn't like Garrett said audibly and publicly that he was afraid to try to arrest Lee on even terms and wanted him out of town when the warrant was issued. Garrett could have replied, if he had been asked, that an attempt to arrest Lee in Las Cruces might have brought on a pitched battle and it was part of his job to prevent unnecessary bloodshed. The barroom debaters never thought of that. But whenever they got together there was a lot of loud talking about whether Lee or Garrett was the better man, and what would happen if the two of them ever got into a position where they would have to shoot it out.

Garrett, it seems, did not intend to let Lee get away. He was simply getting ready to make the arrest on his own terms —or, as Lee put it, he was "trying to get the drop on him." [17] Oliver naturally had no intention of letting anybody sneak up on him, and he could point to McNew and Carr as examples of what happened when one did.

These men were arrested and put in the Las Cruces jail on April 3, the day the bench warrants were handed down. There they had to sit until the law got around to taking action. But when a posse of eight or ten of Garrett's deputies showed up at Lee's ranch almost as soon as he got there himself, he refused to talk to them, though they bore a note from Fall saying that he was "wanted in town." They saw him on the porch putting on his gloves, but he went inside and had Tom Tucker tell them he was not at home. A day later he was in El Paso, where he let it be known that if the court would fix a reasonable bond for him, he would go to Las Cruces by himself. "He did not propose to be taken to Las Cruces and kept in jail for an indefinite period without trial." [18]

So Lee was temporarily out of it when Carr and McNew stood before Judge Parker on April 10, 1898, while the court determined whether or not there was enough evidence to try them for murder.

Albert Fall had bestirred himself during the seven days they had been held in jail. He knew, and they all knew, that the whole affair could be settled once and for all if the prosecution could be convinced that it had no real case. He knew also, as did everybody else, that if the prisoners were held, there would be a weary, long-drawn-out struggle. Now was the time to make a supreme effort, and Fall made it.

First he called in Judge H. L. Warren of Albuquerque and Harry Daugherty of Socorro to help him. Warren was an experienced and respected trial lawyer. Daugherty was the "young and promising" district attorney of Socorro County. Daugherty thought enough of this opportunity to resign from his office. Apparently he anticipated that the case might occupy him—as it did—for some time.

The prosecution also regarded this preliminary passage at arms as a trial of strength which they could not afford to lose. Prosecuting Attorney Bryan of Las Cruces called in W. B. Childers, Republican wheelhorse with a reputation for flights of courtroom oratory, and Thomas Benton Catron himself, the grim and powerful boss of the whole Republican machine.[19]

For six days it went on, witness after witness. The mail carrier—the search parties—Clausen and Lee at the Wildy Well—Dr. Blazer describing his last conversation with the worried Colonel Fountain.

Jack Maxwell was the pivot of the whole case. A sun-burned, scared, inarticulate young man, he was brought in to testify that Lee, Gililland, and McNew had not been at home the day of the Fountain murder—that they had come in that night on fagged-out horses, obviously worried. He seemed sure enough of these facts under direct examination, but when Fall got hold of him it appeared that he wasn't sure of anything. He "succeeded in contradicting his direct testimony and proving himself a good witness for the defense." [20]

On the last day of the preliminary trial Maxwell was brought back again and damaged his side still further by admitting that he had been promised a share of the $10,000 reward.[21] This was the first mention of a fact that was used with telling effect then and later. Garrett had signed a contract with Maxwell promising him $2,000 if his testimony led to the conviction of Fountain's murderers. Much could be said in favor of splitting such rewards, but many people didn't like the sound of it. There was too much suggestion of buying evidence.

When the testimony was all in, Fall moved that the prisoners be discharged on grounds of insufficient evidence. Judge Parker agreed that he did not have enough on Carr to hold him, but he sent McNew back to jail and refused to let him out on bond.[22] Bill stayed behind bars for over a year, as unhappy a man as you could find in the Territory of New Mexico.

This was what Lee feared for himself, and he became as wary as a coyote. When he heard that a new posse of sheriff's deputies was being organized, composed mostly of members of the old Republican militia company with Van Patten at their head,[23] he took extra pains to avoid exposing himself. It was not until July that Garrett's little army got even close to him, and then it was luck rather than sense that got them their opportunity.

The Fight at the Wildy Well

Dᴜsᴛʏ July came to the valley. A brassy sun hammered away at the desert landscape day after day while pack rats and jack rabbits and sidewinders holed up in the earth waiting for night. Whirling dust devils rose lazily into the air at intervals, and occasionally an inadequate rain cloud shed a little moisture on a few square feet of sand before giving up in disgust. Cows, horses, and men moved around as little as possible. Business and pleasure of all sorts slowed down to a walk.

W. W. Cox was not through with his branding yet. On July 11 he had a final go-round in his corral just beneath the granite needles and spires of the Organs. Among those watching from a comfortable seat on the fence were Oliver Lee and Jim Gililland. They had ridden over from Dog Canyon the night before.

Lee was interested in W. W.'s sister-in-law, a Texas girl named Winnie Rhode, and that probably had something to do with his visit. They say that by this time Oliver had lost his early shyness with women, and at first Cox was not very happy to see him around. Winnie was a quiet, gentle girl who had grown up in the Cox family, and W. W. was not going to have any heartbreaks for her if he could help it. However, it soon became apparent that Oliver was serious. As Uncle Bill McCall used to tell it, "Lee shoved the whole stack at her and Cox began to think he was all right." [1]

While the branding was going on, two of Garrett's deputies showed up—Clint Llewellyn and José Espalin. Espalin was the same man who had been known as Walter Good's "Friday" ten years before. He was a tough egg and had been toting a pistol ever since, sometimes (as now) on the side of the law. That he was not too serious about his obligations as a deputy appeared, however, when he made occasion to speak to Lee as he opened the gate to ride away that afternoon.

"*Cuidado*," he said under his breath. "Watch out!"

Having thus declared himself secretly in sympathy with the man he was supposed to be after, he rode over to Garrett's ranch a few miles north of the San Agustin Pass and reported that Lee and Gililland were headed for the Wildy Well.[2] By this act he made himself the Benedict Arnold of southern New Mexico and the cattle people never did forgive him.

Garrett and his men saddled in haste and left that evening just before dark. It was thirty-eight miles from the Garrett ranch to the Wildy Well, and they arrived at daylight—Garrett, Clint Llewellyn, Espalin, Ben Williams, and Kent Kearney of La Luz. Kearney, a husky six-footer who had been a cowboy and a schoolteacher, was new to this sort of business but not a bit frightened.

The place was quiet as a tomb as they dismounted some distance from the house and tied their horses to a fence. There was an adobe dwelling with a wagon shed attached at right angles; a corral, outbuildings, pump house, and a big dirt water tank. A couple of horses were standing in the corral, and Garrett was sure he had caught up with his game at last.

Moving fast but silently, Garrett eased his lanky form through the unlocked door. There were two persons in bed in the main room. He shoved his gun into the ribs of the nearest one and told him in a loud whisper to throw up his hands. The man sat up suddenly, and to Garrett's surprise it was a cowboy named Madison who worked for Lee. In bed beside him was his wife, startled and speechless. Garrett was not merely astonished—he was also embarrassed. Hastily he retreated and rejoined his men at the corral.

There were other people in the house, including a young cowboy named McVey, who seems to have been wide awake in every sense of the phrase. No sooner had Pat got back to his group than this boy appeared in the door, ran around the house, and seemed to be trying to signal to somebody on the roof. The posse got the idea at once. The men were up there, lying behind the adobe parapet. Garrett went back inside and asked Madison to go up and tell them to surrender. Madison declared that he had no idea where Lee and Gililland were.[3]

Disgusted, Garrett went out again and motioned to his men to come on. They would have to get up on the roof of the lean-to wagon shed and do the job themselves. All but Williams and Llewellyn followed Pat onto the shed. Williams took shelter behind a galvanized water tank that stood a short distance away. Llewellyn was detailed to keep an eye on the Madison family inside the house.

It is hard to believe, but neither Gililland nor Lee woke up during the excitement below. Both were still sound asleep when the shooting began. Apparently Kearney jumped the gun. The ethics of the situation demanded that the men on the roof should be called on to surrender. If they refused or offered to fight, it was all right to let them have it. Garrett seems to have ordered the sleeping men to throw up their hands, and Kearney took the words as a signal to fire. On the

witness stand Garrett had to admit that he thought "Kearney
fired too quick," [4] but apparently Pat was not far behind his
deputy in turning loose.

As Oliver Lee told the story later on, he was awakened
when a bullet tore into the roof right under his stomach. In
a split second he had raised his Winchester and fired at Garrett, intending to hit him in the head. Pat ducked so fast that
Lee supposed he had been shot down. Everybody in the posse
but Kearney tumbled off the roof and took cover in the
wagon shed. Kearney continued to stand up and fight until
both Lee and Gililland hit him and he fell to the ground.
Groaning, he was dragged into the wagon shed with the rest.

It had been a lively two minutes. The possemen remembered that Lee laughed as he fought. Now, suddenly, everything was terribly quiet. In a minute Lee called down, "You
are a hell of a lot of bastards to shoot at a man when he is
asleep."

"Are any of you hurt?" Garrett called back from the
depths of the shed.

"No, but you've got yourself into a hell of a close place."

"I know it. How are we going to get away from here?"

To emphasize his mastery of the situation Lee put a few
bullets through the roof of the shed, one of which struck a
wagon tire close to Garrett and bounced off with a vicious
whizzing noise.

"You'd better surrender," Pat said after another pause.

Lee laughed at him. "Pat, don't you think we've got the
best of it?"

"Don't you think I know it?"

"I wouldn't surrender to you anyway. I know you intend to
kill me. You've said so, plenty of times."

"That's a lie, Oliver. You'll be perfectly safe in my hands."

"We've got you where we want you and we don't have to
surrender. You pull off and give us a little time and we'll

promise not to shoot any of you when you get out from shelter."

"I doubt that."

"When I give my word I keep it."

They had to trust him. So one by one the men came out from under the shed, looking over their shoulders at the two figures lying behind their Winchesters on the roof, and made their way as fast as they could without absolutely running to the horses they had tied to the fence outside the yard. Two of them were comic figures. José Espalin had taken off his shoes when the posse crept up to the house. Now he was retreating in his bare feet, dodging grass burrs and having a bad time of it. Williams, who had taken cover under the water tank, had come to grief when half a dozen Winchester bullets went through and deluged him with water. He was half drowned when he crept out and started for his horse.

"Now, Pat," Lee called after the sheriff, "I suppose you'll go away and tell lies about this fight."

"No, I'll tell it just as it happened."

"Well, you fix bond for me and I'll come in and surrender."

Kearney lay bleeding in the lean-to until Pat sent a section crew from Turquoise Siding after him. By then Lee and Gililland had ridden off after exchanging a few words with the wounded man. Garrett brought him to Alamogordo on the train that afternoon.[5]

Kearney was a hardy young man and had no intention of dying. Art McNatt saw him at the family home at La Luz next day and always remembered that brief conversation. "He had holes in him big enough to drive a team through— had lost about all his blood; but he was cheerful. Said he was going to get well and go back and get those fellows. But he died the next day." [6] He was buried at 4:30 in the afternoon on July 14. Lee said that he was the bravest man in the crowd —and that was no mean tribute.[7]

Now the grand jury had another score against Lee and
Gililland, and an indictment was handed down charging them
with the murder of Deputy Kearney. The fat was really in
the fire this time and there was only one thing for them to do.
Quietly but effectively they disappeared from view—went on
the dodge, as the saying was—and the next time Garrett came
to the Wildy Well, they were long gone.[8]

On the Dodge

IF A man has friends enough, he can disappear without too much trouble. Oliver Lee and Jim Gililland had all the friends they needed. They rode off into the hills and were not seen officially again for eight months.

The time might not have been so long had it not been for the Spanish-American war. The clouds of conflict were gathering on the eastern horizon at the time of the Wildy Well fracas, and the whole nation was getting ready to march. The *Maine* had gone down in January. Congress had voted $50,000,000 for "national defense." And when President McKinley refused to rush the country into a fight, the newspapers printed his picture superimposed on the Stars and Stripes under the title "A Blot on the Flag." [1]

Congress declared the Cuban people free and independent on April 20 and called for 75,000 volunteers. Any number of repressed American males leaped at the chance to get away from the dull routine. The West was particularly wild to get into the conflict, and Westerners rose en masse, burning to do bloody and heroic deeds.

In El Paso an organization flourished at this time called the McGinty Club, which fostered all sorts of masculine activity from band work to beer drinking. Anybody who was anybody automatically belonged to it. In El Paso and Juarez an oversize beer schooner is still called a "McGinty" in memory of this organization. One of the most prized possessions of the Club was a brass cannon which was used to dignify all special occasions. So enthusiastic was the membership over the action of Congress that the old field piece was kept booming all day. In the evening the McGinty Club band turned out and helped the people work off the rest of their enthusiasm. The town was described as "boiling" with patriotic energy.[2]

Within a matter of hours the regular troops were in motion,[3] while the militia companies were working feverishly to get in shape to follow. In fact, at the very moment when Garrett was climbing up on Oliver Lee's shed roof at the Wildy Well, the Las Cruces company was in the last stages of pulling itself together. At such a time it was impossible for local affairs to command much attention, and consequently Lee and Gililland were left stranded out in the mountains because their friends were too busy to come to their aid.

Fall in particular was torn by conflicting urges. He wanted to take care of his friends, but he wanted also to be the captain of the Las Cruces militia company. Probably a chance at military distinction was the only consideration in the world that could have taken Fall's mind off Oliver Lee's plight. He had the war fever, and patriotism or ambition, or both, bubbled inside him like yeast.

He first tried making an announcement that he would raise a company of fifty sharpshooters to "act in an independent capacity," but Governor Otero did not warm to the idea.[4] So Fall began to angle for command of the old company of volunteer infantry, a venerable band of home defenders which had long been under the command of Fall's enemy, Eugene Van Patten. At the first sign of impending trouble the volunteers had sprung to arms, begun recruiting, and gone into camp near the courthouse. Every day they drilled to the point of exhaustion, and old and young looked upon them with envy as men destined to do great things.

One week after the Wildy Well battle, Governor Otero, accompanied by Adjutant General W. H. Whiteman and others, came to Las Cruces to swear in the company—the last one in the state to be brought formally into the armed forces.[5] The swearing-in ceremony was not the only thing Otero had on his mind. Van Patten was in command, but everybody except Van Patten himself thought he was too old to remain in charge. Something would have to be done about that.

Albert Fall knew all this and had been taking measures. He had plenty of friends who were ready to support him, and even his Republican enemies, for reasons of their own, were making approving noises. He was overflowing with hope, fear, and anticipation when Otero came in.

The governor went to work with his usual skill at undercover operations. First he got Van Patten to resign from his captaincy on condition that he be given a lieutenant-colonelcy in the National Guard. The necessary steps were taken, and Van Patten was known thenceforward to the end of his life as "Colonel Van."

The Republicans had a meeting the same night that these adjustments were being made and came up with a request that Fall be placed in command of the company. Otero suspected what they had in mind, but he let them present their arguments. At the end of the talk their real purpose appeared when they asked that a condition be tacked onto Fall's appointment: a stipulation that he was never to return to New Mexico. They seemed willing to go to any length to get rid of Albert Fall.

The governor said he wouldn't listen to any such proposi-

tion. "Any man who holds a commission from me is at liberty
to return to the territory whenever he likes. I would not ap-
point a man whom I thought unfit to reside in New Mexico."
At his request the men put their petition in writing,[6] and
"Gilly" Otero promised to think it over.

The conference was held in Numa Reymond's house, where
Fall refused to set foot, but he was waiting outside in the
street when the governor emerged. Otero never said a word,
but he wrote a note to Adjutant-General Whiteman on the
back of a visiting card: "I have just appointed Albert Fall as
Captain of Company H. Administer to him the oath of office
and turn the company over to him. His commission will be
issued when I return to Santa Fe. Miguel A. Otero, Governor
of New Mexico."

As Otero tells it, Fall "jumped for joy" when he read the
card, and "ran every step of the way" to the company en-
campment.[7]

His war service was less than glorious. Like many others,
he never got to Cuba, and he never was able to meet Theodore Roosevelt and form the invaluable friendship which was
the happy privilege of Major Llewellyn, George Curry, and
other New Mexico members of the Rough Riders.

Rewarding or not, Fall's military service kept him out of
New Mexico from the summer of 1898 till the following
spring, and his family and friends had to get along as best they
could. McNew spent the time in the Las Cruces jail. Lee and
Gililland prowled the mountains and deserts of their home-
land, determined not to give up unless they were sure of an
even break.

They were welcome almost anywhere they wanted to go,
and they probably moved around a good deal to keep the offi-
ers off their necks. One of their hangouts was Charley Graham's place on the Jornada, north of Las Cruces, where they
came in occasionally for supplies. When Pat Garrett was in the

neighborhood, Charley would go back into the mountains "for a load of posts" and take them what they needed.

Miss Rina Latham[8] was at the Graham ranch one night when there was a big forest fire in the Sacramentos, and they could see the smoke above the intervening San Andres. One of the men said, "Maybe they're trying to smoke Oliver Lee out."

The next day Lee and Gililland came in to the ranch. They were dressed in old clothes and had beards which had taken at least six weeks to grow. They were introduced, ate at the house, slept in the barn, and departed inconspicuously the next day.[9]

They used to laugh at the tricks they played on their pursuers. Garrett never stopped looking for them. Once he guarded a bridge for a long time, expecting them to cross, but they forded the stream lower down. Again Lee met Garrett face to face on a public road, but his long beard and tattered clothes gave him an appearance so different from his old dapper self that Garrett went by without a second look.[10]

Probably the two "outlaws" spent most of their time in the San Andres with Gene Rhodes, who had a ranch in one of the most picturesque and inaccessible spots in that whole country. Rhodes was the most extraordinary puncher ever to ride those ranges. Before he went East to become a nationally famous writer, he spent twenty-five years cowboying all over the cattle country of New Mexico. He knew more about these people and what made them tick than any other rangeland recorder. He understood their shy kindness, their rock-ribbed reserve, and their special code of ethics. He knew that a man who could kill his enemies could be tender to children, gallant to women, and faithful to a friend. He accepted the fact that you could be loyal to another human being without approving all his actions or analyzing and judging his motives. He sensed a hidden nobility in the most desperate characters and

suspected a hidden weakness in the outwardly ultrarespecta-
ble. In short, he knew and approved of the rules those cowmen lived by, and he became Oliver Lee's friend and supporter.

When and where these men struck up an acquaintance we
do not know, but it would have been hard for them to miss
one another in that thinly settled country. People rode fifty
miles to a dance—paid month-long visits to friends and relatives across the mountains—spent a week in Tularosa playing
poker and catching up on their drinking.

It was geography as much as friendship which brought
them together this time. Rhodes's ranch was well up in the
San Andres—a hidden country of grassy valleys and mountain
slopes clothed in pine and juniper—close beside the trail from
Engle to Tularosa. They call it Rhodes Pass now in his honor.[11]
The Detroit Ranch—the Bar Cross—sent its horses up to winter on Gene's ranch and called him in to help at roundup time.
Otherwise the only travelers along that dim and seldom-used
road were hard-faced *hombres* who watched their back trail
with earnest attention. Gene himself admitted that he had har-
bored many a wanted character, including such big-leaguers
as Black Jack Ketchum.

Loafing around in Gene's one-room picket house, Lee spent
at least part of his time in literary composition. He may have
caught the bug from Gene, who was already experimenting
with stories and poems, and perhaps Gene did part of the
work. At any rate Oliver began sending off Letters to the
Editor which the Las Cruces *Independent Democrat* was
glad to publish, letters which explained what he was doing and
why he was doing it. He wanted people to know that he had
plenty of reason for refusing to surrender to Pat Garrett who,
he said, had repeatedly and publicly threatened to kill him—
even better reasons for staying out of Las Cruces where he had
been threatened with a necktie party. In the issue of August
16 he reached his climax by stating that Garrett had been

brought into the country for the sole purpose of killing him, and that Pat had no intention of even arresting him.

On September 8 old Samuel G. Bean—Roy Bean's older brother—took up the cudgels for Lee, saying that Garrett intended to murder him as he had murdered Billy the Kid.[12]

This was more than Garrett could take, and he got the grand jury to indict editor Bull for criminal libel.[13]

By this time Lee was out of the country entirely. In October he was in San Antonio, Texas, where he took unto himself a wife. The bride was Winnie Rhode, Bill Cox's sister-in-law, and they were married at the house of Jim Hester, an old compadre of Cox's in the Sutton-Taylor feud of twenty years before. After that the record is blank for several months. All we know is that in March 1899 Lee was back in the San Andres mountains and had been there long enough to grow another patriarchal beard.

Fall was home from the wars by now. The uniforms were laid aside; the sabers rattled no longer. It was time to take up where he had left off, and very soon he was pushing a scheme which promised to settle the Tularosa troubles once and for all.

Some old-timers give George Curry credit for the idea. Some say it was cooked up by Fall and his former law partner W. A. Hawkins. Fall certainly did his best to sell it to the politicians in Sante Fe. The plan was to create a new county out of the eastern half of Doña Ana. Tom Catron, the Republican boss, was induced to go along by a promise of support for one of his pet projects. Governor Miguel Otero was persuaded by a suggestion that the new county should be named for him. The deed was done. Otero appointed Lee's friend George Curry as first sheriff of the new county. And then it became obvious that the whole deal had been set up to get Oliver Lee out of his jam—for the western boundary of Otero County was beyond the place where Colonel Fountain had disappeared, and the case would have to be taken over by the new

officials. The long contest between Lee and Garrett was finished—all but the last round.

One slow step at a time the legal minuet moved through its
figures. Lee wrote a letter from his sanctuary at Graham's
HG ranch. Tom Tucker carried it to Sheriff Curry. Curry
carried it to Governor Otero. Otero learned that Lee would
come in and surrender to any sheriff but Pat Garrett if he
could be assured that he would not be placed in the Las Cruces
jail. The governor thought he could agree to these conditions, and Curry went off to tell Judge Frank Parker at Las
Cruces. Parker likewise was agreeable. In the utmost secrecy
final arrangements were made.[14]

On March 13, 1899, Lee and Gililland left the HG ranch,
accompanied by Gene Rhodes, and got aboard the south-
bound Santa Fe train. The fugitives were still dressed in non-
descript clothes, and their eyes still looked out from heavily
bearded faces. It was well they had something to hide behind.
The first man they saw in the day coach was Captain Hughes,
returning from Santa Fe with a prisoner. Worse than that, Pat
Garrett was in the smoking car. Lee saw him just in time and
did not go in. Later Pat walked down the aisle and passed them
while the men held their breaths, waiting to be recognized.
He looked the other way.

Rhodes got off the train at Rincon and wired Judge Parker
that they were coming. At Las Cruces they walked out of the
station past Ben Williams, who was looking very glum, and
surrendered at the judge's house. Parker deputized Gene
Rhodes and James Simpson to guard them, and they handed
over their guns.[15] Since there was no jail as yet in the new
county-seat town of Alamogordo, George Curry took them
up to Socorro "to await the further order of the court." [16]

The Defense Rests

ABOUT one side of the lives of its mighty men, the legendry of the West has little to say. The Indian skirmishes, the long migrations, the lynchings, the gun fights—such dramatic episodes get all the attention, and the fact that the mighty men spent a lot of time in jail gets very little.

The constant struggles of the law men to catch up with these individualists were usually successful, with the result that most of them spent weeks, months, and often years behind the bars. To outdoor men, long confinement was a fate almost as bad as death. They dreaded the prospect of it. They suffered under it while it was going on. And they and their friends moved heaven and earth to get them out.

All three of the suspects in the Fountain business were locked up now, enduring the blank and endless hours of confinement, learning the techniques of a hard new way of life. How to pass the time; how to do anything at all for wives and children and animals left to fend for themselves; how to help the lawyers as they moved the pieces in their legal chess game.

It was lucky for Lee, Gililland, and McNew that they had as subtle a player as Albert B. Fall to make their moves for them. They realized this, and they put everything into his hands.

Fall was not the only friend they had. Most of the cattlemen were for them, and so were many interested outsiders. Simple notoriety brings some people over. Good public relations will account for others. And if there is any hint of persecution mixed in with the prosecution, public opinion is always ready to make an issue of it.

In the spring of 1899 Oliver Lee had more friends than he even knew about. Colonel Fountain, on the other hand, was no more than a name to people who had not known him. Nobody seemed interested anymore in dragging the murderers, whoever they were, to justice, for by this time the Fountain case was just an excuse for bringing a great political feud to a showdown. The Democrats, because they hated Catron and the Santa Fe ring, were automatically convinced of the innocence of Oliver Lee *et al*. Every good Republican was just as certain that he was guilty as hell.

The case got a tremendous build-up. It was in court three times, and the evidence should have become almost painfully familiar, but each time there were sensational developments and the promise of more to come. New Mexico and western Texas watched with deep interest.

The first run-through was concluded on March 25, when Judge Parker decided that two of the three indictments on which the men were to be tried would be argued at Silver City. There, the second hearing was held on the third Monday in April, but nothing much happened. The prosecution was anxious to try Lee at once—get the big fish first. The lawyers were afraid that if they spent all their ammunition on McNew or Gililland, the defense would be able to devise a means of getting Lee out of the trap. But McNew was tried first, and the prosecution, rather than tip its hand, decided to let him go. When Judge Parker refused a continuance, the first two indictments were dropped. The one remaining—the charge of murdering Henry Fountain—was to be heard in May at Hillsboro, the busy little mining town on the eastern slope of the Black Range.

Such caution provoked speculation about what the prosecution was holding in reserve and brought much notoriety to the defendants. When the three men stopped over in El Paso on their return from Silver City, they were trailed by a gallery of curious people. All their acquaintances wanted to shake hands and be seen with them.

One bold reporter approached Lee and asked him, "Is it true that the little boy's bones have been found, and that the prosecution has Colonel Fountain's skeleton ready to produce as evidence against you at the proper moment?"

"No," said Lee. "There is nothing in it that I know of. Fountain may be dead, but we don't have to prove that he is alive to clear ourselves. The prosecution must prove that he is dead and that we killed him, and that cannot be proved. It will be impossible for them to secure a conviction." [1]

Such talk made something between a gladiatorial combat and a circus out of the trial at Hillsboro. People came from far and near to watch the battle of the lawyers, and the little county-seat town found itself unprepared to handle the crowds that threatened to sweep it off its foundations. For Hillsboro, though it was the center of considerable mining activity, numbered no more than two hundred permanent residents. The Little Corner Saloon, the Union Hotel Bar, and the Parlor Saloon expected to be able to handle their end of the business, but the Union Hotel was about the only place where visitors could be entertained. The seventy-five witnesses who had been subpoenaed would more than fill it, and a serious shortage of rooms was expected.

The generals on both sides, however, solved the problem by setting up their own accommodations. The witnesses for the Territory were installed in a tent town on the north side of Hillsboro with a cook, waiters, and guards. The defense set up a similar village at the south end of town, called the Oliver Lee Camp, where a chuck wagon dispensed meals to all friends and supporters.

It was a picturesque spot for any gathering. Hillsboro had grown up at the base of the Black Range, where foothills began to rise sharply toward the green summits. Bench after bench, the land fell away eastward toward the green meandering thread of the Rio Grande Valley. There was plenty of water at that altitude, and the Middle Percha, which looped and twisted through the center of town, was a respectable little creek. Mexican gardeners dug in the rich dirt of the bottoms under monstrous cottonwoods. Houses and stores and saloons were buried in shade. A big smelter overhung the town on the north; on the south, each on its separate hill, sat the brown brick schoolhouse, the brown brick courthouse, and the brown brick jail, all well patronized at this time. Old inhabitants of Hillsboro still look back on it as an idyllic spot, only slightly smudged by the mines and miners which kept the place going.

There was no railroad. To get to a train, the inhabitants rode the stage to Lake Valley. Telegraphs and telephones were unknown—until Oliver Lee came to Hillsboro to be tried for his life. To make sure that the news of this great spectacle reached the outside world promptly, the Western Union Telegraph Company ran a wire from Lake Valley to Hillsboro and provided two operators to man the key.

The community pulse rate began to go up several days before the trial opened. Accused and accusers arrived. Witnesses showed up. Reporters and correspondents from the El Paso papers, the Hearst papers, the Associated Press, and smaller organs moved in with pencils sharpened. Among them was H. D. Slater, newly come from the East to work on the El Paso *Herald*, which he was later to own. The trial was an absorbing and eye-opening experience for him, and his dispatches were the most complete and accurate of all the stories filed.

Among the witnesses was Jack Fountain, just in from Colorado, where he had been working. On the stage from Lake Valley he found himself riding with Lee's friends Jack and Tom Tucker and Bill Carr, all heavily armed, as was to be expected. The trip was peaceful enough, but trouble started for Jack the minute he got off the stage. Fall brought him before Judge Parker and asked that he be put under a peace bond, declaring that the defendants and defense witnesses went in fear of their lives from him.

"Is there any reason why this bond should not be imposed?" Parker inquired of him.

"Your honor," Jack said, "I am just a young boy and have not had much experience, but I will say that I never said I intended to kill any of these men, and don't say so now, though they deserve killing. If the court pleases to hear me, I will state what I did say."

"You may make your statement."

"I said, if my father's bones were ever found and identified (and I think I know how to identify them positively), there is one man I would kill first, if I were not killed myself."

"Who is that man?"

"Albert Bacon Fall."

Parker put the boy under a $500 bond.[2]

By that time the champions on both sides had arrived, and they were an impressive lot. Appearing for the prosecution were District Attorney R. P. Barnes of Silver City, William Burr Childers of Albuquerque, and Thomas Benton Catron of Santa Fe. Defense counsel included three fine lawyers, Harvey B. Fergusson of Albuquerque, Harry M. Daugherty of Socorro, and Albert Bacon Fall of Las Cruces. There was a feeling in the air that this was to be a duel between the old champion and the young one—Catron and Fall—and most of the bets seemed to be on Fall.

Friends of Oliver Lee from all over the Territory had come in for the trial—some of them ready to act if necessary. Will Keleher declares that in the courtroom were three cowboys who had made up their minds to get Lee out of the country if the verdict went against him. They had a mount saddled and waiting outside the courthouse and had arranged for relays of horses to be ready on a trail through the mountains that would take a fugitive into Mexico.[3] Even stranger things might have happened in Hillsboro than the ones that actually took place, though these were bizarre enough.

The proceedings got under way on May 26, 1899, with the selection of a jury, Fall making as much difficulty for the other side as he could. Judge Parker ruled that all three men could be tried at once, but the prosecution decided to charge only Lee and Gililland with the murder of little Henry Fountain. An interpreter was provided, since some of the jurymen spoke only Spanish. Then, with the trial ready to begin, everything had to be postponed. Jack Maxwell was missing.

Maxwell was the star witness for the Territory. His absence "created consternation among the attorneys for the prosecution." [4] Not convinced that he was lying on a bed of pain at White Oaks, as he said, they sent Garrett in haste to corral him.

Meanwhile the feeling between the factions was very tense. Groups of partisans elbowed each other on the narrow streets and exchanged black looks. Lee and Gililland were safe enough in their cells in the jail, but just in case of trouble Lee asked for guards. Parker let him have two, one of whom was Gene Rhodes.

The parade of witnesses began on Monday morning, May 29. First up was Governor William T. Thornton, sometimes known as "Poker Bill." He told of his trip to Las Cruces—the blood-soaked sand—his offer of reward—the finding of the horse with the bloody side.

Cross-examining, Fall acted like a man in complete command of the situation. He spoke in a low voice, looked over his glasses, rumpled his hair, and seemed to find the whole affair amusing and a little exasperating.

Then came the trailing party—Albert Fountain and his father-in-law first. After that Theodore Heman, foreman of the Lincoln County grand jury which had indicted Lee and Mc-New. He produced his indictments in order to establish a motive for the murder. Then Barela, the stage driver, told his story.

The next morning, Tuesday, Jack Maxwell was on hand, but he seemed to hate being there. Deputy Sheriff Latham had picked him up at Alamogordo and brought him in willy-nilly. Now all eyes were on him, and everybody was wondering if he would stick to his story that Lee, Gililland, and McNew had come in to the Dog Canyon ranch five or six hours after Fountain met his end, worn out and worried. He did not stick to his story.

"I have known Oliver Lee when I see him for five or six years," he testified, "and Mr. Gililland about the same length of time. My ranch is not very far from Lee's. On February 1, 1896, I was at Dog Canyon ranch and spent the night there. I got there just before sundown. When I got there I found Mr. Lee, Mr. Blevins, Mr. Bailey, and Ed, the colored man. I ate supper there that night and slept in the house with Mr. Blevins."

They read back his testimony from the McNew preliminary trial at Las Cruces in 1898, over Fall's objections. It was obvious that Maxwell had "forgotten" a good many things.

Then Fall cross-examined and ran Maxwell hard. He got into the record the fact that Maxwell's testimony now was the same as formerly "except as to dates," that Maxwell had been guarded all through the preliminary examination of McNew at Las Cruces, and that he had left immediately thereafter for Colorado Springs. "I left Las Cruces on the train with Mr. Childers," he admitted. "He paid my fare and got me a job."

"Did you not tell Bud Smith after you got back that Mr. Childers had told you you had better go away as the defendants or their friends would kill you?"

The prosecution objected frantically; the objection was overruled; and the answer was "Yes."

Then Fall began his favorite game of significant questions.

"Did Mr. Childers tell you what he would do to you if you failed to testify?

"Did you not tell Bud Smith a week after February 1, 1896, that they need not accuse Oliver Lee or any of these boys of the murder of Colonel Fountain, for you were there and saw Lee setting out grape vines with Mrs. Lee, and the other boys were also there at work?

"Is it not a fact that this is the first time you have been able to fix the day of the week when you got to Dog Canyon, or when you left there, or the day of the month?

"Didn't you write a letter to Jack Tucker telling him that you would make a good witness for the boys as you could swear that they were forty miles away when Fountain disappeared?

"Isn't it a fact that you told Pat Garrett and Mr. Perry that you knew certain facts and would not swear to them until they had given you two thousand dollars?

"Didn't you tell me that Mr. Perry told you that unless you gave evidence convicting these men you might be hung yourself?"

"No sir! No sir! No sir!" Maxwell dodged and denied but had to make some admissions, such as the fact that he had written a letter to Jack Tucker.

Then Fall turned to Maxwell's own personal record. Born in Alabama—six years in Texas—then to Colorado. In the Panhandle of Texas he was known as J. B. Alexander. Obviously no very settled citizen!

The fact that Maxwell had a contract with Garrett and Sheriff Perry of Roswell promising him $2,000 of the reward money in case of conviction was made to look very bad. Fall showed from evidence given in at McNew's preliminary trial that the names of the three men on trial were specified in the contract. That hurt. The jury could not miss the suggestion of collusion, and the dispatches that went out after Maxwell's ordeal said that his testimony was "more damaging to the Territory than to the defense." [5]

Day after day the witnesses submitted to Albert Fall's expert harassment. Poor old Antonio García, young Albert Fountain's father-in-law, got so tangled up he didn't know east from west. Nicolas Armijo proved to be "so little acquainted with the ways of civilization that it took him fully ten minutes to remember the present month and year and he did not even profess to know the day of the week." [6] Fall brushed these men aside with the implication that such morons could not be taken seriously.

When bigger game crossed his sights, he was prepared—as he showed when Dr. Francis Crosson took the stand. Crosson stated that he had made a microscopic examination of the blood-soaked earth and of the hair clipped from the side of Fountain's horse, going on to use "scientific terms and language which balked the interpreter and caused much hilarity in the courtroom." [7]

Fall was not impressed. He went into the specific gravity of blood, the time it takes to dry, and the effect of fibrine content.

"What effect would salt in the earth, if there was any, have on your experiment?"

"I don't know. I didn't examine the earth for salt."

"And yet you swear that this blood was human blood."

"I didn't swear anything of the kind! There is no human being who can tell human blood from any other kind of blood after the red corpuscles have changed construction. But I did swear that my conclusions were that the blood was that of a human being."

"Oh, that's different; that's different. Now is specific gravity any conclusive test of blood? Can you tell by that whether blood is that of a horse, a coyote, a rabbit, or a man?"

"I don't know."

"Will a litmus-paper test enable you to tell whether the blood is that of a man or an animal?"

"I don't know."

"Will you undertake before this jury to taste samples of human blood, dog's blood, or rat's blood and tell which is human blood?"

"No, I wouldn't. Blood testing is so difficult that the best expert in the world would not swear to it." [8]

Fall was kind enough to let him go after that.

Some of the prosecution's witnesses seemed to be playing on Fall's team, especially in this matter of the blood stains. Albert Fountain, Junior, told of finding his father's white horse —the one with the stain on his side. It seemed, he said, "that something wide had been thrown on the horse's back like a blanket, causing him to sweat and his side to be dyed by the blanket or whatever it was. I did not find any blood on the horse." [9]

A few witnesses were heard whose testimony might have been damaging, but Fall had a way with them too. Six days after the trial was begun, "Little Jim" Gould, a cousin of Gililland's wife, was called. Shortly after the disappearance, he said, Gililland had done some talking.

"While out working on the fence he told me that old man Fountain had come from Texas in a chicken coop and prized up hell ever since he had been in New Mexico, but he wouldn't prize up any more. I asked him about killing the child and he said the child was nothing but a half-breed and to kill him was like killing a dog." [10]

Instead of attacking this testimony, Fall attacked Gould.

"Where were you in March, 1897?"

"I was in the Eddy jail."

"Are you a friend or enemy of Mr. Gililland?"

"An enemy, I suppose, now."

"How about McNew?"

"Well, Mr. McNew don't speak to me."

"For a long time prior to the arrest of McNew at Las Cruces all you parties up there in the Sacramentos were going armed for one another and were expecting trouble, were you not?"

"We carried pistols."

"The fact of the matter was you and your father and Kearney expected McNew and others to attack you, didn't you?"

"I was afraid they were going to attack me but didn't know about the rest."

Riley Baker, Gililland's brother-in-law, crept up to the stand and sat down with the air of a man performing a hazardous experiment. His eyes wandered around the room or fastened themselves firmly to the floor. He seemed so abstracted and ill at ease that the judge had to ask him to look at and speak to the jury. He stated that Gililland had once told him that the bodies would never be found and that no one would ever be convicted of the murder. Fall disposed of him by showing that he too was an enemy of Gililland and McNew and that he had acted as a tool and a spy of the law officers who apparently did not have enough nerve to serve their own warrants.

Still hopeful, the prosecution called up Frank Wayne, who lived some twenty-five miles from the Lee ranch and was there looking for a pony just before the day of Fountain's death. He testified, "When I left there Mr. Lee rode out with me and my brother about two miles. When he went to start back he said, 'You boys say nothing about what you saw here, as it might interfere with some of our plans.'"

Just what Wayne saw was not made entirely clear, and Fall forbore to cross-examine.[11]

At last came Pat Garrett, whose testimony was expected to

clinch everything that had gone before. He told nothing that was not already known, spending most of his time describing the fight at Wildy Well and displaying a copy of the contract he had entered into with Maxwell. During cross-examination, Fall absorbed a few blows himself.

"What was the condition of affairs when you first went to Las Cruces?"

"Well, you fellows had been shooting at one another and cutting up."

"What fellows?"

"You and Lee and Williams and others."

"At the time you went to Las Cruces political feeling was running pretty high, wasn't it?"

"That's what they called it."

"What did you say would be your course if given any warrants for the arrest of Lee? Did you not say that you would go after him by yourself?"

"Yes, sir."

"Upon what were these warrants based?"

"Upon affidavits."

"They were issued four terms after Fountain disappeared, were they not, and after the grand jury adjourned?"

"Yes, sir."

"Who made the affidavits before warrants for the defendants were issued?"

"I did."

"When this evidence came into your hands, why did you not apply for a bench warrant?"

"I did not think it was the proper time."

"Why didn't you think it was the proper time?"

"You had too much control of the courts." [laughter]

"In other words you thought that I was the administration."

"You came pretty near to it." [12]

It was about the only time the prosecution scored off Fall, and he did not seem much bothered.

There was more than one passage at arms between him and the mighty Catron. When Major Llewellyn was on the stand, for instance, Fall attacked him in the flank in the matter of his identification of the tracks of the accused men.

"Didn't you testify yesterday that the track you saw at Las Cruces was not the same as any of the three you saw near the blood?"

Catron heaved his great bulk out of his chair. "He did not!" he roared.

There was a brief exchange of "did" and "didn't." "You are stating what you know to be false!" Fall finally told him. "I will apologize for my language to the court, but not to you." [13]

There were other surprises. One afternoon the Hillsboro ladies sent a huge bouquet of flowers into the courtroom to be placed in front of the defendants. At the same time Fall's little daughter Jouett presented another to Oliver Lee. It was good staging before a sympathetic audience.

There was never any doubt about which side the audience was on. At one point, when Print Rhode was testifying that Major Llewellyn had planned to blow up Lee's house with dynamite (a story that the prosecution witnesses denied *in toto*), the spectators "almost burst forth in cheers." [14]

The prosecution closed, having had its few bits of effective testimony unmercifully chewed up by Fall, and the defense opened.

George Curry and Bud Smith swore that Jack Maxwell had told them in private conversation that Lee, McNew, and Gililland were at home the day of the murder. Albert Blevins, a T. and P. fireman from Toyah, Texas, added the information that he came to Lee's ranch the afternoon of the murder and found the defendants there. Mrs. Lee, Oliver's mother, white-haired and dignified, told the jury that her boy had been at home the day of the catastrophe.

Then Lee himself undertook to explain his actions. He said he was busy about the ranch while the crime was being committed and did not even know about it till several days later. When he did find out that he was suspected, he went at once to Las Cruces and offered to surrender. He refused to give up later, he said, "because of mob talk and information that I would be subject to violence." [15]

Mr. Barnes led off when it came time for final arguments, and kept at it till noon, to the extreme consternation of the court interpreter. He made it flowery, quoted from the *Pickwick Papers*, and whipped up soaring metaphors. The last straw was piled on the interpreter's creaking back when Barnes wished to insinuate that Mrs. Lee's alibi for her son was a product of her affection. "She laid a wreath of maternal duty on the altar of maternal love," said Barnes; and the interpreter threw up his hands in defeat.

The *corpus dilecti* was very much on the lawyers' minds. Childers told the jury that the body did not have to be produced.[16] Harry Daugherty for the defense agreed, but maintained that "it is customary to bring into court some part of the body, or something that carries absolute conviction that the crime has been committed. I never heard of a case where men were put on trial before a jury for murder when there was not a scintilla of proof that a crime had been committed." [17]

Fall made the last and climactic appearance for the defense. According to one of his lawyer friends he was worn to a frazzle and had made up his mind to let the other attorneys handle the closing speeches. But Lee would not have it that way. He sent a note after Fall asking him to return to the courtroom.

"I want you to make an address to the jury, even if it is no more than ten minutes long," he said.

"I'm completely beat out. They won't need me. Fergusson

and Daugherty are better speechmakers than I am. They can handle it."

"Fall, they're trying to hang me for something I'm not guilty of, and you know what I would do for you if you were in trouble." [18]

Fall knew well enough what Lee would do for him, and had done. He addressed the jury, and took longer than ten minutes. Nobody who heard that speech ever forgot it.

He talked about the jury system and its great benefits to human beings in trouble—people like the defendants who were being tried far from their homes and friends. Warming up, he attacked the prosecution at front, rear, and center, hitting hardest when he came to the all-important alibi.

"If you believe that man Maxwell told the truth," he said earnestly, "you must believe that Blevins—is a liar; that Joe Fitchett—is a liar; that Bailey—is a liar; that Oliver Lee—is a liar. If Maxwell told the truth, you must believe that these five men and a woman are perjurers, are murderers, for they are implicated in this case. If you believe that Maxwell told the truth, you must believe that George Curry is a liar, and that Bud Smith is a liar. Now take your choice—either all these eight witnesses are liars—or Jack Maxwell is a liar."

The interpreter turned it out in Spanish with fine dramatic power. Fall bore down harder.

"I ask for no white mantle of charity for these men. I desire no vindication. I ask simply stern justice. If the evidence in this case convinces you that these men murdered little Henry Fountain, you must convict. There is no alternative. If you are not so convinced, turn them loose."

Then with a sudden turn Fall lowered his voice and painted a picture.

"You are no doubt surprised to learn that such a state of affairs can exist as that in Doña Ana County. In many streams there is a point at a sharp bend where the water pauses in its flow and forms an eddy. Around the edges the slime gathers, and froth and logs and dead leaves, and all manner of floating filth. The moss and ferns grow dank, and the shadowy places are haunted by creeping things. Snakes come out of their hiding places and bask in the sun on the slimy logs, and if they are disturbed in their retreat, they sting in the heel the man who is so foolish as to venture there. Doña Ana County is just such a dead eddy. Under the territorial form of government the public officers do not hold office by choice of the people, but are appointed by the federal powers. There in Doña Ana County have gathered together, as does the slimy filth on the edges of the dead eddy, a lot of broken-down old political hacks. They bask in the sun of political preferment, like the serpents stretched out on the dead logs. They never got an honest dollar in their lives, and do not know how to earn one except by serving the people, forsooth, in public office. It was in just such a dead eddy as I have described that there arose this plot for the persecution of Oliver Lee."

Subtly he appealed to the sympathies of the poor men on the jury. "These defendants are paying all the expenses of their defense. The Territory does not help them out. They must defend themselves. It costs a lot of money to put sixty witnesses on the stand, but more than all this we do not propose to show our hand until we are compelled to. There are two more cases for us to meet. As long as this persecution persists, we want to have something in reserve.

"Our defense is an alibi, clearly proved. You would not hang a yellow dog on the evidence that has been presented here, much less two men." [19]

When Fall sat down, the courtroom burst into prolonged applause. There was even some subdued cheering in spite of Judge Parker's outraged efforts to restore order.

At eight that night there was a full courtroom for the last round. Tom Catron was to make the final speech, and Catron was worth listening to. His dour and sardonic manner, his grudge against Fall, and his personal eminence aroused much anticipation. He did not let his audience down, though he must have known that his cause was lost. Every suspicious word, every significant movement of the defendants was raked up before he got through; every bit of evidence against them was recapitulated.

Corpus dilecti—the shoes on Lee's horse—Albert Fountain's testimony—Carl Clausen at the Wildy Well. One by one he checked off the points. Eight o'clock. Nine o'clock. Ten o'clock. It was ten-thirty at night when he finished, to the great relief of his audience.[20] The trial had lasted eighteen days, with several night sessions. It was time for all this to be finished, and everybody felt that it would not take long now.

The jury retired at eleven-twenty, expecting to go to bed and complete their work in the morning. At Fall's insistence they were called back—the defense demanded a verdict. They entered the jury room and were out eight minutes. Foreman Alexander Bentley handed the verdict to the clerk, who read out the words: "Not Guilty." [21]

The courtroom came to pieces. The crowd of spectators rose to their feet and cheered and clapped and screamed in relief and jubilation. They all seemed to want to shake hands with Lee and Gililland, and the front of the courtroom became a swirl of excited people. The sheriff could hardly make himself heard as he shouted that court was adjourned. If anyone in that noisy crowd of celebrators remembered that somewhere in the wilds of the Tularosa country Albert Jennings Fountain was lying in an unmarked grave, he kept his thoughts to himself.

The rest was just formality. Parker sent Lee and Gililland back to confinement in the new Alamogordo jail,[22] but in due time the remaining indictments against them were dismissed. The Territory nolle prossed the one case left against McNew. No one was ever actually tried for the murder of Fountain, and nobody knows officially to this day who did it.

They say that when Lee and Gililland rode over to Las

Cruces after they were turned loose, the first stop they made was at Fall's office, and the first question they asked was, "How much do we owe you?" Fall did some figuring on the back of an envelope and presented a bill for $62.25—the actual cash he had spent in traveling and for hotel bills. "I took most of my meals at the chuck wagon during the trial and saved you some money that way," he remarked.[23]

At that, Fall was not the cheapest workman in the legal mill. Tom Catron, it is reported, was so anxious to defeat Fall and send Lee to the scaffold that he offered to head the prosecution for nothing.

Aftermath

The Fountain case was closed, and it stayed closed. The murderers, whoever they were, walked among their fellowmen and no one saw the red stain on their hands. To the end of their lives they were free—perhaps respected and beloved. No man accused them, and probably nobody ever will. It is just as well. The old order changed and new ways of thinking and doing came to townsman and cowman alike. It is best to let the thing stay buried.

But there is never any end to the stories and conjectures that such an affair produces. Close-mouthed with strangers, the cowmen talked a good deal among themselves and some of their talk, distorted perhaps, filtered out to the world at large. Every old-timer had a different theory, however, and the legends multiplied as time went on until it became next to impossible to sift out the truth.

A dozen men with inside information have whispered the names of the killers—always a different set of names. Probably a good many people were involved. The fact that Fountain was followed and spied on by two men, then shadowed by three more, shows careful planning and coordination. It is quite possible, furthermore, that the three men who trailed him to the White Sands did just that and no more. The actual murderers may have been posted at Chalk Hill, ready to carry out their own part of the plot, and they may well have been strangers to the victims. Otherwise, why would it have been necessary to send those riders ahead of the colonel as he came into the trap?

In Texas it was a time-honored custom to hire killers who would not be recognized even if they had the bad luck to be seen. These men would ride off after a job was done and paid for, and that would be that. The gangs, or "mobs," which flourished after the Civil War sometimes even traded work of this sort and obliged each other with payment in kind.

The outsider most frequently given credit for the Fountain job was Black Jack Ketchum, the train robber who was hanged at Clayton, New Mexico, in 1901. Black Jack was familiar with the country and spent some of his hide-out time on Gene Rhodes's ranch in the San Andres. In 1949 Bob Lewis, a former peace officer living at Magdalena, brought the old subject up again for an Albuquerque reporter. "Sam Ketchum told me," he said, "that his brother Tom [Black Jack] Ketchum murdered Colonel Fountain and his son. . . . Sam told me he was an eyewitness to the Fountain killings. . . . There was a third man in the party too, he said, but he would not reveal his name." [1]

The old-timers have remarkably diverse views of what happened to the bodies. One declares that they were burned in the firebox of a steam boiler on a lonely ranch.[2] Another says that they were buried beside a water tank and covered with concrete.

People were always finding bones that could have solved the mystery. In 1900 two skeletons were turned up in James Canyon in the Sacramentos five miles from Cloudcroft. Pat

Garrett declared that they were not the remains in question, but Jack Fountain, it was said, was not so sure.[3]

Las Cruces was stirred up again in 1909 when the Masonic Lodge received a letter with a Texas postmark asking if the reward for finding the bodies was still outstanding. The signature at the bottom of the page was a familiar one in the Tularosa country. A spokesman for the Masons replied that the reward was still available, and a letter came back directing searchers to the area north of the Jarillas. Judge Parker saw the letter and showed signs of considerable excitement. A search party was organized and Albert Fountain, the colonel's son, was sent for. The men were all ready to go when he arrived—their horses tied up to Henry Stoes' fence. Albert was in a terrible state. When they finally asked him point blank if he was going with them or not, he threw up his hands and said, "My God, no! It would kill my mother."

The search was called off and the Masons withdrew their offer of a reward.

The last attempt to solve the mystery came in 1950. Only a little of the story was allowed to leak out to the papers, but that little sounded promising. It seems that an old man who claimed to be one of the killers told a friend, just before he died, where the bodies were buried. They were high up in the San Andres in a lonely spot marked by a pile of stones. To settle any doubts that he knew whereof he spoke, the dying man produced Colonel Fountain's Masonic pin.

In November a party of twelve men, including three of Fountain's grandsons, set off to search for the stone monument and what might lie beneath. They found the stones but nothing else. The earth had obviously never been disturbed. They were not convinced, however, that the bodies might not be in the neighborhood. The old man had put up the marker some time—perhaps years—after the murder and might easily have been off a few feet in his calculations.

His story checked with some of the most persistent of the rumors that had been going around for fifty-four years. "Upon making camp," he said, "the three murderers drew straws to see which of the trio would murder the frail child. One who drew the short straw quickly severed Henry's head with a knife in a moment of impulse.

"They threw his body into a pit of alkali, so that no trace will ever be found.

"Then, after separating, the riders agreed to rendezvous in the high San Andres where Fountain's body was buried in the most inaccessible place possible.

"The riders then took different routes back to their respective homes. Periodically the site of the grave was checked.

". . . the Fountains and the other members of the party are convinced that somewhere within a few feet of the marker is the body of Albert J. Fountain.

"They haven't abandoned the search." [4]

Anything that happened in the Tularosa country in the years that followed Fountain's death was linked to that event if local gossip could find a way to do it. When Pat Garrett was killed in 1908, there were those who said the Fountain business was behind it. The colonel's descendants still believe that Pat settled on his ranch in the San Andres because he thought the victims were buried on it or near it and he hoped to continue the search unmolested.

Again, when Bob Raley, Gililland's brother-in-law, was killed by Bill McNew in the fall of 1915,[5] it was whispered that too much talk about the Fountain case had brought on hard feelings—though the actual bone of contention was a well which both sides claimed.[6]

The speculators got in their best licks when any one of the men on either side came to die. Every one of them, according to the rumors, was on the point of making a deathbed statement about Colonel Fountain. The stories always followed the same pattern. Just as the revelation was about to come, the listeners would be pushed out of the room by some close relative who didn't want them to hear anything.

A fine piece of fantasy got into circulation when Jim Gililland retired from business, sold his ranch in the Mockingbird Gap of the San Andres, and moved to Hot Springs—now known as Truth or Consequences—New Mexico. His diary, they said, was left behind in the confusion of moving, and he came back in great alarm looking for it, but it had been removed by a woman who wanted to know what was inside.[7] Of all men who have ever taken pen in hand, Jim Gililland was probably the least likely to have been bitten by the diary-keeping bug, yet this story has been told and believed.

Bitter feeling stayed alive for a long time—that much is certain—and may not be entirely dead yet, though only a handful of people are left who could possibly be personally concerned. For years there was real danger that something might break out if the right people got together at the wrong place. City dwellers always noted with a feeling of horrified pleasure that when Lee or any of his men came to El Paso, they carried pistols and never sat with their backs to a door or window.

Lawyer Will Burges used to tell about the time Oliver Lee came to his El Paso office to discuss a case and sat back comfortably in an easy chair. His six-shooter dropped out of his pocket, went off, and sent a bullet crashing into the wall. Lee did not seem disturbed, but Burges was considerably startled. When he recovered the use of his tongue, he asked Oliver why he didn't carry five cartridges in his gun, leaving the hammer on an empty chamber.

"Because," Lee answered, "sometimes you need that extra cartridge." [8]

Everybody who lived in the Tularosa country, and some who had merely passed through, had a story to tell which added to the legend. There was seldom any truth in these tales, of course, but people will always believe what they want to.

One such yarn said that there was a tombstone in a cemetery near Ruidoso on which was carved a six-word inscription: "HE CALLED OLIVER LEE A LIAR." You will not find anybody who has seen the stone.

Lee always started a journey before daylight, the legend said—never told anybody where he was going—never sat in a lighted room with the window shades up. Occasional visitors at the ranch reported that he was a light sleeper and that he kept a horse in the barn saddled and ready to go at all times.[9] The most amazing story of all says that he built a tunnel at his Dog Canyon ranch which could be entered by removing a board from beside one of the fireplaces. The other end of the tunnel was in a small outbuilding some distance from the house. Many people say they have seen that tunnel, and perhaps, after many repetitions of the story, they really believe they have.

Occasionally something happened to show that Lee needed to be mighty careful. At the time of the cross-country automobile race from El Paso to Phoenix in November 1919, for example, Johnny Hutchings of Alamogordo entered a Buick roadster and asked Oliver to ride with him. "Because you're lucky," he answered when Oliver asked him why.[10] A good many people had taken their picnic lunches and found positions along the road that Sunday to watch the racers bounce by. Just before Lee and Hutchings reached Lanark Station, half an hour out of El Paso, one of these bystanders put a bullet through the back of the driver's seat, giving Johnny a mortal wound. It is still thought (probably erroneously) that the shot was meant for Lee. Major William F. Scanland, a patient at the Fort Bliss Base Hospital, was convicted and given a prison sentence for the murder. He appealed the case, and while he was out on bail waiting for the final hearing, somebody beat him to death near Arlington, Virginia.[11]

Actually, Lee had to fight his way out of difficulties only

once after the troubles of the nineties. His last battle, about water, occurred in 1907. Somebody was always thinking of proving up on Frenchy's old development in Dog Canyon, which would have meant the ruin of all that Lee had built up. He couldn't stand by and let that happen. J. C. Smith, who came from East Texas in 1899 to teach school and run the first newspaper in Otero County (at Cloudcroft), filed on that water with four other men and held his desert claim for about two years. They were years of trouble and conflicting interests.

On March 20, 1907, the thing came to a head over a fence. A niece of Lee's had a desert claim near the Dog Canyon headquarters, and the boundary line between her land and that of the immigrants was in doubt. One morning James R. Fennimore, his father-in-law Tom Knight, and two of his employees started building a fence on the disputed area. Lee came out to put a stop to it, and there was a long-distance battle with Winchesters. Five shots were fired by the Fennimore party. Lee fired twice, according to newspaper stories, giving Fennimore a flesh wound in the hip.

Lee and his men rode immediately to Alamogordo, gave themselves up and got out warrants for Fennimore, Knight, and the rest. Fennimore did the same for Lee, and neither side did anything more about it.[12]

The men who stand in front of the corner drugstore in Alamogordo and swap yarns think that, when Lee was arraigned for attempting to kill Fennimore, he pointed out that the man had been shot in the region of the hip pockets.

"If I'd wanted to kill him, I'd have shot him in the head," he explained.

This bit of folklore says that the judge, knowing Lee's renown as a marksman, dismissed the case.[13] Regrettably, nothing in the contemporary records indicates that there is a word of truth in the story.

With a reputation like that, Lee was bound to be very high

or very low in the estimation of people who knew him or knew about him. Take J. C. Smith's daughter, now Mrs. C. J. Parker, who heard the shooting during the Lee-Fennimore battle and never forgot her terror. "Lee was the boogey-man of my childhood," she says. "I saw a man shake hands with him in El Paso once, and it sent cold shivers up my spine." [14]

On the other tack, A. M. Tenney, one of Lee's old cowboys, said, "When I was a boy, Oliver Lee was a sort of god, though when I got older I found he had some human weaknesses." [15]

Sixto García of Tularosa worked for him for twelve years, starting when he was just a boy scared to death by the Lee legend. Sixto was still a little disturbed as an old man when he told stories of those far-off times. "He was a demon during the day's work," he told me, "and drove everybody, but especially himself. Sometimes we got through at nine or ten at night, but when the work was done, he made everybody laugh—always had plenty to say. I saw him start to pistol whip three Negroes one time. They were sleeping in a house while their horses were tied in the corral without food or water. I ran, and didn't see how it came out. Nobody had better abuse a horse when Mr. Lee was around. He was the fastest man I ever saw, but he didn't exercise much. He could throw a quarter up and hit it in the air." [16]

His friends and neighbors always swore by him. One way or another he was related to half the country, and the big house he built in Alamogordo was headquarters for everybody in the Sacramento region. Mrs. Lee was famous for her oyster dressing and other culinary specialties. The door was open and his friends walked in, and when they walked out, they were ready to do battle with anybody who spoke slightingly of Oliver Lee.

As time went on, his standing in the community rose in many ways. He was a good cowman and his expanding operations made him more and more prosperous. But it was the Circle Cross which made him a really big operator.

About 1914 he began to negotiate with a group of El Paso businessmen headed by James G. McNary of the First National Bank, who was a fabulous character himself. These men wanted to organize a mammoth ranch enterprise with Oliver Lee as manager. They bought Lee out and set up their organization with a paid-in capital of $800,000. McNary was president and Lee was vice-president and general manager.[17] Headquarters were established at the old Hilton place on the Sacramento River high up under the pines. The circle cross was registered as their brand. And they began to spread out.

Buying up ranch after ranch, they soon controlled the range from the Mescalero Reservation almost to Ysleta, Texas; from the middle of the Tularosa plain to the Cornudas mountains on the east.[18] At its peak the ranch comprised a million acres. There were the usual ups and downs—heavy losses in 1921; more in 1926; several financial reorganizations.[19] But while it lasted, the Circle Cross was the biggest thing in southern New Mexico.

The headquarters became a show place, with a big house and barns, a fine orchard, and even a deer park. The best in machinery and equipment was none too good for the Circle Cross. It seemed that anything so big with so much behind it would have to succeed.

One thing after another weakened the gigantic enterprise, however. McNary's bank got into trouble—a bitter memory in El Paso to this day—and eventually failed, taking the First Mortgage Company down to ruin with it. This did the ranch enterprise no good, but what actually broke it was drought and low prices. Joe Irvin of Marfa wanted to close out his cattle business, and he sold the Circle Cross ten thousand head of four-year-olds for eight hundred thousand dollars. They were driven to the Sacramentos, but there was a drought on, and it became necessary to move them. They were shipped to northern ranges—Dakota and Montana. The drought struck there too. The only thing to do was bring them back to Kansas and sell them. About the time the stock arrived in Kansas, the market dropped. The Circle Cross got back its expenses and lost the original investment of eight hundred thousand dollars.[20]

The great ranch broke up and Oliver Lee lost with the rest of the investors, since he had put his own money back into the company after his original sale. He did save the Circle Cross headquarters, which was his own home place, but it became necessary to sell that, and he looked a long time for a buyer. Many seemed interested, but nobody would take the final plunge. Lee Orndorff of El Paso was handling the sale —or trying to. Finally Oliver asked him point blank: "Lee, why can't you sell this place?"

Orndorff gave it to him straight. "Oliver, I want you to take this the way it is meant. The reason I can't sell it is on account of your reputation. They all know it is your home place and they figure you will shoot any man that goes on there."

Lee was horrified. "Is that possible?" he asked in genuine dismay. "I can hardly believe it." He thought about the situation for a long time and talked to Orndorff about his record more frankly than he ever had before. At the end he said, "Lee, I never in my life willingly hurt man, woman, or child —unless they hurt me first. Then I made them pay." Then he added, "Well, the next man that wants to look the place over, you let me take him up there."

The next man was a doctor from Roswell, whom Lee accompanied to the ranch and entertained as well as he knew how. The man stayed three weeks and eventually bought the place, declaring that his host was the finest gentleman he had ever met.[21]

Lee's friends, of course, didn't care whether Oliver was prosperous or broke. In many ways they let him know how much they esteemed him. Twice they sent him to the State Legislature, where he worked hard for good roads and better schools. Many positions of public trust came to him, and he was called in as referee in a great many cases where the value of land or cattle was in question. His name appeared among the officers and directors of numerous business organizations. For years he was a director of the Federal Land Bank.

He was more and more alone in his last days, and it seemed that he liked it that way. Though he loved to go to cattle-men's conventions and meet his own kind, he found that his own kind was growing increasingly scarce. With the drug-store cowboys and amateur ranchmen, he had little in common. Probably he was happiest on the range with his cattle and horses thinking about the old days—though he said he preferred the new times to the old.

After the stroke came which ended his active life, his family watched over him with loving care and saw to it that he was never by himself for very long. In 1941 he died peace-fully, and the leather-faced riders from the desert and the mountains turned out in a body to see him off.[22]

He never discussed the troubles of the nineties. Neither did his friends. For fifty years and more their united front was never broken. Even after McNew, Gililland, and Lee were dead, it was not broken. One by one they died with their lips firmly closed. That was the way of the old-time cattle-men.

The Bard of the Tularosa

G<small>ENE</small> R<small>HODES</small> started working for cow outfits in 1883, when he was thirteen. He showed up at the headquarters of the Bar Cross at Engle one morning, dragging a saddle he had acquired with soap coupons, and hit the boss for a job. Frank Wallace looked the boy over—a small, wiry, blue-eyed youngster with a shock of mouse-colored hair—and decided to take a chance.[1] Gene went to work as a wrangler and general roustabout, and from then on he spent most of his days on a horse. Before long he was known as a twister who would ride almost anything with hair on it. Persistence was his long suit. When a bronco unloaded him, he got back on and tried it again.

For twenty-five years he rode the ranges of southern New Mexico and made himself known far and wide—not always favorably—among the cattle people. Then he began writing about what he knew and what he remembered. When he died in 1934, he had become the foremost interpreter and defender of the cowman and his way of life. Other "Western" writers sold more books, but for love and understanding of his own people nobody could match him. As long as outsiders are curious about the men in Stetsons and the country they live in, Gene Rhodes will be remembered, for he is the only authentic bard the cow country has produced.

A bard, says the definition, is a professional poet who makes and sings songs about heroes. In so doing, he puts the dreams and ideals of his group into words.

Bard production was low among cowboys, because they were too busy and too self-contained to bother much with telling the world about themselves, and too independent to care whether other groups regarded them with sympathy or not. Most of the writers and artists who have dealt with them have been outsiders who took fire after catching a glimpse of what went on in the cowtowns and round-up camps. Only occasionally has a man on the inside—a Charlie Russell, for instance—made a business of telling about the life he was born to. Most of the time it has been the sons of Owen Wister who sat on the corral fence and reported as best they could how some Virginian managed his affairs.

Eugene Manlove Rhodes wrote fourteen novels and novelettes and sixty short stories of the type we call "Westerns," [2] but with a very impressive difference. While they were uneven in quality,[3] sometimes sinking pretty low, they always rose to remarkable heights when there was occasion to bring in the characters and the talk and the happenings and the landscape of southern New Mexico as it was in Gene's early days. The friends of his youth were his characters, and he believed in them, loved them, defended them. "If I would not be incomparably base," he said, "I must speak up for my own people." [4]

In his mind the cattlemen took rank with the Trojans who followed Aeneas to Italy or the Saxons who overran England: instruments of Destiny, forerunners of new eras. He pictured them spearheading what he called "the Greak Trek."

"The Great Trek," he wrote, "has lasted three hundred

years. Today we dimly perceive that the history of America
is the story of the pioneer; that on our shifting frontiers the
race has been hammered and tempered to a cutting edge."[5]

His stories were not just stories to him—not even fictional
history. They were the poetry and romance of his compa-
triots, their epics and sagas. The hands were the hands of Alkali Ike, but the voice was the voice of Homer.

"You have a fine inquiring mind [says Pres Lewis to a tenderfoot
in *The Trusty Knaves*], and you want to remember that in a thousand years, or some such, historians will publicly offer their right
eye to know what you can see now, at first hand; just as they
puzzle and stew and guess about Harold the Saxon, nowadays.
. . . Here you are, living in the ancient days and the springtime
of the world, with a priceless chance to get the lowdown on how
we scramble through with a certain cheerfulness and something
not far removed from decency, and make merry with small
cause." [6]

It was a long and devious road which brought Gene
Rhodes to such a realization. He was born on January 19,
1869, in a double log house in the town of Tecumseh, Nebraska, where the family had a farm and a store. His father
was Hinman Rhodes, late colonel of the Twenty-eighth Illinois Infantry, a stocky, humorous, courageous man with a
twinkle in his eye and tobacco stains on his beard, who hadn't
done too well since Appomattox. His mother was Julia Manlove, an intelligent, alert, high-strung woman—the driving
force in the family.[7] She was better educated than the average,
fiercely determined in the lifelong struggle she had to wage
against adversity, always resolved that her children's minds
and souls should be fed as well as their bodies. Sometimes
there was no money to buy shoes, but she always managed
to have a few books in the house.

Times were hard. Prairie fires, grasshoppers, and cyclones
added to the burden of life, and such things as debts and mort-

gages were always with them. When Eugene, Clarence, and Nellie (Helen) were still small children, the family pulled up stakes and headed for what they hoped would be a better life, first near Beatrice, Nebraska—then at Cherokee, Kansas, where the colonel set up in the lumber business.

It wasn't much better, but Gene always looked back on those days with pleasure. He read everything from dime novels to the Bible and was already making up stories which he illustrated with pictures cut from almanacs and magazines. There were games around the fire and candy pulls with the neighbors. And he could ride far out in the country with his father, selling sewing machines.

There was an unproductive year at Columbus, Kansas, and then the big move—to New Mexico in 1881. Just what lured Hinman Rhodes to begin a new life in that wild country we do not know,[8] but when his family came out to join him he had a place for them at Engle, a booming little cattle-and-mining town on the Santa Fe just west of the San Andres. He had a job with the Detroit Cattle Company, better known as the Bar Cross, and it was that same company which gave Gene his first riding job.

The Bar Cross, under the field generalship of Cole Railston (who appears under his own name in many of Gene's stories) was a big outfit. The range ran from Doña Ana on the south to San Marcial on the north, a hundred miles of sun-baked, waterless desert hemmed in by the San Andres and the Oscuros on the east and the Rio Grande on the west. The Spaniards, who used to cut across it to avoid a great bend in the river too rough for wagon passage, called it the *Jornada del Muerto*—the Day's Journey of the Dead Man. The Americans who came later called it simply the Jornada. Gene liked to describe its barren magnificence:

Theoretically, the Jornada was fifty miles wide here; in reality it was much wider; in seeming it was twice as wide. From the Red

Lakes as a center you looked up an interminable dazzle of slope
to the San Andreas, up and over a broken bench country to Timber Mountain, the black base of it high above the level of Point
o' Rocks at its highest summit; and toward the north you looked
up and up and up again along a smoother and gentler slope ending
in blank nothingness, against which the eye strained vainly.[9]

The Jornada was always a focal point in Gene Rhodes's
world, but he ranged freely in his stories—to Deming and
Hillsboro and the wild mountain country westward, northward almost to the Colorado line, south to El Paso, and eastward across the Tularosa basin to White Oaks and Lincoln
and Roswell. He named these towns to suit himself (Deming
was Target, Doña Ana was Tripoli, Tularosa was Oasis),
but he saw them clearly in his mind's eye and could describe
them exactly, even when there were miles and many years
between him and them.

He worked for the KY, the KIM, the 7TX, the John
Cross. He dug wells, built roads, drove jerk-line teams. In
1886, when Geronimo was making news in Old Mexico and
Arizona, he was employed as a civilian guide by the United
States troops but didn't see any action. "I was a guide (not
enlisted) for eighteen months," he told his wife. "But I was
east of the Rio Grande. Geronimo heard I was over here
and prudently stayed on the west side." [10]

By this time Colonel Rhodes had started a small ranch in a
canyon in the San Andres in the wildest sort of country and
with not much more than a shoestring to go on. The family
lived in a two-room house and ends hardly approached each
other—never really met. Mrs. Rhodes used to drive a wagon
a hundred miles to Mesilla, load up with apples and other
fruit, and drive back again. She canned her purchases and
made pies to sell to soldiers at the army posts.[11]

There was much about this sort of life to make a boy sensitive, and Gene was sensitive, not to say touchy. He was
sensitive about the poor clothes he had to wear when he

went away to school later. He was sensitive about his unruly blond hair, which rose up in "a crest like a cockatoo." [12] He was sensitive about a speech impediment (he had a cleft palate) which stayed with him through life. Perhaps it was this sensitiveness which made him so pugnacious. He developed into a terrific rough-and-tumble fighter, ready to tackle a buzz saw or a bear, though he preferred to fight men. He liked to wrestle too.

A rumor came to him once when he was living up in the mountains that a fine wrestler named Gene Baird had enrolled at the Agricultural College at Las Cruces. Gene got on his horse, rode the hundred miles to the campus, and looked the boy up.

"I hear you can wrestle," he remarked.

"I can wrestle a little," said Baird.

"Well, I think I can beat you."

"All right, get down off that horse."

So Gene got down and they went at it. Baird knew his business. Gene went over his head a couple of times and landed hard.

"By God, you *can* wrestle," he declared as he got on his horse and rode away, satisfied.[13]

It didn't happen that way often. "If anybody tells you that they beat him," Uncle Bill McCall used to say, "he better show the papers on it." [14]

Behind Gene's prowess lay the fact that whatever he tackled he went at with fury and passion. He was not very big and not very heavy, but he was as tough and muscular as a panther in good condition. A cheerful, humorous soul most of the time, he was easily irritated and sometimes flared up into flashes of searing anger. At such times the bright blue eyes blazed and the quizzical mouth set like granite. When he got into a fight, however, he mostly enjoyed himself and hammered away with great good will. And since he was almost indestructible and never stopped coming back for more, peo-

ple learned to let him pretty much alone—though on more
than one occasion he was shot at.

Once he got into a scuffle with the postmaster at Engle
when he went after his mail. Afterward he walked across
the sandy main street reading his letters and was about halfway over when a gun went off behind him. He kept on reading and walked leisurely ahead. Bang! The air was rent again.
By this time Gene was across the way and turned around to
see who was trying to kill him. His eyes opened wide and his
jaw dropped. "Why," he said, "that fellow was shooting a
shotgun. If I'd known, I'd a run." [15]

The same intensity that Gene brought to his fighting he
carried over into his reading. The result was a high degree of
literacy mixed with pungent colloquialism in his own speech
and in the speech of his best fictional characters.

The combination puzzled his friends and those of his readers who could not imagine a rugged Westerner quoting
Shakespeare. Gene was indignant about it. "I can ride horses
that no one else could stick on, but they never mention that,"
he complained to his wife. "They say, 'He reads' "—adding
bitterly, "I've learned my ABCs; why shouldn't I read?" [16]

Wherever he went he carried a book in the side pocket of
his jacket, doubled back to mark the place. He read while his
horse walked. He read while he was waiting for people to
show up at the house. Once he went off alone after some cows
and didn't come back. After a while his horse ambled in, and
a party set off to look for him. They found him under a
mesquite bush, nursing a broken leg and reading away. He
had been there the best part of two days but appeared cheerful and undisturbed.[17]

Once he squired Kate Doughty (later Mrs. Henry Stoes)
to a dance at Engle, and since there was plenty of time, he
spread a tarp over a mesquite bush to make a little shade and
read to her from *The Autocrat of the Breakfast Table*. She
told me that it was his favorite book.[18]

In 1888, when he was about grown up, he made up his mind to go to college. Why he chose the University of the Pacific in California is a mystery, but there he went, fortified with fifty dollars borrowed from his father. Humboldt Casad and his brother, from the Mesilla Valley, were already there. Their acquaintance with Gene began when he walked into their room and revealed that he had become acquainted with the Casad family back in Mesilla and had promised to make himself known to the boys.

Gene's college career was brief and difficult. He had to work his way, doing all sorts of odd jobs. Apparently window washing was his speciality and Hum Casad always remembered him standing on a ledge outside a window and boasting, "See, I can stand here and 'ing out the 'ag!" One inch more and he would have gone down three stories.

At first he lived on the fourth floor of the dormitory with the Casad boys who, with the others on that floor, carried on a feud with the third-floor dwellers. Then he moved to the third floor and joined the opposition.

Once the fourth-floor boys gave a dinner party for themselves. Gene was naturally not invited, but he decided that he would attend anyway and tried to get in through a window which opened on the roof. Hum Casad opposed this move with some vigor and in a moment Gene was rolling toward four stories of free space. A ledge or gutter saved him, but one wonders how many times in his youth Gene was within an inch of not getting any writing done at all.[19]

Two years of college was all he could manage, and then, broke and discouraged, he had to come home—back to the cows and the horses and the long, lonesome hours of reading. He had already tried his wings as a writer, however. The college paper had printed some of his verse, and he felt that he would one day do more and better.

Before he left for California he had laid claim to a spring in the San Andres in what is now called Rhodes Canyon, six miles from his father's place, and to this spot he returned. He made it a homestead in 1892 and soon thereafter rented his land, with the adjoining country which he was able to control, to the Bar Cross for a horse camp.[20] Periodically he would bring up their fagged-out ponies for a rest, taking fresh ones down to Engle. He built up a horse herd of his own and ran a few cattle. His heart was forever after in that notch in the mountains which in his stories he called Moon-gate Pass—"a great gateway country of parks and cedar mottes, gentle slopes and low rolling ridges, with wide smooth valleys falling away to north and south; eastward rose a barrier of red-sandstone hills." [21]

The pass through Gene's canyon was a highway of a sort —not a main highway but a convenient short cut from the solitudes of the Sierra Blanca to the deeper shades of the Black Range and the Mogollones. Men in a hurry preferred the direct route straight west from Tularosa across the White Sands through Rhodes Pass to Engle, Hillsboro, and maybe Arizona. Gene commented on the advantages of his home country for the men who rode mostly by night:

It was situated in the Panhandle of Socorro County; a long, thin strip of rough mountain, two townships wide and five long, with Sierra County west, Doña Ana to the south, Lincoln and Otero on the east, a convenient juxtaposition in certain contingencies. Many gentlemen came uncommunicative to the horse camp and departed unquestioned. In such cases the tradition of hospitality required the host to ride afield against the parting time; so being enabled to say truly that he knew not the direction of his guest's departure. Word was passed on; the Panhandle became well and widely known. . . .[22]

Some of the men whom he sheltered—and sometimes put to work—were as desperate as they came. Black Jack Ketchum, as we have said, was there for quite a spell. So were two of the Dalton gang, and even (without Gene's knowledge at the time) the notorious Indian renegade the Apache Kid. Bill Doolin was there, and Gene made him the hero of a novel later on.[23]

In 1900 a desperado named Claude Barbee shot Deputy Sheriff Hamilton in Gene's horse corral while the owner was in Tularosa—did it with Gene's gun and rode off on Gene's palomino horse. Not very happy about this, Gene wired Pat Garrett where he could probably catch the killer, but Pat had reasons for being suspicious of any tip that Gene Rhodes gave him, and he missed his chance to catch up.[24]

They buried Deputy Sheriff Hamilton in a coffin made from the planks of a water tank, and he lay in his mountain grave till the flood of 1904 washed away Gene's picket house, corral, and everything else. Gene looked back on that hovel with tender regret. "Long since, the floods have washed out the Bar Cross horse camp," he wrote, "so that no man may say where that poor room stood. Yet youth housed there, and hope, honor and courage and loyalty; there are those who are glad it shall shelter no meaner thing." [25]

People had their troubles up there in the mountains, as elsewhere, and for a while Gene had a feud on his hands. Next to the Rhodeses lived a family named Ritch. William G. Ritch, during his long service (1873-1884) as Secretary of the Territory, was once, briefly, governor *ad interim*, as a result of which he was forever after known in his home country as Governor Ritch. His son Watson was just about Gene's age, and the two boys became principals in a feud situation when the two families fell out in 1887.

It started when the elder Ritch filed a contest on the Rhodes homestead on the grounds that Hinman Rhodes had not lived up to the terms of his Timber Culture entry. Ritch was able to make his point. Rhodes's entry was canceled. Eventually Ritch took over the place.[26]

There seems to have been much bitterness, aggravated by overt acts, on both sides. When two of his dogs were poisoned, Gene blamed Ritch for it and never forgave nor forgot. Forty years later he remembered that grief of his childhood and spoke of it with pain and resentment.

"For that deed, when I grew up I broke that man—literally. I stole over forty thousand dollars' worth of cattle from him. He wouldn't fight. The only way to kill him would be to murder him. I tried to force him to fight." So spoke Gene Rhodes in 1931.[27]

A good deal of the $40,000 was collected in the form of steaks and roasts. It seems that Gene served Ritch beef exclusively to his family and guests. A friend of his once inquired how many Ritch cattle he had eaten as of that date. W. H. Hutchinson, Gene's latest and best biographer, quotes his reply:

"This," said Rhodes meticulously, "makes exactly one hundred eighty-one of his." [28]

It was for such reasons that Gene Rhodes and Watson Ritch carried guns for each other for a good many years. An outsider might wonder why they didn't look each other up and get it over with, but that was not the way such situations were handled. As Gene explained it in one of his stories:

You might be unfriendly with a man and yet meet on neutral ground or when each was on his lawful occasions, without trouble. It was not the custom to war without fresh offense, openly given. You must not smile and shoot. You must not shoot an unarmed man, and you must not shoot an unwarned man. Here is a nice distinction, but a clear one: you might not ambush your enemy; but when you fled and your enemy followed, you might then waylay and surprise without question to your honor, for they were presumed to be on their guard and sufficiently warned.[29]

In town, Gene and Watson acted polite, if not friendly, and no outright cause for resentment was given by either of them. The precarious balance was kept until the outbreak of the Spanish-American War. Then Watson got the war fever

and was ready to go. Not wishing to leave his father unpro-
tected, however, he got in touch with Gene and suggested
that they suspend hostilities. In his old age Watson told me
what happened:

We talked to each other so nobody would have known there
was anything going on—apparently we were the best of friends.
I knew Gene wouldn't shoot me in the back, and wouldn't let
anybody else do it either. He had plenty of chances too. But he
wouldn't bury the hatchet, so I stayed home.

Later on, after Gene had left the country and settled in
New York State, a small herd of cattle went on the market
bearing the old "61" Rhodes brand, which now belonged to
Gene's mother.[30] Watson Ritch bought them. After the purchase was completed, he found that Mrs. Rhodes had a lien
on them. An honest and straightforward cattleman, Watson
immediately arranged for her claim to be taken care of. Gene
heard of it and wrote Watson a fine, friendly letter announc-
ing, "The hatchet is buried." He wrote frequently after that
and came to see Watson whenever he could.[31]

Since his private feud never demanded any desperate deeds,
Gene sometimes went afield looking for excitement. He says
of such people as himself:

They worked like demons of the pit at roundup time, cool spring
or cool fall. But cattle could not be worked in summer. It was too
hot—for the cattle. Nor in winter, which was too cold—for the
cattle. These seasons were therefore set apart by all cattlemen as
a half-life of gentle divertisement.[32]

His own "divertisements" included baseball and poker, and
he would ride a long distance to indulge in either one. Each
offered a convenient route to a fight, if a man wanted one, and
Gene had his share. His experiences provided the material
for many an exciting scene in his stories and for such sen-

tentious observations as "A faint heart never filled a spade flush." [33]

His most famous brawl at this period, however, was the result of a higher artistic urge—namely, the urge to sing. It must have happened in 1892. As usual there was great excitement over the election, and Fountain's Republicans had engineered the appointment of about twenty-five "special guards"—for security. Tom Fountain, the colonel's son, was one of them. In the midst of the tension the Rhodes family came into Mesilla and Gene looked up his friend of college days, Hum Casad.

"We went to see a girl we were both fond of," as Hum told it, "and on the way home as we were passing through the plaza, Gene said, 'Let's wake up the town.'

" 'Well, how do you want to do it?'

" 'Let's sing *Billy Roy* as loud as we can.'

"We could both sing very loud. So when we came under the big cottonwood trees around the plaza—gone long ago—we let out. And about the time we were in full cry several men—deputies—stepped out from behind one of those big cottonwoods. The leader was Anastacio Barela, and Tom Fountain was one of the others. They grabbed our horses' heads. I said, 'Come on, I can talk these fellows out of it,' but Gene wanted to fight—said they were all damn dirty thieves.

" 'Who do you mean?' Barela said, and Gene said, 'I mean you,' and he came down off his horse right on top of him. They had a bloody time. Tom Fountain had his pistol out, and Gene got hold of it. They rolled around on the ground while he tried to get the gun away, and all the time the rest were beating Gene over the head with pistol butts.

"He hollered at me, 'The sons of bitches are trying to kill me!'

"I said, 'Why do you fight back, then?' But he wouldn't stop fighting. Finally they got him down and started to take him to jail. He had something like sixteen marks of pistol butts on his head. I told them he didn't mean any particular harm— just resented having his horse stopped. Barela said, 'You're probably right. He's crazy anyway.'

"They took him to Dr. Price's house. On the way he complained, 'They're jabbing their guns in my ribs.'

" 'Well,' Barela said, 'he's biting and kicking us.'

"It was late at night, but we got the doctor to get out of bed and come to the door. When he got there, Gene was bawling out the first lines of *Billy Roy*. The doctor was scandalized and told him to shut up. Gene went around with his head bandaged for a long time." [34]

At this time Colonel Rhodes was having a precarious time of it as Indian agent at Mescalero. He got the job without the blessing of the Republican machine, which was in the habit of running New Mexico, and he made no concessions to the local representatives of the Republican ring. He always thought that charges were pressed against Gene in order to discredit the family and himself.[35]

On the docket of the district court for 1892 appears an entry charging Eugene Manlove Rhodes with "drawing a deadly weapon" and "resisting an officer." [36] This case was transferred to Sierra County after a year's interval during which Gene stayed out of town. On motion of the prosecution it was dropped.

We can assume that there were other episodes just as lively. For instance, there was one entanglement, date unknown, when a deputy named Walter Danbury "rode after me nearly four hundred miles, just behind me but never quite catching up, from Alma to Roswell. I know I made that ride pretty briskly, but I didn't know that anyone was chasing me. I was in a hurry. And I can't even guess what he wanted me for. There were so many things. Innocent, says you? Possibly, but probably not. Probably guilty as all get out." [37]

"Gene," his wife said, "was considered wild," and he was not displeased with himself therefor.

By now the whole country, from Socorro to El Paso, was beginning to undergo the pangs which culminated in the Fountain murder. Gene saw the trouble through a cattleman's eyes. He seems to have had no part in the affair, however, until Lee and Gililland selected his ranch as a place of refuge. Then he plunged in and "sided" the two men until their acquittal at the Hillsboro trial. Very shortly after that he was on his way east—to get married.

For some time he had been carrying on a correspondence with May Davidson Purple, a widow of Apalachin, New York, who had seen and admired some of his early poems.[38] Now he had a chance at a free ride with a shipment of cattle and appeared at her home on July 18, 1899. Less than a month later they were married, and the cowpuncher from Engle began a new life. He went back to New Mexico four days after the ceremony,[39] but ambition was rising in him now. With his wife's encouragement he began writing short stories which she typed up for him and sent on to the publishers.[40] His production was spasmodic and intermittent. As a rule he put off his writing chores until the cupboard was practically bare, but May kept after him, encouraged him, and offered very practical help, since she was the only soul on earth who could decipher his barbarous scrawl.

In June 1900 Mrs. Rhodes and her son by a previous marriage set up housekeeping in a two-room adobe a quarter of a mile outside Tularosa. Gene spent most of his time at the ranch, and the arrangement was a good deal less than satisfactory. She tried the ranch herself in the winter of 1900, coming back to Tularosa in the spring to be near help when the expected baby arrived. Doctors charged a dollar a mile for trips to outlying ranches in those days.

She held out till 1902. But life in the West was too much for her—and besides she was needed at home when her mother's health became precarious. Three years later Gene came east to join her.

There has been much speculation about the reason for his exodus. Cow trouble, debts, poker, personal difficulty—you hear tales about them all. There may have been a number of underlying reasons, but a personal difficulty was what pulled the trigger.

By 1906 Oliver Lee had begun carrying out a special dream of his. He controlled the water of the Sacramento River high up in the mountains and had made arrangements to pipe it all the way to Orogrande, a gold camp in the Jarillas down on the plain. Some of it went to the railroad; the little mining town used the rest. Rhodes was there working on the pipe line and was indulging in a crap game during a leisure hour when one of the players, a colored man, took exception to something he said. When the argument grew serious, it was adjourned to a nearby backyard. Gene reported that he broke six empty beer bottles on the man's head before he quieted his resentment. Next morning the colored man's brother came in to take it up and there was more trouble.[41] Gene left the country and stayed away for twenty years.[42]

During those twenty years he was always homesick for his blazing deserts and lonely canyons. His stories are the product of a mighty yearning for the big and barren country he called home.

"Your precious New Mexico!" says an Eastern girl in *Pasó por Aquí*. "Sand, snakes, scorpions; wind, dust, glare, and heat; lonely, desolate, and forlorn." [43]

Lonely, desolate, forlorn? [He picks up the phrase in another story.] Not to him . . . To his thought he rode the crowded lists of joy with all his thronging peers, young gods in a young world . . . a blue and gold world, radiant with mountain and dune and plain, the deep-lit glowing stars, freshness of tender dawns and thrilling dusks, long, cool shadows at nightfall, brooding noons and wide, clean skies, the great free winds and the strong white sun, the silences, the wastrel echoes of the hills, the tense passion of the mockingbird's call that woke them in the Blue Bedroom to see the morning made.[44]

Colors—shapes—sounds—everything stayed with Gene Rhodes during those twenty years of exile, and how clearly he recalled them! He could close his eyes and see day breaking on the Tularosa plain:

Low and far against the black base of the Sacramentos, white feathers lifted and fluffed, the smoke of the first fires at Tularosa, fifty miles away. Flame tipped the far-off crests, the sun leaped up from behind the mountain wall, the level light struck on the White Sands, glanced from those burnished levels and splashed on the western cliffs; the desert day blazed over this new half world.[45]

He could hear the familiar talk of his old friends and enemies and he put it down accurately:

"Hear Nate Logan's back again?"
"Yes. Ain't you seen him? He's been here quite a spell."
"Nope. I been presenting. Got in last night."
"He resembles himself a heap."
"Oh, well, you needn't be abusive." [46]

"You'd better tarry a spell and grow up with the country," said Red. "You'd fit in. The cactus is our state flower, with the motto, 'Don't sit on me.' " [47]

"What in name of suffering humanity are you building a fence here for?"
"I find it matchless for the hands and the complexion," explained Bates. He flashed a bleeding finger.[48]

"Speaking of faces, Creagan, old sport, what's happened to you and your nose? You look like someone had spread you on the minutes." [49]

"How you makin' it, Spinal? Gettin' no older fast? You look dusty."

"I am dusty. Dusty outside, dusty inside. Any suggestions to make?"

"I have here," said Andy, "a remedy that is highly spoken of, for such cases." Turning, he slid a hand into his saddle pockets. "Leave me a small dose. Then we'll terrapin down to Tripoli, and maybe get some more." [50]

Most vivid in his recollection were the grim days in the early nineties when the great drought was going into its third year. Time and again he reverts to the "dumb terror" of those days and to the darkness and uproar of the rainstorms which at long last arrived. For twenty years he remembered, and memories were about all he had. From 1906 until 1926[51] his native state did not know him. But he wrote it all into his novels and stories, published mostly in the *Saturday Evening Post*. In between tales he played baseball, raised his family, and farmed—quite happily, in spite of his cowman's prejudice against the "splay-footed, sod-hopping, apple-grafting granger." [52]

Then came 1926, the end of Mrs. Rhodes's responsibilities in New York State, and the long trek back to New Mexico. In October they braked their Hupmobile in front of the De Vargas Hotel in Santa Fe, and the prodigal had returned. By now he was a moderately famous man, with a small but select following of enthusiasts who realized that Gene was unique in his knowledge of the real West and in his talent for interpreting it. New Mexico—most of it—was proud of him.

He kissed Maud McFie Bloom in the post office at Albuquerque, to her rosy-cheeked embarrassment, and told her, "I came all the way from New York just to get back to a place where women can still blush." [53]

The rest of the story is brief and sad. The Rhodeses stayed around Santa Fe for a while, then moved to Alamogordo, where they lived across the street from Oliver Lee. Gene was busy getting together material for what he hoped would be his most important book, a compendium of facts about the men he had known in the old days. The last chapter was to be a defense of Albert Fall.

By now, however, Gene had a bad heart condition and was not any too prosperous. Judge Fall offered him the use of the "Rock House" on his Three Rivers Ranch—a house which had belonged to Mrs. Susan McSween Barber, a famous figure in the Lincoln County War. In 1930, a victim of bronchitis, he decided to try California, and there, in a small house in Pacific Beach, he died on June 27, 1934.

In accordance with his wish he was brought back to the San Andres to take his long rest. They buried him at the top of Rhodes Pass, where the water runs east and west. He lies under a big red boulder from the corral at his old ranch, in a nook where golden sunshine filters through the branches of pine and juniper and the peace of far places flows over everything like an invisible sea.

He said once that his autobiography would be found in his books, and this is simple truth. It is also true that much of the history of his time and place can be found there likewise. Most of the episodes which he recounts actually happened, and three quarters of his characters are drawn from life, usually appearing under their right names. It is not clear how much of what he tells actually happened to him, but a good share of it probably did. For a sample, take Uncle Bill McCall's story of a disagreement that happened a long time ago—Uncle Bill did not remember just when—at Flat Lake. Gene was there, and so was Jack Chandler, a man with a reputation sufficiently large to cause the boys to take the cartridges out of his gun in case there should be trouble.

Trouble came. Gene and Chandler fell to sparring and fisticuffing. Finally Chandler said, "I can't beat you with my fists, but I can shoot it out with you."

"It's all right with me," Gene told him.

They found out then that Chandler's gun was empty and he had no shells in his pocket. Gene's gun was loaded—five cartridges.

"I'll divide with you," Gene said.

"That gives you three and me two."

"No, it gives you two and me two, and I'll throw one away."

He tossed one cartridge off into the bushes and was ready to turn two over to Chandler, but their friends got them off to bed before any damage was done.[54]

Gene used that situation in *Copper Streak Trail* when Pete Johnson gets into a shooting match with a couple of cowboys who hope to trick him into emptying his gun. Old Pete tricks them instead.

"See here—you!" said the big Texan. "You talk pretty biggity. It's mighty easy to run a whizzer when you've got the only loaded gun in camp. If I had one damned cartridge left it would be different."

"Never mind," said Johnson kindly. "I'll give you one!"

Rising, he twirled the cylinder of his gun and extracted his three cartridges. He threw one far down the hillslope; he dropped one on the ground beside him; he tossed the last one in the sand at the Texan's feet.

Jim, from Texas, looked at the cartridge without animation; he looked into Pete Johnson's frosty eyes; he kicked the cartridge back.

"I lay 'em down right here," he stated firmly. "I like a damned fool; but you suit me too well."

He stalked away toward his horse with much dignity. He stopped halfway, dropped upon a box, pounded his thigh and gave way to huge and unaffected laughter. . . .[55]

Mrs. Rhodes tells of a few other such transcripts from Gene's own adventures, but there would be hundreds more if we only knew all the escapades of the "locoed puncher from Engle."

This is, of course, interesting, but it is also important when we remember that Rhodes was not just a fiction writer. He was the historian and defender of a people and a way of life. It helps to know that he was frequently telling the literal truth and that much of it happened to him. We feel more like trusting him when he warms to his great task of analyzing those old-time American cattlemen.

First of all, he thought they were a separate breed—not better, not worse; just different from other people. "They got different ways," says Andy Hinkle to his friend Spinal Maginnis after a trip to the East. "Nine or ten complete set of ways, all different from the rest."

"But you think our ways are best?"

"I would never say so. I think our ways are different. So they don't understand each other or us, and we don't understand them. One thing I noticed, Spinal, that I didn't like at all. The people are disarmed. Everybody but the police and the criminals. That's bad. That's always bad. All down the long road the slickers have schemed to get the people disarmed—and then they done 'em dirt." [56]

The split between "Them" and "Us" seemed to Rhodes to show up most clearly in the way local government was handled. In towns like Hillsboro, where the cattlemen were pretty much in control, he noted that the administration was relaxed, informal, and in the hands of a "natural aristocracy" who did the thinking for the community. This sort of government was in accordance with the folkways, and it worked. Cowtowns "had very little ruling and needed less." [57] Trouble came when outsiders—politicians—moved in and set up their own codes for their own profit.

In Gene's thinking—as in Albert Fall's and Oliver Lee's—Las Cruces was a prime example of what the politicians could do to a good town. "In Doña Ana County taxes were high and life was cheap. Since the Civil War, Doña Ana had been bedeviled by the rule of professional politicians." [58] The result was hard times for the "little people" in whose cause Gene was always passionate.

Knowing his cowmen as he did, Gene was not surprised at their willingness to take matters into their own hands, to follow their own unwritten law. And since the unwritten law came first, the rancher was generally in opposition to the "law-abiding" citizens somehow, as Gene was well aware. Jeff Bransford "knew Fleck only slightly; but Fleck's reputation among the cowmen was good—that is to say, as you would say it, very bad." [59]

Naturally Gene's heroes are almost always cowboys, and his villains are almost always town men. When a cowboy does go wrong in the Little World that Gene wrote about, he usually retains some redeeming grace—"some wild touch of generosity, of loyalty, of unshrinking courage" which wins him "grudging admiration; yes, even love and tears." [60]

Put all these pieces together and you have Rhodes's basic belief: *The cowman is a rough and ready frontier citizen, and he lives by a set of principles which the town dweller does not understand. Often this puts him outside the formal codes of law; but when the chips are down, he is ready to sacrifice himself for a woman, a friend, or a principle.*

In the process of illustrating his special views, Rhodes moved all over the cattle country of the Southwest, but the geographical center of the universe was somewhere near Rhodes canyon in the San Andres; he was most at home on the Jornada to the west and in the Tularosa country to the east. *Bransford of Rainbow Range* (first called *The Little Eohippus*) moves between the Sacramentos (Rainbow Range) and Arcadia (Alamogordo). "Consider the Lizard" is about a train robbery at Tularosa. *Beyond the Desert*[61] circles the foot of Sierra Blanca (Star Mountain) and renames Tularosa La Huerta (The Garden). *Pasó por Aquí*, his best-known and possibly his best story, is set right on top of the scene of Colonel Fountain's murder at the point of the White Sands,[62] though Fountain's name is not mentioned.

And that brings up one last troublesome point about Gene Rhodes. The Tularosa country was his country. Its heroes were his heroes. His outlaws, with their hearts of gold, were modeled on characters he knew. He names the names and describes the adventures of many of his cowboy friends. Why did he never mention Gililland, McNew, and Lee? Why did he never use the Fountain case as a basis for fiction? He very pointedly does not discuss it, though his views, as we have seen, were those of Fall, Lee and Company.

Here and there he introduces a situation reminiscent of something that happened in 1896—a hero who won't give up to a sheriff because he is afraid of being assassinated—a village ready to turn to lynch law—a body hidden under the dam of a new dirt tank. But there ought to be more, considering how close Rhodes was to the principals on one side of the feud.

Part of the explanation is the fact that he was discouraged from dipping into the Fountain business for material. In 1914 he thought of making a fictional episode out of the part he played in the surrender of Lee and Gililland. His publishers wrote to Albert B. Fall to ask if it would be all right, and Fall said No. "The old animosities have been buried and we must let them lie." [63]

Two years later he used the Fountain case as background— not foreground—for a story. *The Desire of the Moth* tells how Sheriff Matt Lisner of Las Uvas (Las Cruces) tries to revive the troubles of the nineties in order to increase his power. He is aided by José Espalin—presumably the same Espalin who smirched himself in the cattle country by tipping off Pat Garrett just before the Wildy Well fight. The real Espolin, however, was large and corpulent, while this one is "a little dried-up mannikin" with glittering black eyes and the general effect of a spider. Lisner and Espalin are anxious to do away with Kit Foy—"about thirty, above middle height, every mold and line of him slender and fine and strong"— who of all Rhodes's characters most resembles Oliver Lee. Foy was the leader of his party in 1896; now he suspects that the old trouble is being stirred up for political reasons, and he is right.

Deputy Anastacio Barela, the same Anastacio who helped to run Gene in during his singing escapade at Mesilla in 1892, refuses to plot against Foy. "I'll have nothing to do with your fine plan. 'Tis an old stratagem to call oppression law, and resistance to oppression, lawlessness. You tried that in ninety-six, didn't you? And I never could hear that our side had any the best of it or that the good name of Doña Ana was in any way bettered by our wars. Come, Mr. Lisner—the Kingdom of Lady Ann has been quiet now for nearly eight years. Let us leave it so. . . ." [64]

Gene Rhodes would come no closer than that to using the Fall-Fountain trouble. The knowledge that his friends back home did not want him to use it had weight with him, undoubtedly, though he could be painfully frank about his old acquaintances when he wanted to. That two of them threatened to shoot him on sight is proof enough. The best explanation for his silence, however, may be the simple truth that men of his time and place just didn't talk about their troubles to strangers, and they were more than ordinarily reticent about the Fountain killing. It was too serious; it involved too many people; and those people were not the kind one wished to trifle with. We have Gene's own word for it that "the safe plan to use in dealin' with any rumor about feuds and wars is not to believe all you hear. You needn't disbelieve it; just don't believe it. One of the wisest ways I know of to put in a pleasant afternoon is not repeating town talk about the Morgans." [65]

There might be another reason. It could be that Fountain's death upset some of Gene's most cherished beliefs. In his "Little World" that sort of thing didn't happen. People killed their enemies in fair fight, but they didn't plot ambushes and murder eight-year-old boys. They righted their own wrongs, but they gave their lives for women and children. Therefore the Fountain murder was not characteristic. It did not follow the rules. It was not really true—though it was a fact. "It takes at least three trees to make a row, and it needs at least three facts to make a truth," says a Rhodes character, significantly.[66]

He knew that his concept of truth sometimes went counter to the facts, and it worried him. Once he tried to explain it: "It is charged to me that I suppress certain sorry and unsavory truths when I put remembered facts to paper—that I pick the best at their best, and shield with silence their hours of shame and weakness—these men I loved. Well—it is true. I take my own risk by that; but for them, it is what they have deserved." [67]

So he left Colonel Fountain and his little boy out of it and went on painting his cowboys as he knew they really were. Over and over he picked out the core of good in the "bad" man; pictured him calmly choosing death so that a woman or a child might not suffer. The very men who liquidated this noble outlaw called him "good leather" and promised to go to his funeral with their hats in their hands.[68]

To the end of his life he went on singing—mostly in prose —of the "gay, kind and fearless" [69] cavaliers who were to him the type of the cattleman. And he summarized his views—in verse—in the best poem in our language about cowboys. He called it "The Hired Man on Horseback," and in it he told about the cheerful heroism with which the cowhand faces his hard and dangerous life while other people are enjoying themselves:

There is no star in the pit-black night, there is none to
  know or blame
And a hundred yards to left or right, there is safety there
  —and shame!
A stone throw out on either side, with none to guess or
  tell—
But the hired man on horseback has raised the rebel yell!

And so on to the end of the old cattleman's life, when "The
last man on horseback rides on into the night":

Cossack and Saracen
Shout their wild welcome, then,
Ragged proud Conquistadores claim him kind and kin,
And the wild Beggars of the Sea leap up to swell the din;
And Hector leans upon the wall, and David bends to scan
This new brown comrade for the old brown clan.
The great-hearted gentlemen who guard the outer wall,
Black with sin and stained with blood—and faithful
  through it all;
Still wearing for an ornament the scars they won below—
And the Lord God Out-of-Doors, He cannot let them
  go!
They have halted the hired horseman beyond the outer
  gate,
But the gentlemen adventurers cry shame that he should
  wait;
And the sour saints soften with a puzzled grin,
As Esau and Ishmael press to let their brother in.
Hat tip-tilted and his head held high,
Brave spurs jingling as he passes by—
Gray hair touseled and his lips a-quirk—
To the Master of the Workmen, with the tally of his
  work! [70]

Pat Garrett's Last Ride

CARL ADAMSON came to the Garrett ranch about five o'clock in the afternoon. It was February 28, 1908—a crisp New Mexico winter day. The sun had already dropped behind the long rampart of the San Andres, which rose westward behind the house. The steep upward slope was washed with soft shadow; the canyons were rivers of deeper black.

Pat Garrett came out to answer Adamson's "Hello the house," grunted a greeting, and walked beside his visitor as he led his horses toward the corral. Garrett was fifty-eight years old now, and his hair and mustache were graying, but the old man hunter still held his six feet four inches erect and walked with an easy stride. His somber, deeply lined face with the suggestion of Indian blood in its sharp planes and high cheekbones was dark with care and worry.

Mrs. Garrett watched disapprovingly from the door. She did not like Adamson, in spite of his jolly red face and hearty manner, and wished he had not come. She was growing more and more frightened—more hopeless about the difficulties into which Pat seemed to be sinking, like a man in quicksand. On his last trip to El Paso he had even received an anonymous letter threatening his life.[1] After the fashion of Mexican women, she kept her thoughts to herself, but she did not trust Adamson, and it was in her mind that his visit meant more trouble.

She knew that money was at the bottom of it. None of Pat's schemes had turned out well since Teddy Roosevelt had refused to reappoint him to the office of collector of customs at the port of El Paso. He had moved his family to this lonely ranch—hadn't been able to pay his taxes—finally borrowed $3,500 from his neighbor W. W. Cox. Some of the Garrett cattle had been placed in Cox's pasture under Cox's brand in order to get them out of the way of creditors. When Pat was unable to pay what he owed, Cox refused to give up the stock. He offered to buy the ranch, but Pat swore he would not sell. There was some bitterness between the two men.

Wayne Brazel was a worse problem. At Cox's suggestion Pat had leased him a big pasture—to run cows, he assumed. But Brazel surprised him by bringing in a big herd of goats which Pat, like any cattleman, hated and despised. Adamson had come along wanting to lease land so he and his partner could winter a herd of Mexican cattle on the ranch. It sounded like a good deal, but there were those goats in the way. If they could be disposed of, the bargain could be made. Adamson was talking about buying the goat herd himself just to get rid of it, and Pat was eager for him to do so.

They were deep in discussion as they came back to the house, talking earnestly, with overtones of exasperation in their voices.

"So Brazel ran his count?" Adamson was saying.

"Yes, and it came out better than eighteen hundred head."

"That's too many goats. We can't pay for more than

twelve hundred; we ain't got the money. And if Wayne Brazel wants four dollars a head, we can't pay for *that* many."

"Carl, you know how I'm fixed. I've got to get those damn stinking blatting pests off my range. They're ruining me and the whole ranch. Brazel says he'll move if he can sell his stock. You're willing to buy. There's got to be some way to swing this deal. Can't you borrow the money to handle six hundred head more? Can't your partner help you?"

"Miller? I doubt it. He's got a ranch in Oklahoma but we spent all our ready cash on them Mexican cattle—all but what it will take to lease this ranch. We like the place fine. It's just what we want for holding the bunch till we get them in shape for a long drive next fall. But we can't buy all those goats and lease the ranch too. Don't you know anybody that wants goats?"

"No, I don't. And there ain't much time to look around if you expect those cows to be delivered in El Paso on March fifteenth."

"That's a fact. But they don't know me in Las Cruces, and they do know you. You ought to be able to do something yourself."

"My God, man, I'm in over my head now. I had to borrow from Cox to pay my back taxes, and now he's run a brand on my cows that I've been keeping in his pasture. I can't move a foot." [2]

"We'll go to town in the morning and see what can be done. Miller is there now and we'll see what he says."

"Jim Miller! You say he's from Fort Worth. Maybe I know him. Well, we'll see about it in the morning."

They went inside and sat down to supper.

Breakfast the next morning was even gloomier than the meal the night before. Garrett ate in stony silence as did Frank Adams, his foreman. Mrs. Garrett moved about wordlessly and sadly. Little Oscar came in scowling like a thunder-cloud and dragging a bandaged leg. He was supposed to go into town with his father, but he had slipped on his mother's freshly scrubbed floor, knocked over a bucket of lye water, and come out of it with a badly skinned and burned knee. Adamson, for once, was without a joke. They all seemed relieved when it was time to get up and go.

Mrs. Garrett watched them drive away, her husband sitting straight-backed in the buggy with his shotgun, muzzle down, beside him. He rode with his chin thrust forward and his hat pulled low over half-closed eyes, like a man squinting at far horizons. She stood there while the buggy grew smaller under the vast sky, diminished to the size of a child's toy, and dropped into nothing on the other side of a hill. It was a four-hour drive to Las Cruces. They would be there by noon. She sighed, turned back to the small house where there was always so much to be done, and plunged into the morning chores.

A long and devious road had brought Pat Garrett to this last morning—a road which began on June 14, 1850, in Alabama and led westward to Louisiana six years later. Colonel John L. Garrett had six children and plenty of money in those years, and he let his boys develop according to their own ideas. Patrick Floyd preferred business to school and went to work in his father's plantation store.[3]

The Civil War came, and bad days succeeded. Colonel Garrett died—his wife followed. The plantation went to pieces. At the age of eighteen, in 1868, Pat gave it up and pulled his freight for Texas.

Dallas County—new land—immigrants—cattle drives—cotton patches! Then a farm in south Texas where a man couldn't even plant a crop without grubbing enough roots and stumps to start a wood yard. One year on shares was enough of that. Pat edged westward, learning to rope and ride with the best of them, developing his skill with pistol and rifle.

By 1875 he was ready for a rougher life and threw in with a party en route to the buffalo plains. For three winters he joined in the great slaughter, dropping buffalo by the hundreds while the skinners stripped off the hides and left the carcasses to rot on the prairie.

His first big trouble came in '77. He was in partnership with another buffalo hunter named Glenn and was camping with a crew of roustabouts and skinners on McKenzie Lake, where the town of Benjamin now stands. When they had been in camp for some time and nerves were as taut as a trace chain, Garrett quarreled with one of the hunters named Joe Briscoe and a fight ensued. Briscoe came at Garrett with an axe.

Pat was not anxious to fight. He ran around the tent trying to get away, Briscoe following with blood in his eye. As he ran, Pat saw the stock of his old buffalo gun showing under the canvas. He grabbed it and faced about.

"Briscoe, you stop where you are, or I'll kill you!"

Briscoe kept coming, and Garrett blew him into the outdoor fireplace.

One of the men hitched up a team of mules and drove over to Uncle George Knox's camp where John Meadows (who tells the story) was working. Uncle George came back with the driver.

"You'd better go on in to Fort Griffin, Pat," he advised. "Leave a guard here and go give yourself up. You've got nothing to fear if you take a couple of witnesses."

Instead of leaving a guard, he took the whole force into Griffin with him. When they got back, after Pat had been released without even having to put up a bond, they found an awful mess waiting for them. The Indians had come in and cut most of their stock of hides to ribbons. There wasn't enough left to pay the men their wages, so they broke up camp, took what hides they could find, carted them to Griffin, and divided the proceeds. What Pat's men thought of him may be learned from the fact that they made him take an equal share with the rest of them.[4]

Then it was westward again. He lived an unwritten chapter of his life in Sweetwater,[5] where some people are still said to claim kin with him. The wild town of Tascosa in the Panhandle came next,[6] and finally in February, 1878 he rode into Fort Sumner in the Pecos Valley.

Fort Sumner was the focus of a gathering storm. John Chisum's great herds were being systematically whittled away by rustlers, both professional and part-time. Major Murphy and Chisum were feuding. Stolen cattle from the Panhandle were crowding Pat Coghlan's slaughter pens at Fort Stanton, where he filled his government beef contracts. Lincoln County was full of dangerous characters who would kill a man "to see him kick."

Pat did all right in this lead-weighted environment. The first cowman he asked for a job said he was sorry but he didn't need a man.

"That's too bad," Pat told him, "because I came here for a job and I've got to have one."

As Pat's friend Emerson Hough tells it, the cattleman was impressed by this unusual attitude.

"What can you do, Lengthy?" he inquired.

"Ride anything with hair on it, and rope better than any man in your outfit."

"All right, get in." [7]

Pat got in; and when his cowboy job gave out, he tried running a restaurant—then became a partner in Beaver Smith's store and saloon.[8]

That was when he began to be friendly with a young fellow called Billy the Kid. They say that Pat was known as Big Casino and Billy as Little Casino in the Fort Sumner gambling halls and that each was ready to stake the other when luck ran the wrong way.[9] The Mexicans had another nickname for Garrett. They called him Juan Largo—Long John.[10]

Soon after his arrival he married Juanita Gutierrez, a Fort Sumner girl who died shortly after. On January 14, 1880, he married her sister Apolinaria (or Pauline) who bore him eight children and was much beloved by all who knew her.[11]

Being now a settled resident of Fort Sumner with a wife and two nicknames, he was drawn into the life of the community. Since he was a good shot and obviously not afraid of anybody, he had no difficulty in becoming a deputy sheriff. In the elections of 1880 he was persuaded to run against his boss, Sheriff George Kimbell.

It was a hot campaign. Garrett announced that if elected he would put Billy the Kid and his gang out of business. Billy himself worked against Garrett; his friends sent out a stream of threats and warnings; but Pat won the election. Then everybody waited expectantly for something to break loose.

Pat took his time. One by one the minor outlaws found their way out of the county or into jail. The new sheriff was never one to worry about the technicalities of the law, but he was proud of his reputation for keeping his word, even to the outlaws. Years later, Theodore Roosevelt remarked that Pat Garrett did not uphold law and order in southern New Mexico—he introduced it.[12]

In due time he got around to Billy the Kid. On July 14, 1881, Garrett, John W. Poe, and Kip McKinney came to Fort Sumner on a tip that Billy might be there visiting a sweetheart. In Pete Maxwell's darkened bedroom, Pat fired the shot that ended the Kid's career as a gunman.

Overnight Long John became famous. He acquired a new title—"Slayer of Billy the Kid"—and entered the ranks of frontier nobility. Wherever people discussed the exploits of Western gunmen—wherever the *Police Gazette* was read—

Garrett's name was known. It was only in his own country that he lost ground. There, however, the ethics of the scene in Maxwell's bedroom were much debated and Pat was severely condemned. Many a man who would have done exactly as he did under similar circumstances opined positively that it was plain murder to shoot the Kid without warning—and that the deed was so much the darker because the men had once been friends. The feeling was strong enough to prevent Pat's renomination for the sheriff's office.

To keep the pot boiling he stocked a ranch on Eagle Creek in the Sierra Blanca and did well enough for a couple of years. In 1885 he gave up the ranch to organize a company of Texas Rangers and discourage cattle thieves who operated along the Texas-New Mexico line. Five months later he abandoned this project to become manager of the V V outfit, a huge new ranching project put together by Captain Brandon Kirby, an Englishman with considerable capital, and a Scotchman, James Cree. Garrett lasted only a few months in this job. John Meadows asserted that he and Garrett were discharged at the same time and neither of them ever knew why.[13]

Without breaking his stride, Pat plunged immediately into another venture. He acquired some land on the Hondo River below Roswell and dreamed of developing a great irrigation project with Pecos water and artesian wells. Years later his dream was realized by others, but Pat himself got only as far as organizing a company and building a ditch.[14] Unhappy over his defeat in the race to become sheriff of newly organized Chavez County, he closed out all his affairs in New Mexico and moved to Uvalde, Texas.[15]

For five years he lived there, breeding race horses and dabbling in county politics. A particular friend of his was a young lawyer named John Nance Garner. If Colonel Fountain had not lost his life in 1896, Garrett might have lived out his days in Texas and slept under the Uvalde live oaks. Life had a few more unexpected turns for him, however, and the next chapter brought him back to Las Cruces at the invitation of Governor Thornton to try to solve the Fountain mystery.

The Fountain case did his cause no good. He never did arrest the men he wanted—they came in when they got ready. In one or two encounters, like the fight at the Wildy Well, Pat and his men did not come off with first honors. The Fall-Lee combination was more than he or anybody else could handle at that time. Later on he had business dealings with these men and met them in friendly fashion, but the knowing ones around Las Cruces and Alamogordo had a feeling that the enmity was not dead, and maybe never would be.

The best break Pat ever had came his way in 1901 when Theodore Roosevelt made him collector of customs at the port of El Paso, over determined opposition from the staunch Republicans. Pat had been a Democrat all his life up to the time of his return to Las Cruces, and the Republicans (especially the ones who wanted the job themselves) held this against him. Important people were on his side, however—people like Thomas S. Hubbell, Solomon Luna, and General Lew Wallace, all of whom paid personal calls on the President in Pat's behalf.[16] Roosevelt had a weakness for colorful personalities and needed little prodding to give Garrett the job.

He moved his family to El Paso and became an important figure in barroom circles. There is no getting around the fact that Pat Garrett was most at home among the sporting element. He drank a good deal more than was good for him, played a lot of poker, bet on horse races, and cultivated such friends as Tom Powers, the genial, one-eyed proprietor of the Coney Island Saloon. He wore striped suits and did the best he could with his job.

His best was just barely good enough. Garrett in the brush running down a bandit was one thing. Garrett behind a desk in the collector's office was another. Criticism bubbled to the surface from time to time, and there was talk once of having him removed from office—talk possibly inspired by one of the disappointed office seekers. He finished his term, but Roosevelt refused to reappoint him. It was said that the President took offense when Garrett brought his friend Tom Powers with him to an official banquet in San Antonio and placed him directly behind the President in a group picture.[17]

The long trail finally led back to the Tularosa country—to the lonely ranch on the flanks of the San Andres. It was a pleasant enough place as desert ranches go, the small house standing in a sheltered spot between two hills at the very foot of the range five miles north of the Tularosa road. There was a spring up the hill a little way, providing water for stock and a garden. The broad Tularosa Valley made a giant-size front yard, with the Sacramentos, thirty miles away, for a fence.[18]

Pat had a little money at first, and he invested it in good horse flesh, hoping to get back into his former business of breeding race horses. But the old, quiet, confident Pat Garrett was gone; a restless, irritable, aging man had replaced him. A year before his death he stopped drinking, but he still played poker and did not like to lose. He quarreled with his neighbors, ran short of money, and found no peace.[19]

One complication followed another. First there was the money he borrowed from W. W. Cox and the trouble he had in paying it back—then the loss of the cattle that Cox was holding—the leasing of his pasture to Wayne Brazel, Cox's nephew—and now this trouble about the goats. Carl Adamson and his partner; debts; frustration . . .

That partner of Adamson's was on Pat Garrett's mind as the buggy snailed up the long slope to the top of the San Augustin Pass. J. P. Miller of Fort Worth! That must be Jim Miller who used to live at Pecos—relative of John Wesley Hardin, the Texas killer. Miller had a record himself—killed his brother-in-law in East Texas somewhere—shot Bud Fraser through a saloon door at Toyah—others since. They said he would kill anybody for money and had maybe twenty notches on his gun. Pious fellow, though. Always dressed like a preacher and went to church. Made a lot of influential friends that way. It was queer about his having a ranch in Oklahoma. If it was the same Miller, he was a hotel man when he wasn't assassinating somebody. The whole business was queer.

They topped out on the pass with the Rio Grande Valley spread out before them and the Tularosa plain behind, half a world in one eye flight. Neither of them had any thought for that tremendous panorama. The road dipped downward; the horses broke into a trot; and just then they saw Wayne Brazel ahead, bound for Las Cruces like themselves.

He was just an ordinary cowboy to look at—rough clothes, wind-reddened face under a beat-up Stetson. A quiet fellow, not a bit pugnacious, and liked by everybody. He carried a Winchester in a saddle scabbard, but that was just part of a riding costume in those days.

The old topic started up again, and it was still going when they stopped at L. B. Bentley's store and post office at Organ mining camp. Bentley could see that Garrett was angry. Long afterward he used to tell how Pat's jaw shook as he talked. The last thing he heard as the party left was Wayne Brazel saying plaintively but firmly, "But Pat, I *can't* get those goats off!" [20]

Three hours later, a little after noon, Brazel rode up to Henry Stoes' house in Las Cruces, tied his horse to the fence and called Henry from his lunch. "I just killed Pat Garrett," he said. "He's lying under a lap robe about five miles out. I had to do it. It was him or me. Will you come with me to the sheriff's office?"

They went downtown to look up Felipe Lucero.

Adamson told his story at the preliminary hearing before Justice Manuel Lopez on March 3. There was a big crowd— so big that many would-be listeners could not get in. Brazel, seemingly quite unconcerned about what was going on, sat looking out the window while Carl talked. Carl was quite comical and made the spectators laugh several times, but Wayne did not respond to his humor.

"I knew Pat Garrett about three weeks," Adamson said. "I met him at his ranch. Brazel, I met about a week ago. On our way in that morning, just the other side of Organ, we saw Brazel talking to someone in the road. He passed us on horseback—had a Winchester on his saddle. We only spoke. No, we didn't exactly travel together. Sometimes he was close; sometimes he was behind.

"When we were getting close to Las Cruces I asked him if his goats were kidding. Garrett said, 'How does it come you signed a contract for twelve hundred goats when you've got eighteen hundred?'

"Brazel said, 'I don't think I've got eighteen hundred.'

" 'Well,' I said, 'I don't know if we want eighteen hundred goats or not. We might break up the deal. I didn't want the twelve hundred, but I bought them to get possession of the ranch.'

" 'If I don't sell the whole bunch, I won't sell none,' Brazel says. 'If I have to keep any goats I'll stay on the ranch.'

"Pat got pretty mad at that. 'I don't care whether you give up the ranch or not. I can get you off anyway.'

" 'I don't know whether you can or not.'

"About that time I got out to relieve myself. Garrett took the lines. I heard him say, 'Damn you, I'll get you off now.' He was starting to get out of the buggy with his shotgun in his hand when Brazel shot him. He staggered back and fell. He stretched and groaned a little after he fell, and that was all. I took a lap robe and covered him up, and we came on in. Brazel gave me his six-shooter." [21]

By nightfall the day of the murder the whole territory knew that Garrett was gone—and that all the tale had not been told. Up at the little mountain town of Capitan the

News ran the story and remarked that the account given by Adamson and Brazel was "received with a great deal of incredulity." The editor pointed out that a bullet had entered the back of Garrett's head, coming out over his eyebrow, and a second shot in the breast "could have been fired only when the body was prone on the ground; for the bullet struck near the fourth rib, ranged upward and lodged in the shoulder." [22]

Some people thought Garrett had been shot in the head with a pistol and in the body with a rifle. They observed further that when the sheriff and the coroner got to him, Pat still had a glove on his right hand, as if he had not been expecting to use his trigger finger.

It was whispered also that a horse—and presumably a horseman—had waited just off the road for a long time. The ground was trampled, and horse droppings were scattered about. The whisperers also said that Pat himself had been the one to go behind the bush, and that his trousers were still unbuttoned when he was found. These signs pointed to cold-blooded murder. Not one man in ten believed that it all happened just as Adamson said. [23]

But if Wayne Brazel was not the killer, who was? Bill Isaacs, who shared his room with Brazel during the court proceedings, always believed that Adamson was brought in to do the job for money. It was all carefully worked out. Brazel carried a pistol and a rifle, but the pistol was Adamson's—not his own. They had swapped guns before the journey began. When Garrett started to get out of the buggy, Adamson shot him through the head with Wayne's pistol. Then they exchanged weapons again. [24]

The version which is almost universally believed in the cattle country gives Jim Miller credit for the murder. He was seen in Las Cruces the day it happened. It was his horse which stood so long just off the road, and it was his bullet that got Garrett in the back of the head. Dee Harkey in his book

Mean as Hell says Miller was riding a horse from the Harkey ranch in the Pecos Valley and that he rode it to death getting away after the murder.[25]

As more facts came to light, it was learned that Miller and Adamson were related by marriage and that Adamson had been in trouble before. There was no ranch in Oklahoma. The Mexican cattle deal was probably nonexistent. It looked more and more as if the goat and cattle business was just a series of phony negotiations prolonged until Garrett could be caught off guard or provoked into a fight.

It is still believed by many old-timers that Miller confessed to committing the Garrett murder just before he himself was finally eliminated. He was involved in the grudge murder of Gus Bobbitt, an Oklahoma farmer, in the spring of 1909. The law caught up with him and he was placed in the Ada jail. At two o'clock in the morning of April 19 a mob cut off the electric power in the town, took Miller and his accomplices out of their cells, and hanged them in a disused livery stable. As he stood there with the rope around his neck, says the legend, he confessed that he had agreed to kill Garrett for two thousand dollars—that he had lain in ambush and fired the shot which penetrated Garrett's body—that Garrett turned on Brazel, thinking he had done it, and that Brazel thereupon shot him in the head.[26]

If you ask the men who lynched Miller, they will tell you there is no truth in the legend. An outspoken Oklahombre still living in Ada says he is willing to make affidavit that Miller confessed nothing before he was strung up—"And I ought to know," he says, "because I hung him." [27] Moss Wimbish, whose father was county attorney in 1909 and handled the legal steps taken against Miller, confirms this statement.[28] Even the old men at Ada, however, are pretty sure that Miller had a hand in the Garrett murder.

As for Wayne Brazel, he never wavered in his assertion that he fired both shots. He told Harris Walthall, an El Paso attorney, that when Garrett reached into the buggy after his shotgun there was a look on his face that he had never seen on a human countenance before. It was a killer look, and Brazel knew he had to do something.[29] He repeated the tale over and over to Bill Isaacs while he stayed at his place during the trial, and always told it the same way. Finally he said, "Bill, you don't believe a damn word of my story, do you?"

"No," answered Bill, "but it is a good story. Keep saying it over and over and you will believe it yourself. I can't. You're no killer."

They buried Pat Garrett on March 5 at three o'clock in the afternoon. The body had been lying at the Strong Undertaking Parlors in an oversize casket which had to be sent up from El Paso. Constant streams of people came to look at him, noting that his features were "only slightly discolored" and staring curiously at "the small bullet hole through the left eyebrow, a little to the left of center and the swollen and blackened condition of the flesh surrounding the eye." While the funeral was delayed for Garrett's brothers John and Alfred to come in from Louisiana, the family received telegrams and letters from President Roosevelt, Emerson Hough, and a hundred other old-time friends and found a place for more flowers than Pat had ever smelled in his lifetime.[30]

At the graveside in the Odd Fellows' Cemetery the ceremonies were brief and, to many, painful. Pat had been a freethinker, or agnostic, a far-off disciple of Robert G. Ingersoll (they called such people atheists in those days), and had wanted no religious ceremony at his funeral. It was decided that his favorite page from the Great Agnostic's works—the eulogy delivered by Ingersoll at the grave of his brother—should be read as the coffin was lowered. Tom Powers, the faithful El Paso saloon man, volunteered to read it.

Life is a narow vale between the cold and barren peaks of two eternities. We strive in vain to look beyond the heights. We cry aloud—and the only answer is the echo of our wailing cry. From the voiceless lips of the unreplying dead there comes no word. But in the night of death Hope sees a star and listening love can hear the rustling of a wing.

Pat had liked that.

Somebody else read a page by William Jennings Bryan to counteract the Ingersoll, and they left him to his long rest.

Mrs. Garrett and her younger children went back to the ranch, sad and disconsolate. Adamson pranced off to El Paso, where he was to meet Jim Miller. Brazel was left to face the music. On April 13 he appeared before the grand jury and was indicted, but Governor George Curry, who had come to Las Cruces immediately after the killing, recommended that he be admitted to bail. In Curry's opinion, and he knew the background as well as any man could, having served as the first sheriff of Otero County, Garrett's death might have been the fuse to touch off more trouble. To lock Brazel up, he thought, "might be a source of ill feeling among his cowpuncher friends." [31]

Brazel's friend Bill Cox immediately circulated among the ranchmen and merchants and raised the required ten thousand in less than an hour. Cox said he could have raised a hundred thousand, and he actually turned in pledges for eighteen thousand. The names of some of the best citizens of Las Cruces appeared on the bond. Brazel and Cox rode out to Cox's ranch in a mood approaching triumph. [32]

The last round was almost a joke. Brazel had his trial on April 19, 1909. The prosecution, led by Mark S. Thompson, tried feebly to prove that Garrett's death was the result of conspiracy. The defense attorneys, Albert B. Fall and H. B. Holt (the latter a personal friend and legal adviser of Oliver Lee, W. W. Cox, and others of their party), argued that Brazel had fired in self-defense. The prosecution did not press the points which would have counted most heavily against

Brazel—the wound in the back of the head; the upward-ranging shot in the breast—the gloved right hand. And Adamson, the only witness, was not even called to the stand.

It was all done in one day. Brazel told his story at the beginning of the afternoon session, and the case went to the jury at 5:20 P.M. Fifteen minutes later the verdict of not guilty was brought in.

By this time W. W. Cox had already bought the Garrett place.[33] The family was out of the country. With Pat six feet under ground, it would seem that the chapter was closed. But it is hard to write *finis* to the career of a man like Pat Garrett, even when he is dead. With all his weaknesses and all his mistakes he still stands up tall and sturdy among the sons of the frontier.

It is true that he was no hero. He was no great shakes as a husband and father. The refinements of life meant little to him. He gambled and drank and fought. But he was no coward and no hypocrite, and there was a lot of salt and yeast in him—more than enough to balance his deficits. Hollywood has belittled him. Storytellers have lied about him. Yet his name is inscribed for future generations among the law bringers.

Maybe for that reason Pat Garrett's last ride is still discussed and explained in the cattle country, and men still wonder just how and why he died.

Three Rivers: A Fabulous History

Twenty miles north of Tularosa there is a magic valley. It goes by the name of Tres Ritos—Three Rivers—from the mountain streams draining the western flank of the Sierra Blanca which join forces at the foot and meander downward through fertile acres, turning into crops and cash on the way.

If you like ranch country you would fall in love with Three Rivers, as Pat Coghlan did in 1873—as Albert Fall did sixteen years later—as Thomas Fortune Ryan III did in 1939. You turn off the highway from Alamogordo to Carrizozo at Three Rivers Station, which is just a store and filling station between the tracks and the highway. The San Andres loom up, a blue shadow on the western horizon, the White Sands a glittering line at their feet. Out on the plain rises a black and sullen ridge of volcanic rock, last outpost of an ancient lava flow, with the Hatchet Ranch headquarters at the southern tip, tiny beneath a flourish of green cottonwoods.

The road strikes eastward between low, converging hills that are like the wings of a fish trap. In Albert Fall's time it followed a concrete-lined ditch shaded by a row of majestic trees, with long fields of cotton and alfalfa on the left. Hard times, absentee ownership, and the long drought have left the fields to tumbleweeds, and the cottonwoods to the inroads of time and change, but the road goes on to the green oasis which has offered refreshment since the first weary traveler crossed the gray desert between the Sierra Blanca and the San Andres.

The house that Coghlan built, with its three-foot-thick adobe walls—the house that Albert Fall loved and enlarged— is gone now. There is a big red barn, a huge earth tank, a caretaker's house, a power house, and Tom Ryan's rambling, Spanish-style home under the magnificent grove of pecan trees south of the old headquarters. All is quiet and spacious and remote from everything but sun and space and the looming shadow of Old Baldy soaring twelve thousand feet into the blue New Mexico heavens, mantled in snow and purple clouds during the winter, naked and gleaming above the timberline the rest of the year.

A country road skirts the ranch buildings and rises mile after mile past ruined adobe *casitas* once inhabited by Mexican families who worked on the ranch, past new wells and clearings, to a sort of pass leading into a wonderful bowl-shaped hollow six or eight miles across. Down the middle runs the green thread of the tree-lined river. Off to the left you see the Rock House where Mrs. Susan McSween Barber lived when she was known as the Cattle Queen of New Mexico —long after her first husband perished outside his blazing house in Lincoln before the guns of Murphy's warriors.

Beyond the barbed wire at the eastern limits of the ranch are the red frame buildings of the Shanta Indian community. And still beyond, the mountain begins its final uplift—tremendous ridges and canyons clothed in the somber green of pine and spruce—red clay slopes above—and the mighty peak of Old Baldy brooding over all.

You turn to watch an Indian boy and girl riding double on a spotted pony on their way to the post office at Three Rivers village, and you catch your breath at the great sweep of desert country spread out before you. The enormous gray plain flows away to the blue hedge of the San Andres. Your eye follows as the range merges in a long decrescendo with the Organs and the Franklins to the south—with the Oscuros and the Burritos to the north. On a clear day you take in a panorama of three hundred miles of heaven and earth, and it puts you in your proper place. As Gene Rhodes said, "Right smart of a universe and very little of us. That is about the proper proportion. This is no place for delusions of grandeur." [1]

To this magic valley in 1874 came the first of the mighty men who have possessed it. He was an Irishman named Patrick Coghlan, born at Clonakilty, County Cork—a fine figure of a man, big and strong, red-faced and hearty, a lover of fun and women and children and horseflesh. The first chapter of Three Rivers history belongs to him.

It is well over a century and a half since Pat Coghlan first saw the light of Irish day on March 14, 1822, and there is nobody left to tell who his people were, how he got his little education, why he decided to come to America in 1845. He was not a man of great intellect or sagacity. In fact, he was easy prey in later years for the men of figures and calculations. Neither was he any too scrupulous about the way he ran his kingdom during the days when he had a kingdom to run. But he was of a stirring disposition, full of energy and jollity and fine plans and ambitions. So when he was twenty-three he crossed the Atlantic and set foot in the New World. For two years he scrambled for a living, we don't know how. Then in 1845 he enlisted in the United States Army.

His service brought him to Texas (he was discharged at San Antonio in 1852), and Texas looked good to him. For some reason he was especially drawn to Mason County, where the thrifty Germans had settled in large numbers. Probably he had been stationed at Fort Mason and noted the possibilities of that green and fertile land. He bought a farm at Cherry Springs; lived there three years; moved to Mason, where he ran a store and traded in cattle. In 1862 he married a girl named Ann Crosby. A little later he moved westward into newer country and settled on an irrigated farm in Menard County eighteen miles from Fort McKavett. His idea was to raise vegetables, feed, and melons and sell them to the soldiers at the Fort.

Always restless, he soon got tired of that venture, and in 1873 he turned up in New Mexico, where he lived for a while on the Block Ranch in the Hondo Valley between Tularosa and the Pecos. Then he became a citizen of Tularosa and began acquiring land at Three Rivers.[2] It seems that the Magic Valley spoke to this wandering Irishman and told him that he had come home at last.

By this time Coghlan had accumulated considerable money, probably not always by the most approved methods. Stories drifted back from Texas about his driving off other people's cattle, though these may have been just malicious rumors.[3] He always had plenty of friends and did a rushing business. Naturally he had money to spend, until he fell into the clutches of the bankers and moneylenders—but that came later.

In those days a man who wanted to rule a kingdom was obliged to move slowly. It was a question of getting possession of the water holes and streams, and these were usually held by old Mexican families or tenacious squatters of one kind or another. Sometimes these people could be bought out or forced out, but either method took time and money. Empires were not set up overnight.

Coghlan went ahead as fast as he could, beginning with property in Tularosa. In 1874 he bought from Perfecto Armijo all the town lots which were not occupied or in use,[4] and he continued to acquire block after block until people said, without too much exaggeration, that he owned half the town.[5] He was by all odds the big man in the community and enjoyed being described as "the king of Tularosa."

There was still the magic valley to be acquired, and he got his foothold there by buying out Joe Wingfield's ranch and Bar KL cattle.[6] In time he acquired more land and cattle from Juan Chávez and others,[7] and coveted a good deal that he did not get, for some of the first comers did not want his money and did not choose to move. Among these were Susan Mc-Sween Barber and her husband George Barber, who settled there in 1883. Shortly after her arrival Mrs. Barber decided to manage without her husband, but she carried on in the midst of Coghlan's domain and was a match for him or any man.

Another immovable family was George Nesmith's. George was an honest Scotchman who had marched into New Mexico with the California Column in 1862 and was one of the men who went in with Dr. Blazer after the war in the purchase of La Maquina, thenceforward known as Blazer's Mill, just outside of Mescalero. In 1876 Blazer bought out his partners and Nesmith went off to pitch his tent at Three Rivers.[8] He must have stood in well with the Indians, for he lived through some perilous times in a mighty exposed position.

Coghlan tried in vain to get Nesmith's land, and at last he decided that he might as well make the man useful. Our honest Scotchman became a sort of general caretaker for the place; his wife handled the cooking, gardening, milking, and similar chores.[9]

For a time things went well enough. But the Nesmiths were conscientious and observing, and before long they took note of many things that scandalized their Presbyterian blood. For the time being, however, they said nothing because there was nobody to say anything to.

Coghlan divided his time between his headquarters at Three Rivers and his headquarters at Tularosa. The latter soon became famous throughout southern New Mexico. Pat had an adobe store and saloon on the main street flanked by a pair of huge wooden gates which led into a spacious wagon yard, with sleeping rooms attached for those who could afford to abandon their bedrolls.

His second-in-command, who actually managed this many-sided enterprise, was one Morris Wohlgemuth—an obliging soul who was credited with doing much of Pat's dirty work. He was the one who sold a saddle to a cowboy one time, first taking off the stirrups which, he said, would cost extra. The cowboy was so overcome that he pulled his gun on Morris and was ready to kill him had Wohlgemuth not changed his mind.[10]

Coghlan's residence was around the corner to the west of his store, and in it he lived as royally as he knew how. He drank good liquor and smoked expensive cigars, drove a spirited team of *caballos grullos*, took trips to Texas or California or Ireland when he felt like it, and did as he pleased with regal good humor.

His fellow townsmen bowed before him. Mrs. Coghlan, a thin, nervous little woman, was *la Madama*—not *la Señora*. And when she and her husband appeared on the street riding in their carriage behind a colored coachman and high-stepping buckskin horses, everyone stood aside and almost stopped breathing.[11]

But people who sit on thrones, no matter how low, often become presumptuous and forget that no man's will is law forever. This mistake, Pat Coghlan made. He began making it before he assumed the purple, and his rise made him reckless.

His worst mistake was a business partnership he formed with a young man known as William Bonney, alias Billy the Kid, who came out of the Lincoln County War in a mood to even the score with a society which in his view had done him wrong. He eased his mind, profitably, by setting up a two-way rustling operation. He would collect a herd of horses or a bunch of John Chisum's cattle in New Mexico and drive them to the Texas Panhandle for sale. Then he would round up a bunch of Panhandle stock for disposal in the Tularosa country.

Pat Coghlan had the contract to supply the army post at Fort Stanton with beef—supposedly from his Three Rivers ranch; but the cattle he butchered in his slaughter pens seldom wore the Coghlan brands. And when Billy made a particularly good haul, Pat would trail the herd off to Arizona or Old Mexico.

Among the big Panhandle ranches suffering from this system was the mighty LX spread, in whose employ at this time was the noted cowboy detective Charlie Siringo. In February 1881 Siringo went on detached duty to see what could be done about it. He and Tom Emory rode over to White Oaks first, and then came down to Stanton, where they found "Dad" Peppin, sheriff during the Lincoln County troubles, in charge of Coghlan's beef business. A lot of fresh hides were hanging on the corral fence, and among them Siringo found five bearing the LX brand. When this fact was verified and witnessed he turned to Peppin.

"Don't you butcher any more of those Billy the Kid cows," he said. "You're in trouble enough now."

"All right," Peppin promised. "I won't unless I get new orders from Coghlan."

The next move was to corner Coghlan, and this involved some difficulty, for some of his stolen stock had been re-stolen and he was off in pursuit of the thieves. Siringo caught up with him at the post office in Las Cruces.

"My name is Siringo," he said. "I've been sent from the Panhandle to take over the cattle you bought from Billy the Kid."

"You won't get 'em," growled Coghlan, turning a fine shade of mahogany red and swelling up ominously.

"Oh, yes, I will! I've got a crowd at White Oaks ready to

move in, and our instructions are to take them by force if that's the only way we can get them."

Pat thought it over and changed his tactics. "All right," he agreed. "I'll let you take any Panhandle cows in the brands you represent. But my herds are scattered all over the mountains and I don't want you fellows riding in there and disturbing them. We'll have new grass by the first of April, and if you'll wait till then, I'll help you round up every hoof on the range."

"That suits me," Siringo told me. "But you'll have to promise not to butcher any more."

"That goes. I'm having trouble enough now. That herd that Tom Cooper stole got away clean. We followed them into the Black Range and only got back a few of the broken-down ones."

All of which, as Siringo found out later, was "taffy." Coghlan was just playing for time.

The detective back-trailed to Tularosa and actually had the nerve to spend the night at Coghlan's ranch, where Mr. and Mrs. Nesmith treated him, as he says, "like a whitehead," and saw him off in the morning. Against their advice he took a short cut over the mountains to White Oaks, bringing a Mexican along to put him on the trail. We will let him tell the rest of the story.

"About an hour after bidding the Greaser adieu, I came to where the trail made a short curve to the left, but I could tell from the lay of the ground that, by keeping straight ahead, I would strike it again. So I left it, and lucky for me that I did, for there was someone laying for me not far from there.

"I hadn't gone but a rod or two when bang! bang! bang! went three shots in quick succession, not over fifty yards to the left; and at the same time my mule gave a lunge forward, on the ice-covered stones, and fell broadside, throwing me over a precipice about eight feet to the bottom. My Winchester and pistol both were hanging to the saddlehorn, but I managed to grab and pull the latter out of the scabbard as I went off, and took it with me.

"The first thing I done on striking bottom was to hunt a hole. I found a nice like nook between two boulders and lay there with cocked pistol, expecting every second to see three Indians or Greasers peep over the ledge on the hunt for a dead Gringo—as the Mexicans call an American.

"After waiting a few minutes, I became impatient and crawled on top of a small knoll and, on looking in the direction the shooting had come from, I got a glimpse of what I took to be two half-stooped human forms retreating through the pinyon brush at a lively gait." [12]

Siringo found his mule, only slightly scarred, and rode on to White Oaks, where he expected to wait till the first of April, according to his agreement with Coghlan. On the evening of March 10, however, he had a letter from George Nesmith telling him that Coghlan was getting rid of the LX cattle on the place as fast as he could. Next morning a very angry Charlie Siringo struck out for Fort Stanton, where he found the hides of freshly butchered LX cattle in full confirmation of Nesmith's tip.

It took him till midnight to ride cross country over the mountains to Three Rivers. "Mr. and Mrs. Nesmith got out of bed," he says, "and gave us a cold supper; and he also gave us a few pointers in regard to his employer's doings, etc."

Coghlan had almost got the best of it. Siringo and his men found only eight LX cattle on the ranch, but they figured they had enough evidence to send Pat to the penitentiary and so informed their employers.[13] As a result, John William Poe, sheriff and deputy United States marshal at Roswell, rode over to Three Rivers and put Coghlan under arrest. Mrs. Poe, in her life of her husband, shows the erring Irishman no mercy:

Before Coghlan had become aware of an officer's presence on his place, John William had him under arrest. Like the coward he was, Coghlan begged for mercy. He offered John William large sums to be liberated; but John William was always inflexible when it came to a question of right or wrong. So it came about that, in the course of time, Coghlan was indicted by the grand jury at Mesilla.[14]

The case did go to Mesilla on a change of venue. It was set for the first Monday in April, 1882, and at the appointed time Poe, Siringo, Pat Garrett, and others were on hand to witness against Coghlan.

Among the others sent for were Mr. and Mrs. George Nesmith, who were subpoenaed and forced to come in. They realized now what they had done, and Mrs. Nesmith especially was scared. She complained to her neighbors that she had a premonition that something dreadful was about to happen.

"I am afraid to go by the White Sands," she confessed. "So many terrible things have happened there. It's so lonely out there. I feel just terrible about taking this trip." [15]

She started out, however, she and George and their eight-year-old adopted daughter, attended the trial and got back safely.

From the first the trial was a battle of wits rather than a battle of evidence. Coghlan was badly scared and well aware that he was only one step from a cold prison cell. There were eight indictments against him, Siringo says—the most dangerous being the charge that he had gone on butchering LX cattle after Siringo had identified his brand and issued a warning.

His only hope [says Siringo] was to sugar the prosecuting attorney, and that no doubt was easily done, or at least it would have looked easy to a man up a tree. You see, Coghlan was worth at least a hundred thousand dollars and therefore could well afford to do a little sugaring, especially to keep out of the penitentiary.

At any rate, whether the attorney was bought off or not, the trial was put off, on account of illness on said attorney's part, until the last days of court.

When the case came up again Mr. Prosecuting Attorney was confined to his room on account of a severe attack of cramp-colic. Judge Bristol was mad, and so was Poe. They could see through the whole thing now.

That night Coghlan made a proposition that he would plead guilty to buying stolen cattle knowing they were stolen, if the one case in which he had killed cattle after being notified not to, would be dismissed, or thrown entirely out of court.

It was finally decided to do that, as then he could be sued for damages, so the next day he pleaded guilty to the above charges, and was fined one hundred and fifty dollars besides costs.

Fountain, our lawyer, then entered suit against him for ten thousand dollars' damages.[16]

Again Coghlan got off with less than he deserved. During the September term of court in 1882 judgment was rendered against him on two counts in favor of the Panhandle outfits, one for $2,257.79 and the other for $120.80.[17]

Long before these cases were settled, Coghlan was in still worse trouble. Mrs. Nesmith's fears had proved to be well founded. On August 17, 1882, she and her family were murdered as they passed the White Sands. Three weeks later a couple of prospectors out hunting mules noticed an abandoned wagon some distance off the Tularosa road. It was surrounded by buzzards, and a wolf or two sneaked away as they came up. They noted that blood had oozed over the axles and wheels and collected in pools on the ground.[18]

It was the Nesmiths. The bodies were unrecognizable, but Mrs. Nesmith's trunk and George's silver watch told the tale. There was no indication of who had done it, but their friends noted that Nesmith's new overcoat was missing. It turned out that the murderers had defeated themselves by failing to let well enough alone.

A certain Mrs. Tucker of Las Cruces had made the overcoat but had miscalculated her materials and run out of lining. She used a piece of dress goods to finish it, thus leaving a conspicuous mark of identification. Word got around that a Mexican had been seen at the village of Doña Ana wearing such a coat, and an officer went to see about it. The Mexican had departed for Mexico, however, taking the garment with him.[19]

He did not come back for four years. But he did come back, and the law was waiting for him. The country finally learned that two men named Maximo Apodaca and Rupert Lara had waylaid the Nesmiths. Apodaca had killed the man and his wife. Lara was going to dispose of the child, but she begged for her life and he couldn't do it. Only when Apodaca pulled a gun on him and threatened him with death if he refused did he go ahead and shoot the little girl.[20]

An earnest attempt was made to pin the murder on Coghlan. Rupert Lara said that a man with reddish hair and beard had met them just outside Tularosa and hired them to do the job.[21] The prosecution assumed that Pat had provided the money, though a story went round that the serviceable Morris Wohlgemuth had made the actual arrangements.

To settle the matter, the accuser, Lara, was asked to pick the contact man out of a line-up of nineteen citizens. Coghlan and Wohlgemuth stood up with the rest, but after four years the assassin could not identify the man who had employed him. In fact, he put the finger on Marshal Dave Woods and Henry J. Cuniffe, who could not possibly have been involved in the crime.

Lara was hanged. Apodaca confessed and got off with a life sentence. Conscience was too much for him, however. He jumped out of his fourth-story jail window and finished himself. He said he had heard that baby cry ever since he killed her.[22]

Gene Rhodes always thought the case against Coghlan

was a frame-up and advised an interested acquaintance to let the story alone "until you can get it straight." Remember, he said, "a dead man's reputation is at stake." [23]

Trials cost money, and so much litigation hurt Coghlan badly. The hard times which came at the end of the eighties took further toll, and he had to borrow money to live as he wanted to. The interest rates which obtained in those days were simply suicidal.

On April 16, 1886, Coghlan executed a mortgage deed to Numa Reymond and Martin Lohman of Las Cruces for $15,000.[24] In 1892 he went in deeper, signing a promissory note to Reymond for $26,795.48 at twelve-per-cent interest. By 1897 the note was worth $32,000 to W. W. Cox, who bought it and sold a third each to Oliver Lee and Fitzgerald Moore. A month later foreclosure proceedings were begun, Pat Garrett acting as agent. Coghlan's cattle—1,025 cows and ninety-six horses—were rounded up and Cox, Lee, and Moore bid them in. They paid $22,500 for the cows and $500 for the horses.[25]

In the final decree, which was handed down by Judge W. H. Pope in July 1906, Cox, Lee, and Moore were awarded $13,123.65 plus accumulated interest at twelve per cent. The lawyers got $3,000. Garrett collected $1,236.95. The Three Rivers property was adjudged to be security for the payment of the sums. These figures are useful in showing what happened to people who fell among bankers in those days.

Some of Coghlan's old friends declare that he didn't understand interest and had no notion that his property was being eaten up by the ruinous twelve per cent. The probable truth is that he just didn't like to be bothered with figures and avoided facing financial facts. Once he had signed the first note, his days were numbered at Three Rivers.

Six months before the final decree, he had given up his magic valley. On January 26, 1906, he signed a warranty deed to Albert Bacon Fall, who had bought up the note originally held by Numa Reymond.[26] How Fall satisfied Lee, Cox, and

Moore, we do not know, but that was undoubtedly the easiest part of the transaction.

Coghlan lasted a few years longer, a pale and palsied version of the old king of Tularosa. His wife died in 1903 and he was left alone. It is said that he had divorced his first wife some time before and that this was her sister. Mrs. Fall, who knew both women well, used to tell that the second Mrs. Coghlan was a devout Catholic and was much concerned about the validity of her marriage in the sight of God. She called Mrs. Fall in once when she was sick and told her that she hoped above all things that she might outlive her sister in order to be Pat's wife in reality. She asked Mrs. Fall to pray that this might happen. Mrs. Fall said she was afraid she might not be effective in that way, but she knew a woman in Las Cruces who was very good at praying and would ask her to do it.[27]

The fact is that Pat outlived both his wives and dragged on in reduced circumstances until January 22, 1911. He had been in a declining state for two years and had to rely on his friends for care. When at last he faded out, there wasn't much left to divide. The poor relics of his former wealth, including ten beds from his hotel, one pistol, and fifteen dollars' worth of books, were valued at less than $300. The few parcels of land still in his name came to $4,300. A nephew and two nieces survived him and should have had a little from his estate. When all the bills were paid, however, the remainder was only $319.20, and that went to a Mrs. E. B. Taylor, who appeared from remote regions and claimed that Pat owed her $1,382.26. Her claim was allowed and she swallowed that pitiful remainder, thereby frustrating Mary C. O'Houran of Greenock, Scotland, Mary C. O'Cleary of Klonakilty, and Dr. Lawrence O'Cleary of the same place.[28]

They buried him in El Paso, an almost forgotten man, and few indeed were those who remembered his virtues. Mrs. Jim Baird was one. "He was a powerful man physically," she wrote; "an all-around athlete of his time, and had a lively disposition. He never turned a deaf ear to the cry of the poor; always a great lover of children; never too busy to talk to them in their sports. Peace to his ashes. May the sod rest lightly on his breast." [29]

Albert Fall first saw Three Rivers in 1889 in the course of a horse-and-buggy trip to Roswell. He had just been admitted to the bar and probably had picked up some court business which he hoped would better his circumstances—and God knew those circumstances needed bettering.

For some reason he chose to go around the west side of the mountain by way of White Oaks, and instead of stopping at Tularosa he went on to Three Rivers. In those open-handed days, Coghlan expected to entertain travelers, and travelers expected to be entertained.

The ranch had never looked more seductive. The long drought had not yet struck in. Peach and apricot trees had produced enormously, and the apple orchard was still heavy with fruit. The mighty cottonwoods dreamed above Coghlan's massive adobe house and wide-flung corrals, and the vast bulk of the mountain added a fantastically beautiful backdrop. Fall looked at all this grandeur, and a thought was born far back in his mind—a thought which was full grown by the time he got back to Las Cruces.

"Emma," he said to his wife, "Pat Coghlan's place is the prettiest spot I ever saw. It's the sort of place I've always wanted to own. Emma, some day I'm going to have that ranch." [30]

Emma, up to her neck in cooking and children and money troubles, probably listened tolerantly as she did to all her husband's schemes, but hardly realized that this was a prophecy and not just a dream.

It took time, but everything played into Fall's hands. When Coghlan, broken and defeated, signed the warranty deed in

1906, in effect he handed over his crown to a new king of Tularosa.

To Albert Fall the ranch was more than a home. It was a place where he could rule and plan and develop to his heart's content. He always had some scheme afoot for making Three Rivers bigger and better. Of course he wanted all the land that joined his, and he got most of it. Mrs. Susan McSween Barber, for instance, who had held her acreage since 1883, sold to Monroe Harper on July 3, 1902, and Fall finally got it from Harper in 1915.[31]

For Emma and Albert Fall there was no joy like coming back to their little empire, though sometimes it was many months between visits when Albert was at the height of his success. They loved the fertile acres and the barren slopes, the cottonwoods and the clear stream of mountain water, the Indian petroglyphs at prehistoric camp sites, the Mexican workmen who raised their families in adobe *casitas* tucked into the garden spots along the stream. They even loved their neighbors.

And since it was his kingdom, Albert Fall made his own laws and saw to it that they were not questioned. There was the matter of water rights, for instance. Pete Crawford sold him half of his parcel of land with all the water rights, and Fall immediately transferred the water to the railroad company for $75,000. There has been considerable doubt about the legality of this transaction, but nobody said anything while Fall was alive.[32]

The rest of his supply he stored in a great earthen tank near the house and used to irrigate broad fields of cotton and alfalfa. Mrs. Fall was a persistent planter of trees and shrubs, always bringing back something to put in the ground whenever she made a trip somewhere, and everything she planted grew. What had been an oasis in Coghlan's time developed into a desert paradise in Emma Fall's, with a vegetable garden, a rose garden, and even a conservatory.

The house had enormously thick walls, which gave the interior a dim and heavenly coolness in summer and a cozy warmth in winter. It was a casual, shirt-sleeves sort of mansion, for the Falls were not fussy about their housekeeping, but gradually it attained a museumlike quality as they brought home gifts and keepsakes from faraway places.

The Fall children loved it as much as their parents did. Jouett was seven when the family came there to live, and she never forgot what a thrill it was. She learned about its history from Candelario Duran, whose parents had given him to Pat Coghlan when he was just a baby. "Candy" loved to tell stories which made the children's eyes pop. One was about the time he saw a dead man brought in and put in the basement —a redheaded cowboy with silver spurs. He wasn't in the cellar next morning, but once when a heavy rain washed out the river, a pair of silver spurs and some bones came to light. Candy thought it was the same man. "There are many more buried on the ranch," he would say.

By now Fall was the biggest man in southern New Mexico, and his influence was felt from El Paso to Santa Fe. In 1905 he opened a law office in El Paso and built his big red-brick house on a hilltop—white-columned and dignified as befitted a Kentuckian—but he kept his New Mexico residence.

His prestige as a lawyer grew apace. Clients came long distances to consult him. Railroad men, mining men, lumber men flowed through his offices in a steady stream. He tackled his biggest job when he became head man for Colonel William C. Greene's far-flung mining, cattle, and railroad interests in Mexico. Money flowed in, and much of it Fall plowed back into his ranch, enlarging the house, filling the library with books, developing more farm land, building a concrete ditch to water the two-mile-long avenue of trees between his ranch house and the station.[33] In time his little kingdom grew into a ranch empire of hundreds of square miles, and everything —for a while, at least—was according to his desire.

Those were the days when Albert Fall was nobody to trifle with. Dignified and commanding, he went his imperious way, his sharp tongue and sardonic eye cowing the lesser men who infrequently opposed him. His appearance was a combination of the old-time Southern statesman and the new-style Western empire builder. He dressed in dark, formal-looking clothes, wore his brown, wavy hair rather long, and topped it all off, not incongruously for him, with a great, broad-brimmed black Stetson. He was always seen puffing a cigar and swinging a cane, and the cane was known to be a weapon as well as an ornament.

Many people loved Fall, and many more feared him. He was a fighter, hard to his enemies, generous to his friends. One had to be either for him or against him. And since one never encountered him when he was not promoting something or other, it was a case of get on the bandwagon or get out of the way.

Fall was the most ambitious man who ever rose to the top in New Mexico politics, and one of the most successful. He was not content, either, with the rewards that his own community, or even his own Territory, could offer. He wanted to go on into the national arena—to the very top if possible.

Everybody knew, and who better than Albert Fall, that one day the Territory of New Mexico would be the State of New Mexico. Who knows how many prominent New Mexicans daydreamed about being one of the first senators from the new state and trimmed their sails accordingly! Fall was one of them and figured his chances were good.

He took his first step in 1902, when he left the Democratic party. The move was a bombshell in New Mexico, where he had fought the Republicans during the bloody nineties with words and with bullets.

Why did he do it? He said it was because he could not support William Jennings Bryan and his free-silver policies. His former political associates growled that it was because he hadn't been nominated as a delegate in Congress in 1900.[34]

Fall was probably glad of an excuse to join the Republicans anyway, since they were the stronger party and could do more for a man who wanted to go to the Senate. His friend Oliver Lee jumped the fence with him and went on to construct a political career of his own within the boundaries of the state.

By sheer ability and political know-how, Fall pushed himself into the front ranks of his new party. In 1902 he was elected to the territorial upper house. In 1907 he was attorney general for a time under Governor George Curry. In 1912 the first legislature sent him to Washington as one of the two senators from the newly created state. Three Rivers saw him only briefly thereafter for many years, though he came back at intervals and never stopped strengthening the bulwarks and bastions of his private empire.

In the same year that he went to Washington, Fall arranged for an ultimate and final expansion of his ranch. His son-in-law Mahlon T. Everhart borrowed money from the Thatcher brothers of Pueblo, Colorado, to buy up the patented land and water holes of the old Bar W outfit, which controlled the northern ranges of the Tularosa Valley west of Carrizozo. The new company also brought the Hatchet brand into its range of nine hundred thousand acres and soon combined with Fall to bring the total acreage to over a million.[35]

Even this tremendous expansion did not satisfy the insatiable Fall. The minute he got to Washington he set afoot schemes to magnify Three Rivers still further, casting his eye eastward this time toward the Indian lands on the slopes of the Sierra Blanca. In Fall's view the reservation was a great sweep of natural resources going to waste.

His favorite project, the one he always came back to, was a proposal to make a National Park out of the Mescalero tribal lands. He wanted it all developed for the benefit of the white man, and his plans included the construction of a sanitarium not far from his own headquarters. *The Quarterly Journal of the Society of American Indians* commented bitterly in 1914 that this

would include the construction of a road through that portion of the reservation over to the railroad station, a distance of some twelve miles or more. Curiously enough, the sponsor for the Bill is the senator from New Mexico, who has a large ranch, and his line comes right along the reservation line. Of course, he might say he is doing this for the benefit of the Indians, but evidently it will benefit this senator more than it will the Indians.[36]

The indignant author went on to suggest that it would be just as reasonable for the Indians to lay claim to Fall's ranch and introduce a bill to make a national park out of Three Rivers.

Nothing came of this first attempt, but on January 5, 1916, Fall tried again, with elaborations. His new bill proposed to allot lands "in severalty" to the Indians and to convert the rest of the reservation into a summer resort where white citizens might take up parcels of one acre for homes and cottages and miners might pay one hundred dollars' rental for claims. Thus, most of four hundred seventy thousand acres would be available for manipulation by white promoters, and three million dollars' worth of timber would be taken out of the hands of the Indians.[37]

Again Fall was defeated, but he kept on trying till he left Washington in 1923.[38]

His first great personal disaster came in 1918, when his son Jack and his daughter Mrs. Mahlon Everhart died in the influenza epidemic. Jack had been active with his brother-in-law Everhart in managing the ranch. His death was a staggering blow to the senator and took away much of his incentive toward building an empire in New Mexico. Politically, however, he was still moving upward. In 1921 he became President Harding's secretary of the interior.

For two years he remained in the Cabinet, resigning in March 1923 because of feeble health and feebler finances. Most Americans who remember him at all believe that he resigned because of the Teapot Dome scandal; but that episode broke out several months after his retirement. Fall had been anxious for some time to return to private life, and his reasons were bona fide. He had a history of tuberculosis, chronic bronchitis, pleurisy, arthritis, and heart trouble. His personal finances had been wrecked by the Mexican revolution, which had wiped out investments south of the Border. Back taxes and debts had accumulated around his Three Rivers property like barnacles on a ship.[39] It was high time he started taking care of himself and trying to make some money.

To raise cash, he sold a third interest in his ranch to Harry F. Sinclair, the oil man, for $233,000 and borrowed $100,000 more from his old friend Edward L. Doheny. With this money he paid his back taxes, repaired his roads, planted trees, installed a fifty-thousand-dollar power generator, and made his house habitable again. In addition he bought the Harris-Brownfield ranch for $91,500.

Then came October 1923 and a request to appear before the Senate Committee on Public Land and Surveys and explain his handling of naval oil leases during his tenure as secretary of the interior. Men who wanted to make headlines found that Fall was a wonderful subject for investigation, and Fall helped them along by trying to conceal his dealings with Sinclair and Doheny and perjuring himself in his panic. If he had told the simple truth, he might have come out with only a few scars, but Senator Walsh and his committee pursued him ruthlessly, and in the end he was broken and discredited.

Fall's side of the story has never been given an adequate hearing, but the facts have been assembled and will some day be printed. Historian David S. Stratton, doubting his "alleged criminality," thinks he made some bad moves but was the victim of politicians who needed a scapegoat in an era of political shenanigans.[40]

His role in the granting of Naval oil leases was "hardly decisive." The reserves in Colorado, Utah, Wyoming, and California were set up to provide oil and gasoline for the Navy in case of need. The oil had to be stored, either above ground or below, and Fall thought it ought to be stored above ground in a location accessible to ships. He found that the Elk Hills reserve was being depleted by drillers around the margin of the field, and this gave him additional reason for feeling that the country would lose by leaving the oil in the ground. There was a war scare on at the time. Everybody thought trouble with Japan was in danger of breaking out almost any minute; and Fall thought that Pearl Harbor was the place where supplies would be most needed.

Edward L. Doheny of Pan American Oil Company, Fall's old crony, was one of those favored in the awarding of contracts for handling the oil. Harry F. Sinclair was another. The Doheny contract was spotlighted by the investigators and made to appear particularly bad. The "sinister" feature, however, was not the contract itself—Doheny's offer was the best one made—but rather the *sub rosa* way in which the transaction was handled.[41] Fall had sold out, the newspaper headlines said. Doheny's loan was really a bribe. The oil man had paid off and got what he wanted.

The fact that Doheny's hundred thousand was a real loan and not a payoff was proved beyond doubt by the fact that, when Fall could not repay the money, he lost his ranch to the Doheny interests. That, however, came later. Fall and Doheny were indicted and tried on several counts. They were acquitted of conspiracy in 1926, but charges of giving and receiving a bribe still hung over them. In the fall of 1925 the ex-secretary came into court to answer in this matter. A nurse and a doctor were with him, and he was helped into a cushioned chair. On the second day he began spitting blood, and the court had to recess for three days. It was a sad spectacle, made sadder when Fall was convicted, sentenced to a year's imprisonment, and fined one hundred thousand dollars. He appealed the decision, but two years later the verdict was upheld.

Doheny fared better when he came to trial in 1930. He was acquitted of giving the bribe. The affirmation of Fall's conviction the following year set up a ridiculous situation. Fall was adjudged guilty of accepting money which Doheny was declared innocent of having given him.

On July 31, 1931, Fall left his Three Rivers house to go to prison. He traveled in an ambulance, and his cell was the prison hospital. They let him come back six months later to his solitudes and the loyal friends who had always stood with him. "Nobody around here believes Judge Fall ever did anything wrong," remarked his protégé and admirer Albert Burch. "They know him too well. And even if he had, they would still be for him. Mr. Fall built up this country." [42]

The case had cost Albert Fall seven years of his life. It had taken the last of his strength and all his money. Now, with a sort of poetic justice, he found himself in the same trap that had caught Coghlan long before. His property was valued at three quarters of a million, but he had no way of raising the money necessary to pay off the Doheny loan. [43] The great ranch enterprise fell apart, and in 1935 Doheny's agent notified the Falls that the place had been sold and they would have to move.

Fall declared flatly that he wouldn't go. He said Doheny had agreed to let him retain the ranch house and one hundred acres no matter what happened; and if the ranch should be sold, he was to have all money in excess of the actual indebtedness. He said he knew that Doheny was not well and that this was all the work of Mrs. Doheny and R. M. Sands, vice-

president of the Petroleum Securities Company, which Doheny headed. Mrs. Doheny had always disliked Mrs. Fall, and
now she was holding the whip.

There was no way out. Mrs. Fall, who was operating a
restaurant in El Paso and a store in Three Rivers, fought as
long as she could to put off the day of departure—all to no
purpose. Her husband could give her no help. He sat in his
wheel chair on the porch of his Three Rivers house, watched
the ducks and geese, and traced the clean line of the Sierra
Blanca high against the pale blue sky. He read day and night,
sometimes all night, drowning out the voices of the present
with a chorus of voices from the past; losing himself in history
and biography; sometimes turning to the opiate of a Western
story.

Marshall Hail of the El Paso *Herald-Post* went up to see
him and asked him what he thought would be his place in
history.

"Some of my friends believe I will be completely vindicated," he replied. "They believe the world will see that I
did what I thought was best for my country. Others insist
that I will go down in history in an unfavorable light.

"I don't know. I think perhaps I will be vindicated.

"The unfortunate thing was that my health broke and I
could not do my own fighting. If I could have, perhaps the
result would have been different." [44]

When the Japanese attacked Pearl Harbor in 1941, he felt
that the vindication had been at least partially accomplished.
His plan to store oil in the Hawaiian Islands looked a good
deal more reasonable now, he thought.

The end was long in coming for Albert Fall, and soon after
the close of his Three Rivers dream he began a round of
visits to hospitals—William Beaumont at El Paso, the Veter-
ans' Hospital in Albuquerque, and finally Hotel Dieu in El
Paso once more.

There he lay for many weeks, propped up in bed. His only

reading now was the newspaper. His cheeks became swollen and red, looking like shiny apples. His hair was white and there was only a faint spark in the watery, red-rimmed eyes. They never told him when Mrs. Fall died in a room across the hall, but he seemed to know.

When his time came, he went quickly. His heart stopped while he was reading his paper.

There was an impressive Catholic funeral attended by big and little people from all over the Southwest. Many kind and charitable words were said, but all who came were conscious of a glory departed—a great opportunity missed—a triumph turned into tragedy. So much given! So much accomplished! So little at the end!

For a while, after Fall lost out at Three Rivers, the old ranch was kicked around like a football. The Doheny interests sold it to the Palomas Cattle Company, a big outfit with many ranches scattered around. The Palomas people held on only a short time, disposing of most of the property to four men well known in the cattle industry—Will Ed Harris, A. D. Brownfield, Truman Spencer, and Jesse York. The Four Horsemen, or the Big Four as the newcomers were sometimes called, broke up the range by selling off several parcels to other ranchmen. Albert Burch, who had been very close to the Falls, got about twenty sections in the southeastern portion. Three Rivers itself was picked up in 1941 by Thomas Fortune Ryan, who still owns it.

Ryan was in the service at the time of the purchase and had not seen the property for a long time. He knew enough about it, however, to feel that ninety thousand dollars was not too much to pay for the Magic Valley, so he signed the papers and went on with his soldiering.

Tom's father, W. K. Ryan, was an Eastern capitalist interested in all sorts of business enterprises, including railroads. He had come to the Southwest in 1903 to build the North-western, which angles off from Juarez to the foothills of the Sierra Madre, touches the Mormon stakes, and arrives at last in Chihuahua, where Tom was born.

Tom went east to grow up, but the Southwest was in his blood. In 1924 he came back to live, more or less permanently. His start as a cattleman came in 1929, when he bought a thousand head of stock from Oliver Lee. Fifty dollars for a cow and calf—fifty thousand dollars.[45]

Always interested in airplanes and a major stockholder in one of the big airlines, Tom Ryan went into the Air Corps when World War II arrived. He flew many missions, including the evacuation of prisoners of war from Japan after the surrender. When it was over, he came back to New Mexico and settled down to ranching on his sixty thousand acres. With six hundred head of good stock, plenty of room for them to roam around in,[46] and money enough to provide for all emergencies, life should have been beautiful.

But even for a man with plenty of money, ranch life has its hazards. This, Ryan found out as soon as he set foot on his property. The old house was going to ruin. Repairs had been neglected after the Falls left; the roof leaked, the walls had been damaged, his architect told him it would be easier to build a new house than to restore the old one. So he tore down all but one wing—Albert Fall's library—and that still stands off by itself. Where Fall's adobe palace once rose, there is now a half acre of unoccupied ground. A new sixty-five-thousand-dollar hacienda rises in modest grandeur under the crowding shade trees just south of the old site.

Ryan had a worse shock coming. He found that he had bought sixty thousand acres but no water. His deed did not include any water rights, not so much as a glass to drink. The subject was not even mentioned in the legal papers, and Ryan was, literally, high and dry. He hired a lawyer to look into the matter and found that the water situation at Three Rivers was a mare's nest which went back to the time of Albert Fall.

The way it was set up, Joe Shanta and his Indians got what they wanted to use. The Southern Pacific got seventy-five thousand gallons a day, thanks to a deal with Judge Fall. The rest—if there was any—should have been the property of the new owner, but since the deed assigned him nothing, he was entitled to nothing.

Ryan got along as well as he could for a while, but it was obvious that if he meant to stay he would have to find his own water, and he prepared to go underground after it. He laid down seven hundred feet of pipe before he sank the first well. Luck was with him. He hit a vein at two hundred fifty feet. Encouraged, he went up the valley and tried again, connecting at two hundred feet. Then he drilled three more holes and got nothing. "If I'd turned that process around," he says with a grin, "I'd have given up." [47]

He has come to consider his place not so much a refuge as a vital force in the Tularosa country. Like Fall and Coghlan before him, he would like the ranch to be self-contained and patriarchal, as it was in the early days. He would like to see the Mexican families back in the adobe houses with garden and orchard and pigpen. At the same time he has the urge to build up good will in the community and be of service to his neighbors.

He has put up a "Bataan Lodge" in the middle of his acres, where the survivors of the Death March, many of whom he ferried out of Japan, can come and hunt in the season. [48] Another enterprise which he sponsors is the annual Kids' Rodeo, which draws contestants and spectators from a hundred miles in all directions. Fifteen hundred people crowd in for the event. Ryan has dedicated a new A. B. Fall Arena. The Tularosa Lions Club provides the free barbecue, and everything is relaxed and friendly.

Step by step the ranch has moved ahead. Telephone service, an improved road to the headquarters, rural electrification, a good landing strip—such improvements have made a modern enterprise out of Three Rivers. But some of the old traditions and families remain. Several Mescalero Apache families continue to live in the Shanta Community just beyond the east fence. Domingo Montoya, born on Three Rivers seventy-odd years ago, still tills his acres. Pete Crawford, whose father came with the First Cavalry at the time of the Lincoln County War, has spent most of his years on the ranch likewise. And Ricardo Portillo can show you the gravestones of his ancestors who lie in the little cemetery next to the newly renovated Three Rivers Chapel.

As the years go by, the spell of the magic valley lies more and more in its memories.

Frontiers in Space

THE city desk of the *Herald-Post* is a focal point for all the funny business that happens in El Paso, but it seemed to Chester Chope, the managing editor, that something funnier than usual was going on. It was July 16, 1945. The weather was hot and the air was full of rumors. First there was a telegram from Don Lusk, a good newspaperman at Silver City, New Mexico, reporting an earthquake in that area—glass cracked in downtown windows—a sound like great claps of thunder—heavy temblors shaking the earth. "Hmmm," said Chester to himself, "might be something in this."

He mentioned it to city editor H. A. Michael on the other side of the desk. Michael was skeptical. Rumors were always flying around, and most of them were pure hot air or damn lies anyway.

"Well," Chester argued, "remember that story about the airplane abandoned over North Dakota with five thousand gallons of gasoline aboard when the crew bailed out? It could be something like that."

"I still don't believe it's anything," said Michael.

Chester called reporter Mary Beck over to the city desk so they could start checking by telephone. Right away there was a call, Mrs. H. E. Wieselman of 901 Ochoa Street reporting a strange experience east of Safford, Arizona, that morning. Just before daylight the tops of the mountains near the New Mexico line were suddenly illuminated by a strong reddish-orange light. "It was just like the sun had come up and suddenly gone down again," Mrs. Wieselman declared.

"Call up Fort Bliss," said Chester, "and see if they'll give out anything."

The security officer at the fort had nothing to report, but thought it might be a good idea to call the colonel in Albuquerque. They called him.

"Yes," he said, choosing his words carefully, "there has been an explosion on a military reservation north of El Paso. An ammunition dump exploded." No, he couldn't say just where it was or what the circumstances were. Nobody had been injured. Civilians? Well, it might be that weather conditions affecting the content of gas shells exploded by the blast might make it desirable for the Army to evacuate temporarily a few civilians from their homes.

More incredible reports kept coming in. A ranger in the Gila National Forest said a shock had been felt throughout the Mogollon mountains and wanted to know if there had been an earthquake.

"This might be something big," Chester said.

"I think you're nuts," Michael growled, but his typewriter began to clatter as he got to work on the story.

A minute later Mike had a call himself—this time from a friend of his named Ed Lane, an engineer on the Santa Fe. "Hey," he said, "I just had a front seat at the greatest fireworks show I ever saw. I was on a siding at Belen, coming in to El Paso. Just before daylight there was a tremendous white flash, then a red glare all over everything. Then I saw three smoke rings thousands of feet in the sky. Haven't any idea what it was. The smoke rings swirled and twisted as if they were moved by a great force. The glare lasted about three minutes and then everything was dark again, with dawn breaking in the east."

Mike was not convinced yet. He got Ed Lane's report into the story, but he reduced "thousands of feet" to "high in the sky."

By now word of these marvels had penetrated to the composing room. E. R. Carpenter, the foreman, came up to let the desk know that he had been driving down Piedras Street at 5:30 that morning with Louie Ratliff and Jack Coulehan and had seen the whole sky ablaze with light.

"*Now* you tell us," Chester howled—"five minutes before we go to press."

He put a good big head on it—ARMY AMMUNITION EXPLOSION ROCKS SOUTHWEST AREA—and turned it loose for the home edition. Before the ink was dry, a man slid up to the city desk and flashed a badge.

"I'm from the Albuquerque Security Office," he told them. "I'm here about that explosion story. We don't want you to say anything about it."

"To hell with that," Chester snapped. "We've got this information on a release from the colonel himself."

"Don't run it," said the man.

"It's on the street now. We can't stop it."

"Well, don't print any more. The security of the country is at stake if it gets out."

Chester looked at Mike and there was a brief but heavy pause.

"O.K." he said.

After Hiroshima, Chope and Michael learned that they had scooped the country on the first atomic explosion and didn't know what they had.[1]

The wild, unvisited country was never the same after that

sixteenth of July and never will be again. Squads and companies and regiments of soldiers moved in, followed by small armies of scientists and technicians. Military installations took over the whole area. Beside every road rose warning signs: "*Peligro.* Danger. *No Entre.*"

Behind each new invasion was the thought Perry Altman had voiced in 1884: "Oliver, this country is so damn sorry I think we can stay here a long time and never be bothered by anybody else." The isolation and barrenness which made the place a haven for harried Apaches in prehistoric times and for discouraged Texans in the eighties now attracted another kind of pioneer—the scientist laboring to perfect new weapons for the defense of his country.

The Bomb was exploded in a rough and secluded part of the Jornada del Muerto near San Marcial on the old Bar Cross range. The Alamogordo Air Base reservation extended across the crest of the Oscuros at this point. Here, however, the scientists paused only a little while. The Tularosa country from El Paso northward, more accessible but almost as undisturbed, was the key area after 1945.

In the beginning was Fort Bliss, an old cavalry post which boomed during the war, along with the Biggs Field Air Base nearby. The horse cavalry became the mechanized cavalry. In 1940 an anti-aircraft-artillery training center was set up. Firing ranges of various kinds decorated the flanks of Mount Franklin and swallowed up the sandhills east from Fort Bliss almost as far as the Hueco range. Housing developments and shopping centers pushed out into the valley where once the coyote and the jack rabbit had the country to themselves. The trainees from greener districts cursed the dust and heat, but this land of cloudless skies and unmuddied roads was an ideal spot for making soldiers, and by 1943 fifty-three thousand young men were sweating it out in the training areas.[2]

They did not have the country to themselves for very long.

The awful facts about the atomic bomb stampeded Congress into spending large sums for research. The army organized the Guided Missile Division of the Ordnance Research and Development program. The Navy and the Air Force were not far behind in setting up similar programs of their own.[3] And they all descended on the Tularosa country, to the astonishment and dismay of the scattered inhabitants.

Fort Bliss kept ahead of all competitors as the nerve center of rocketry in the Southwest. What was once the headquarters of the Seventh Cavalry—the last stronghold of polo-playing lieutenants—developed in a few years into the biggest anti-aircraft and guided-missile school in the United States—probably in the world. Its population, military and civilian, was close to thirty thousand. A faculty of nearly two thousand officers, enlisted men, and civilians taught groups of specially selected American and foreign students to handle the weapons which have revolutionized war.[4]

Holloman Air Force Base, created very soon after Fort Bliss became rocket-minded, was the second great installation to move into the missile field. It began in 1942 as a place to train bomber crews for the British Royal Air Force. Tar-paper shacks and wooden barracks were thrown up ten miles from Alamogordo in the midst of the blank and barren Tularosa plain. A bombing range was laid out to the north. Intended first as a short-term project, it turned out to be more useful than was expected and soon became an important training center for American airmen.[5] For a while after the end of World War II it was abandoned, and the empty wooden buildings peeled and blistered in the merciless desert sun. By 1947, however, it was again in operation as an Air Force Research and Development Center, specializing in ground-to-air and air-to-air missiles. In 1952 it was given independent status as the Holloman Air Development Center. Renamed later the Air Force Missile Development Center, it soon became a major focus of experimental activity.

White Sands Proving Ground, now the White Sands Missile Range, was officially brought into being on February 20, 1945, as an Army Ordnance project. The Germans were leveling whole blocks of London with massive missiles when the war ended, and we were ten years behind them in know-how. Lieutenant Colonel Harold R. Turner, hawk-nosed, portly, and efficient, was sent out to find a location and set up facilities for testing rockets. After making a nationwide survey, he decided that southern New Mexico was an almost ideal site. It had sparse population, infrequent highways, and year-round clear weather. Tularosa Valley was by nature a corridor long enough to give the missiles a good run. It was cut off by screening mountain ranges from outside interference, and the high peaks on either side were ideal for setting up observation posts. Construction was started east of the Organs at a good rifle shot's distance from W. W. Cox's old ranch house in July 1945[6] and has never stopped since that time.

The lonely pastures were soon crisscrossed with roads and trails. Dozens of radar stations and observation posts dotted the country. New equipment, new housing, new personnel were added as the effort to catch up with the German rocket men gained momentum.

Many Germans put their shoulders to the American wheel. In the front rank of our invasion forces in Europe was a group of officers whose job was to round up German scientists and their equipment. Their campaign was sometimes called "the Battle of the Brains." All sorts of specialists responded to the offer of asylum and work in the United States. Dr. Wernher von Braun and his associates at the great rocket works at Peenemünde gathered up their files and made a dash for the American lines just ahead of the Russians. As quietly as might be, 118 of them were brought to the Ordnance Research and Development Center at Fort Bliss, and the work of learning how the Germans did it went on there until in 1950 the whole group was moved to Huntsville, Alabama.

Led by von Braun, a vigorous young aristocrat who had started his rocket studies in his teens,[7] the Germans at White Sands worked with twenty-five captured V-2s and rebuilt many others from salvaged parts. At first their movements were restricted, but little by little they gained more privileges, brought their families over, and prepared to become American citizens. Once every two weeks or so they assisted in launching a German rocket and spent the rest of the time helping to develop new American models.

The tempo of activity never ceased to rise. The armed services, finding themselves in the midst of the age of rockets, put terrific pressure on developmental agencies, assembly lines, and testing facilities to turn out many new types of rockets. As a result, a boom set in throughout the Tularosa Valley like nothing seen in those parts before. What was once the lonesomest country imaginable now sprouted towns, camps, observation stations, firing areas, and outposts of a dozen different kinds. Soldiers and civilians arrived in increasing numbers as new projects necessitated new personnel.

The Holloman Air Force Missile Development Center soon employed seventy-five hundred people.[8] Alamogordo, ten miles away, expanded at the rate of three hundred new residents a month.[9] Crews worked hard at getting the bugs out of new missiles, testing the performance of old ones, thinking up models which would fly farther, faster, or more accurately. There were Falcons, Matadors, Rascals, Aerobees, and experimental types whose names were unknown off the base. There was even a program of "Human Resources Experiments," made famous by Colonel John P. Stapp, "the fastest man alive," and by Lieutenant Colonel David G. Simons, "Mr. Man-High." Stapp used a rocket sled to test the reactions of the human body in machines of the jet age. Simons and his associates rode huge balloons to investigate the great emptiness a hundred thousand feet over our heads.

Assisting in the experiments was a small zoo of chimpanzees, rats, mice, frogs and rabbits, some of which accompanied rockets into space and returned safely to earth.[10]

Activities at White Sands expanded at an even faster rate than at Holloman. In 1958 its permanent personnel numbered eight-seven hundred and its budget had risen to one hundred sixty million dollars. It had all the facilities of a small city —theater, school, houses, clubs, stores, recreation facilities, newspaper. Nike, Honest John, Little John, Sergeant, Lacrosse, Hawk, Dart—such names identified the missiles which gave this strange community its reason for existence. Everybody's business was missiles—making, firing, testing, or improving them. Where it would end, nobody knew, but new construction would run into more millions every year. Nothing was too good or too fantastic for the rocket men.[11]

The lonesome cowboys of 1885, or even 1935, could not recognize their home ranges. In fact, they were never allowed on them without a permit and a good reason. Only the fringes of the country were still in private hands. Fort Bliss and its Hueco Range reached almost all the way across the southern part of the valley. Adjoining Fort Bliss on the north and occupying one hundred seventy-eight thousand more acres was Biggs Air Force Base, and installation of the Strategic Air Command which constantly lengthened its runways and expanded its facilities to keep up with developments of the new age. Eight thousand officers and men lived on the base, and hundreds of families were scattered out through El Paso.[12]

North of Biggs Field and occupying most of the country between the Alamogordo road and the Sacramentos was the McGregor Range, extending eighty-five miles north from the Texas line, where training in handling Nike anti-aircraft missiles would henceforward be concentrated.

From Fort Bliss northward the west side of the valley likewise became a great military reservation for over one hundred fifty miles. When the Alamogordo Bombing Range was combined with the White Sands Range for joint coordinated use, the northern half of the valley became a single unit devoted to missiles and nothing else. Alamogordo, Tularosa, Three Rivers, Carrizozo were perched on the edge of this vast testing area. It is hard to believe that such a transformation could take place in ten years—from the last lonesome frontier to a great technical community with a population of many thousands.

Such a tremendous, violent, and sudden expansion could not be accomplished without some dislocation. The men who were dislocated were the descendants of the Texas cattlemen who had come in the eighties and possessed the land. They had fought many a fight to keep their holdings, and now the time had come to make a last stand. They were few in number, but they had got there first and were notoriously hard to uproot. The government could not go into the rocket business, however, without getting rid of them, and land acquisition was begun when the Alamogordo base was activated in 1942. After the war, when the base was reopened, condemnation suits were filed which eventually gave Holloman and White Sands over two million acres—a strip of land thirty to forty miles wide and over one hundred miles long.[13] A good deal of this was public property already, belonging either to the Federal government or to the state of New Mexico. The ranchers filled out their patches of patented land by leasing and developing this public domain.

The expansion of the firing ranges was catastrophic for most of those ranchers. At first the compensation offered for their private property and improvements was extremely small, and many of them had to leave their homes and the work of many years, accepting rentals which they could not possibly live on. Others were allowed to stay on their lands under a system of co-use. On firing days they were expected

to get themselves and their livestock off the range—a difficult arrangement at best. They were good Americans, however, and though they availed themselves of their inalienable
right to grumble, they cooperated. When the first Ameri-
can-assembled rocket was launched at White Sands Proving
Ground in March 1946, they could see some purpose in their
cooperation.

For two years after that, the rocket men were satisfied to
go on with their experiments without asking for more land,
and they were getting spectacular results. There was more to
it, of course, than assembling and firing missiles. In the interest
of future developments it was necessary to gain as much
knowledge as possible about the reaches of space beyond the
earth's atmosphere, where only a rocket could go. Instead
of explosives, the war heads were loaded with gadgets for
the study of everything from temperatures to cosmic rays.
As many as twenty-eight "telemetering" instruments radioed
their readings back to the control room while a rocket was in
flight.[14]

Up and up they bored into the sky—100 miles—132 miles—
157 miles—coming down ten, twenty, fifty miles away. A
two-stage rocket, a V-2 with a smaller missile fixed in the
nose, ascended 250 miles, so high that the crew had to aim it
off the reservation to compensate for the turning of the earth
beneath. In 1948, experiments began in controlling the missiles
in flight.[15]

Before the early models had been worked over, there was
some question about where the rockets would land. One ec-
centric V-2 got out of control and headed for Alamogordo,
landing in the foothills beyond town. Another came down in
barren country south of Juarez, Mexico, with a terrific explosion.[16] No one was hurt, and no real trouble was encountered
again until February 1957, when a Matador missile went out
of control at Holloman and headed north on its own. It was
eventually found in ranch country west of Albuquerque.

There were a few strays later, but no damage was done. Any rocket which showed signs of going off course was immediately destroyed.[17]

In 1947 the missile men were ready to unveil the Neptune, and in 1954 a Viking model broke the record for single-stage rockets, climbing up to 158 miles and attaining a speed of 4,300 miles per hour.[18] In 1957 a Navy Aerobee Hi pushed the upper limit to 190 miles.[19]

As their missiles became bigger and more powerful, the rocket men understandably began again to think about finding more room. That brought on a series of controversies that lasted from 1948 onward—the last stand of the Tularosa cattlemen. Gone were the days when they had to unite against Indians or rustlers or big operators, but their existence was still threatened, this time by their own government.

In 1948, contracts had run out. It was time to negotiate new ones. The government proposed to continue the leases and extend the range thirty-three miles northward, displacing forty additional families. This time the cattlemen agreed that it was time to fight. Their opportunity came when the Department of the Interior decided to hold a public hearing at Las Cruces on August 2, 1948.

The witnesses included top men from the government and the armed forces. Secretary of the Interior Krug sent Roscoe E. Bell, assistant director of the Bureau of Land Management, to speak for him. Present also were Major General John L. Homer of Fort Bliss, Colonel Harold R. Turner, formerly of White Sands, Brigadier General Philip G. Blackmore, then in charge of the Proving Ground, and Colonel Paul Helmick of Holloman Air Force Base. Opposed to them and jamming the federal district courtroom, was a crowd of exasperated ranchers and miners.

"It is imperative that the area in question be reserved for the use of the Department of National Defense," General Homer stated, "if this country of ours is to be insured of its safety." [20]

Ten ranchers and assorted miners took the stand to argue
against him. John W. Harliss of Bingham said, "The government might as well cut my throat as take away my ranch.
Ranching is all I know." E. G. Hill of Carthage choked up as
he described his fifty-year-long battle to make a good ranch.
"I can't run it on Saturdays and Sundays under the co-use
plan," he declared.

Charley Madrid, an Indian, got up like a thundercloud. "I'm
used to being pushed around, but these fellows aren't. They
are not money lovers. They love our country, but by God
you'd better pay them fairly if you take their land. We are
treating our displaced persons worse than foreigners in the
same position." [21]

The campaign staged by these embattled cowmen did some
good. The authorities in Washington reduced their demands
and offered better terms to the displaced ranchers. In June
1951 Hal R. Cox, son of pioneer settler W. W. Cox and owner
of a good ranch just north of the San Agustin Pass, accepted
the terms offered him.[22] He was the last holdout, and his ca-
pitulation seemed to indicate that there would be peace and
stability at last.

For three years the remaining Tularosa cattlemen went
about their business undisturbed, though they had premoni-
tions that the axe might fall again. In 1954 it did. The Mc-
Gregor range was already under lease as a Fort Bliss artillery
range. Now the Army asked to have this area, plus 353,347
acres more, withdrawn permanently from public and private
ownership for Army use as a Nike training area. A total of
682,000 acres would thus be taken over, and about two hundred persons were affected. They were given twenty days to
show cause why they should not be dispossessed.[23]

The ranchers were up in arms once more. They demanded
a Congressional hearing and tried to find someone in high
place who would do something about their plight.[24] Again
they were helpless. Rockets were the weapons of the future.

The center of American rocket training was the Tularosa desert. A few individuals must not stand in the way of the program.

As if to prove the urgency of the Army's need for elbow room, the 259th Field Artillery Battalion, equipped with Corporal and Nike rockets, was ordered to Europe to join the North Atlantic Treaty Organization.[25] At the same time the great cities of our country were being ringed with Nike installations as a protection against air raids. It was on the expanded McGregor range that the Nike crews would learn their business. The ranchers in the shadow of the Sacramentos had to go.

Among those whose property was condemned were Oliver Lee's sons Hop (Oliver, Jr.) and Don. Included also were old-timers like Sam Fairchild, who came to the country in a covered wagon in 1887, the Lewises from Crow Flat, and the Grays from Orogrande. Some whose property was not directly affected would be hurt by the closing of Highway 73, which cut across the basin from the Jarillas to the south end of the Sacramentos. For some it would mean a two-hundred-mile trip to get to the county seat.[26]

The House Armed Services Committee sent representatives to Alamogordo, where a public hearing was held on June 23 and 24, 1955.[27] The upshot was that most of the cattlemen saw the futility of resistance and prepared to clear out.

One salty old cowman, however, was not about to move. This was John Prather, still vigorous at eighty-two, a mild-appearing old man with an almost permanent "sun grin" and thick-lensed glasses. The Prathers came from Texas in 1883 and settled in the Sacramento country. About 1905 John and his brother Owen moved to the high, lonesome range land south of the Sacramentos, miles from anywhere. Owen went in for sheep raising, but John built himself a cow ranch which eventually took in four thousand acres of deeded land and twenty thousand acres of state and federal land.

John Prather built up his spread with grit and muscle. Following a team and scraper, he scooped out tanks to catch rain water. He sank a 1,050-foot well, built fences and roads, put up a comfortable rock house.[28] After fifty years of this the Army came with its missiles and its high-ranging guns and told him he would have to give it all up. To John Prather this seemed like a violation of the most basic principles of right and justice. The land was his. He had occupied it for fifty years. His headquarters was only a mile and a half inside the line which the army had drawn. The thought of abandoning his eight sections where the grass grew as high as the top of a car was too much for him. After the condemnation proceedings at Albuquerque in July 1956 he announced simply, "I'm not moving," and let it be known that anybody who tried to put him off was liable to get hurt.

When the specified ninety days were up, the U. S. District Court at Albuquerque ordered the ranchers off by March 30, 1957. John Prather said, when asked what he was going to do, "I'm going to die at home." [29]

U. S. Marshal George Beach said he would see that the ranchers vacated. John Prather remarked, in answer to a query, that he expected to finish out his first hundred years on his home place.[30]

By now it was becoming obvious that one determined man who thought he was right could confound the United States government—at least for a while. The Army couldn't afford to make a martyr of John Prather. He was "the kind of man who built the nation the missile men were expecting some day to defend." Word of his valiant stand was getting around the country. Assistant Secretary of the Army General Hugh Milton revealed that Secretary Brucker was thinking the Prather situation over.[31]

Word came down that the gentle approach was to be tried, and the old rancher had an invitation to come to Fort Bliss and confer with the commanding general. General Robert Wood, a man of considerable personal charm, got on very well with Prather and made him a proposition which must have been some temptation. He could have better than $200,000 for his property and could keep his ranch house with fifteen acres as long as he lived. Prather said he would go home and think it over. They asked him if he wasn't afraid to live in the midst of all that shooting. He said, "I am not afraid of missiles. I've raised mules all my life." [32]

Hopefully the Army prepared to step up its training program in the area and announced that there would be dedicatory exercises and a rocket shoot open to the public on April 26. Secretary Brucker, who was to be in El Paso for a "Rocket Symposium" staged for leading industrialists and Army officers, was to be in attendance. The announcement, however, set off a reaction which threatened to blow the Army right out of its own Rocket Testing Ground.

Congressman Clair Engle of California, who had long viewed with alarm the land grabs of various government agencies, finally took action. He announced that the Army was currently asking for 12,800,000 acres of the public domain at various places in the United States. "It makes your hair stand on end," he said, and proposed legislation which would make Congressional approval necessary for withdrawal of tracts containing more than 5,000 acres. [33]

At once the Army's expansion of McGregor Range in southern New Mexico was spotlighted as a particularly horrible example. State Land Commissioner Murray Morgan declared that he would file suit to block the transaction unless the government came through with arrangements to exchange acceptable tracts of public land for the state lands which would have to be sacrificed. [34] He and other New Mexico officials pointed out that almost half the state was now owned by federal agencies—that each new acquisition was taken off the tax rolls, leaving the commonwealth smaller and poorer—that New Mexico's loss would be Texas' gain, since

Fort Bliss and El Paso would get the Army payroll and New Mexico would get nothing but shrinkage. It was "practical annexation of New Mexico by Texas." [35]

Statesmen with sensitive noses immediately picked up the scent of injustice and began to object to what was going on. Among them was Senator Clinton Anderson of New Mexico. He blasted the Army for moving into lands to which it did not have clear title and demanded that the generals keep their hands off until the Senate Interior Subcommittee had a chance to do something about the Engle bill.

Gracefully yielding to circumstances, Secretary Brucker, General Wood, and their spokesmen expressed deep regret over the misunderstanding, called off the dedication of the McGregor Range, and suspended training activities in the area.

It became obvious at once that the remedy was worse than the disease. The range was already operating on a tight schedule with new Nike "packages" (units) lining up for training and old ones coming back for firing practice. Even a short interruption of these programs meant great waste of time and money. With a minimum of delay the Department of the Interior issued a permit allowing the Army to use the government acreage involved, and the state of New Mexico cooperated by accepting an offer of $31,000-a-year rental for its share of the territory. The R-Cat targets began flying once more, and the slim white Nikes roared into the New Mexico sky to intercept them, while plans went forward to start training in handling new weapons such as the Army's low-level missile, the Hawk. [36]

The one obstacle in the way of progress was John Prather. He would not move. He would not even discuss moving. August 1 was the final date set for his evacuation, and as the day drew near, people in and out of the Tularosa country began to wonder whether Prather would win, lose, or compromise.

The old man left nobody in doubt about what he intended to do. He was going to stay put.

"We've fought a hard battle against low cattle markets and droughts and depressions and big cow outfits for fifty years," he said, "and we don't know anything else to do but fight. And I've always figured I had a right to be buried here at home, where I've always worked. You think I want a bunch of Army officers running right around my grave all the time, making a beer garden and hunting lodge out of my home?" Later he added, "We used to carry six-shooters to keep what was ours. I don't think it's a sin for a man to use a gun to protect his property and I don't think the Army would force me to do it." [37]

The Army wouldn't. But the men at the top could not allow their program to be crippled by John's stubbornness without making a final effort to get rid of him. They checked the play to the civil authorities. On August 6, 1957, District Judge Waldo Rogers of Albuquerque issued a writ of assistance which would enable U. S. Marshal George Beach to evict John Prather from his ranch.

That was a Tuesday. On Wednesday morning three deputy U. S. marshals—Dave Frescas, Demetrio de la O, and Mike Gonzáles—armed and embarrassed, drove into Prather's yard. The deputies caught him on his way back to the house from working with his cattle, and they stood there for three hours threshing it out. The old man had only a knife to defend himself with, but he kept it in his hand and defied the officers to lay a finger on him. They talked—and talked. At one point Prather told them that if they would let him get his guns, he would settle the matter once and for all. "I'd like to live a while yet," he told the three unhappy officers, "but I'm not moving, by damn, and if it's time for me to die, I'm ready. Just let me get my gun and we'll square off and have at it. I'm ready any time you are." [38]

About 3:30 in the afternoon the deputies gave up, accepted a cup of coffee from Mary Toy, John's housekeeper, and left the ranch.

By this time the eyes of Texas, New Mexico, and the Pentagon were on John Prather. By midafternoon, Army officers were dismounting from jeeps, reporters were flying in, and Prather's kinfolks were arriving to back him up. Before nightfall a little army of twenty-five people had forted up in the ranch house waiting for the big push.

"I will kill the first man that steps into the door of my house," Prather is reported to have declared. "I'm staying here, dead or alive." [39]

One completely courageous and determined man was all it took. The officers did not come back. Judge Rogers, on recommendation of the Army, issued a new writ exempting Prather's ranch house and fifteen acres of land from seizure, and it was understood that the embattled ranchman would be let alone if he made no further trouble.[40]

It was a victory for the code of the Texas cowman. John Prather's psychology was the psychology of the eighties. He reacted as his forebears had reacted against any invasion of their independence and property rights. He was still fighting the battle of the little cattlemen against the big ones—the same battle which had cost so many lives sixty years before. He was the last of his kind. None of his neighbors had tried to hold out to the bitter end. John probably wouldn't have tried it either if he had been forty years younger.

The Army did the best it could under these difficulties. Since much public opinion was on the side of the old ranchman, service personnel were instructed not to discuss the Prather case. Instead of arguing the point, the Information and Education officers undertook to let the public see for itself what was going on in the world's largest guided-missile center. Invited guests at McGregor Range firings saw the

Nike-Ajax in action and realized without being told that when awe-inspiring Nike-Zeus was ready to go into full operation, the Army would simply have to have more room whether John Prather and his cows were inconvenienced or not. Briefing officers underlined the point by showing that on account of "land-acquisition difficulties" the training area for anti-aircraft artillery and guided-missile crews occupied a strip of desert nine by thirty-six miles—not fourteen by forty-two as it should have been.[41]

The need for land extended far beyond John Prather's holdings. There was talk about adding more territory to the White Sands Missile Range,[42] and acquiring a new testing site on the Jornada across the San Andres range—Gene Rhodes' old home territory.[43] Late in 1959 a forty-mile extension was actually added at the northern end of the Range to facilitate testing the Nike-Zeus and other long-range vehicles. The ranch families involved moved out on firing days without much complaint.[44]

It was not so with John Prather. He never gave in. "If they come after me, they better bring a box," he declared. "I am staying till hell freezes over." And he did stay until old age forced him to leave the ranch for medical treatment. When he died in an Albuquerque hospital, his ranch became government property.[45]

Meanwhile the once-lonely reaches of the Tularosa country continued to attract a growing horde of scientists and technicians who swarmed over the mountains and drove jeeps and trucks across the cattle ranges of not so long ago. These men looked far beyond the military use of rocketry. They wanted to go into space. They talked quite calmly about lunar probes and space stations and the inevitability of visiting other planets. Wernher von Braun, leader of the German rocket men and a speaker and writer of considerable power, pleaded for a program which would "open up a road to the stars."[46]

Little by little his dream came closer to reality. In 1956 off-range firing programs began and missiles commenced to move hundreds of miles across the land from Utah to Texas, to impact on the White Sands Range.[47] Army, Navy and Air Force groups worked independently and together. Four Directorates were established to supervise operations: NRO (National Range Operations), ARMTE (Army Missile Test and Evaluation), ID (Instrumentation Directorate), and AA (Army Air Operations). In 1970 some of the Air Force Research and Development programs were moved to White Sands Missile Range and to Kirtland Air Force Base, Albuquerque. At the same time Holloman became the home of the 49th Tactical Wing (a NATO group).

A new focus was given to White Sands activities when NASA, founded in 1958, erected a multi-million-dollar plant at White Sands and began the effort which put the first man on the moon in 1969.

When the Apollo program ended at the beginning of the seventies, the space shuttle and related activities took its place. An astronaut shuttle flight training program was begun in 1976 and several shuttle subsystems underwent testing. In another area, WSMR became involved during the seventies in energy research, using its "thermal radiation facility" (solar furnace) to gasify both coal and oil shale by solar heat for the first time. In 1977 the Range was designated as host to a "tri-service high-energy laser facility," funded at $34 million.

Space activities never took second place, however, and when von Braun's vision of "a highway to the stars" eventually becomes a reality, a spaceport may occupy what used to be W. W. Cox's pasture. When that day comes, the Tularosa country, where the Old West made one of its last stands, will still be frontier—the frontier which borders on the unknown regions beyond our universe.

Sparse

ΠΠΠΠΠΠΠΠΠΠΠΠΠΠΠΠΠΠΠΠ

Sources

Seventeen years of time, documentary sources of many kinds, and the recollections of dozens of men and women have gone into the making of this book. Sources actually quoted are listed below. I owe a great debt, however, to many people whose words I have not used but who have helped with information, photographs, letters, and just talk.

For such assistance I offer thanks to Clovis Aguilar of Tularosa, Charles F. Teed and Evan Heywood Antone of El Paso, E. W. Bowers of Clarksville, Texas, Bud Rouse and Gabe Brillante of White Sands Missile Range, Miss Julia Buchanan of El Paso, Miss Ann Bucher of El Paso, Mrs. Lansing Bloom of Albuquerque, The Rev. Ross Calvin of Clovis, Dr. Arthur L. Campa of Denver, Verner Clayton of Tularosa, Mrs. Edith Crawford of Carrizozo, Porter Day of Three Rivers, Miss Rita Faudoa of El Paso, Miss Erna Fergusson of Albuquerque, the late Col. Maurice G. Fulton of Roswell, Miss Elizabeth Garrett of Las Cruces, Mrs. George Haile of Alamogordo, Carroll Johnson of Three Rivers, Mrs. Paul

Klopfer of La Luz, Mrs. Mary Lee of El Paso, Mrs. G. W. Linnenkohl and the late Mr. Linnenkohl of Alamogordo, J. D. McGregor, Jr., of El Paso, James G. McNary of Albuquerque, R. N. Mullin of Chicago, Guy W. Moore of Arlington, Va., W. M. Osborne of Norfolk, Va., Miss Inez Richmond, assistant librarian, Ada, Oklahoma, Irving Schwartz of El Paso, Miss Helen Shields of Alamogordo, Tom Stephens of Roswell, Mrs. Sam Tanner of Piñon, Mrs. Walter Vanderpool of Denton, Tex., Moss Wimbish of Ada, Oklahoma.

I owe special thanks to the late Mrs. Katherine Doughty Stoes of Las Cruces, who opened her extensive historical collection and helped in a hundred additional ways; to the late Margaret Fountain Guion, daughter of Colonel Fountain, and to Mrs. Manuel Aguirre, his granddaughter, long-time friends and advisers; to the late Mrs. Lucy Gililland Raley, who lived much of the history in this book and never lost her courage and serenity; to Bess Cooper Barton, daughter of Jim Cooper, who provided much information about her father; to the late Oscar L. Garrett, Pat Garrett's son, for debating the facts of his father's life and death with me; to John O. Camden, general manager of Pinkerton's National Detective Agency, who kindly gave permission to quote the invaluable Pinkerton reports used herein; to the late Maury Kemp, whose counsel and friendship I shall always cherish; to Mrs. Helen Farrington Kister, former librarian, and the staff of the El Paso Public Library, without whose help such books as this could never be finished; to Mr. C. E. Burns of Alamogordo, whose assistance in getting together the picture section was priceless.

Among those who have read the manuscript wholly or in part and offered useful advice and criticism, the following people have my grateful acknowledgment: Mrs. Tom Charles, Mr. Dick Gililland, Mrs. Mary Lee, Mr. Irving Schwartz, Dr. David S. Stratton, the late H. B. Holt, Mrs. George Brunner, Mr. T. F. Ryan, Mr. A. B. Cox, the late Lee Orndorff, the late Oliver M. Lee, Jr., and Mrs. Lee.

To these good friends, present and absent, and to the others listed below under "Interviews," my deepest gratitude.

Books and Articles

Blazer, A. N., "Blazer's Mill," *New Mexico*, Jan., 1933.

Bradford, Giles, *A History of Mitchell County*, M. A. Thesis, The University of Texas, 1937.

Bronson, Edgar Beecher, *The Red-blooded Heroes of the Frontier*, Grosset and Dunlap, New York, 1910.

Charles, Mrs. Tom, "Thomas F. Ryan Rebuilds Tres Ritos Ranch," El Paso *Times*, Dec. 30, 1951.

———, "Historic Dog Canyon," El Paso *Times*, March 2, 1952.

Coan, Charles F., *A History of New Mexico*, The American Historical Society, Chicago and New York, 1925, vol. 7.

Coleman, Max, "Frontier Sheriff Played Important Role," *Frontier Times*, Nov., 1935.

Collier, John, *The Indians of the Americas*, W. W. Norton Co., New York, 1947.

Curry, George, *George Curry 1861-1947 An Autobiography*, ed. H. B. Hening, The University of New Mexico Press, Albuquerque, 1958.

Dobie, J. Frank, "My Salute to Gene Rhodes," Introduction to *The Little World Waddies*, Carl Hertzog, El Paso, 1946.

El Paso Troubles in Texas, House Executive Document no. 93, 45th Congress, Second Session, Washington, 1878.

Fergusson, Erna, *Murder and Mystery in New Mexico*, Merle Armitage Editions, Albuquerque, 1948.

Gregg, John Ernest, *The History of Presidio County*, M. A. Thesis, The University of Texas, 1937.

Harkey, Dee, *Mean as Hell*, The University of New Mexico Press, Albuquerque, 1948.

Harper, Richard H., "The Mescaleros in Danger," *Quarterly Journal of the Society of American Indians*, vol. III, no. 4, Oct.-Dec., 1915.

Hough, Emerson, *The Story of the Outlaw*, in *Frontier Omnibus*, Grosset and Dunlap, New York, n. d. (copyright, 1907).

Hutchinson, W. H., *A Bar Cross Man*, The University of Oklahoma Press, Norman, 1956.

———, editor, *The Rhodes Reader Stories of Virgins, Villains, and Varmints. By Eugene Manlove Rhodes*, The University of Oklahoma Press, Norman, 1957.

Illustrated History of New Mexico, The Lewis Company, Chicago, 1895.

Keleher, William A., *The Fabulous Frontier*, The Rydal Press, Santa Fe, 1945.

Kelly, Florence Finch, *With Hoops of Steel*, Bowen Merril Co., n.p., 1906.

Meadows, John P., "The Round Mountain Fight of 1868," Alamogordo *News*, Jan. 30, 1936.

——, "My Association with Pat Garrett," Alamogordo *News*, March 12, 1936.

Mills, W. W., *El Paso. A Glance at Its Men and Contests*, The Republican Office, Austin, Texas, 1871.

——, *Forty Years at El Paso*, privately printed, 1901.

Orcutt, Eddy, "Passed by Here," *Saturday Evening Post*, v. 211, August 20, 1938.

Otero, Miguel A., *The Real Billy the Kid*, Rufus Rockwell Wilson, New York, 1936.

——, *My Nine Years as Governor of the Territory of New Mexico, 1897-1906*, The University of New Mexico Press, Albuquerque, 1940.

Poe, Sophie A., *Buckboard Days*, The Caxton Printers, Caldwell, Idaho, 1936.

Read, Benjamin M., *Illustrated History of New Mexico*, Privately printed, 1912.

Rhodes, Eugene Manlove, *West Is West*, Grosset and Dunlap, New York, n. d. (Copyright, 1918, the H. K. Fly Co.).

——, *Stepsons of Light*, Houghton, Mifflin Co., Boston, 1921.

——, *Copper Streak Trail*, Houghton, Mifflin Co., Boston, 1922.

——, *The Trusty Knaves*, Houghton, Mifflin Co., Boston, 1933.

——, *The Proud Sheriff*, Dell Publishing Company, New York (copyright, Houghton, Mifflin Co., 1935).

——, *The Little World Waddies*, ed. William Hutchinson, Carl Hertzog, El Paso, Texas, 1946.

——, *Best Novels and Stories*, ed. Frank Dearing, Houghton, Mifflin Co., Boston, 1949.

Rhodes, May Davison, *The Hired Man on Horseback*, Houghton, Mifflin Co., Boston, 1938.

Siringo, Charles A., *A Texas Cowboy*, J. S. Ogilvie Publishing Co., New York, 1946.

Sniffen, Matthew, "Conditions among the Indians of the Southwest,"

Quarterly Journal of the Society of American Indians, vol. II, no. 1, Jan.-March, 1914.

Sonnichsen, C. L., *Ten Texas Feuds*, The University of New Mexico Press, Albuquerque, 1957.

———, *The Mescalero Apaches*, The University of Oklahoma Press, Norman, 1958.

Stratton, David H., *Albert B. Fall and the Teapot Dome Affair*, Unpublished Ph. D. dissertation, University of Colorado, 1955.

Twitchell, Ralph Emerson, *The Leading Facts of New Mexican History*, vol. 2, The Torch Press, Cedar Rapids, Iowa, 1912.

Manuscripts

Clayton, Jane, *Tularosa*, MS in the files of Tularosa High School.

Cooper, Jim, Account Books, in possession of his daughter, Mrs. Bess Cooper Barton of Carnegie, Oklahoma.

District Court Minutes, Doña Ana County, Doña Ana County Court House, Las Cruces, New Mexico.

District Court Minutes, Otero County, Otero County Court House, Alamogordo, New Mexico.

Fountain, A. J., military record, from Muster Rolls of Company E, First California Infantry, photocopy from the General Services Administration, The National Archives, Washington, D. C.

Lee, Mrs. Mary, *Life of Albert Fall*, MS.

McNatt, Mrs. A. A., *Memoirs*, MS dated June 17, 1949.

Mescalero Indian Agency Correspondence Files, Mescalero, New Mexico.

Otero County Deed Record, Otero County Court House, Alamogordo, New Mexico.

Pace, Laura Hannah (Mrs. Walter Vanderpool), *History of Tularosa*, MS.

Reports of Pinkerton Operatives J. C. Fraser and W. B. Sayers to Governor W. T. Thornton of New Mexico, March 5-May 13, 1896.

Reports of Texas Ranger Captains in the Adjutant General's Files (AGF), State Library, Austin, Texas.

Frank Rochas File, Probate Records, Doña Ana County Court House, Las Cruces, New Mexico.

St. Patrick's Cathedral Parish Records, El Paso, Texas, unsigned letter dated July 25, 1916, on the history of the Tularosa Catholic Church.

Mrs. Katherine Doughty Stoes, Las Cruces, New Mexico, MS notes.

Newspapers and Magazines

Alamogordo *News*
New Mexico Sentinel (Albuquerque)
Austin (Texas) *Weekly Statesman*
Weekly Austin Republican
Capitan (New Mexico) *News*
Cheyenne (Oklahoma) *Star*
El Paso *Daily Herald*
El Paso *Herald-Post*
El Paso *Times*
Flake's Daily Bulletin (Houston)
Flake's Semi-Weekly Bulletin (Houston)
Fort Griffin (Texas) *Frontier Echo*
Las Cruces 34
Life
Mesilla Valley Independent
Mesilla Valley Democrat
Rio Grande Republican
Time
Tularosa Valley Tribune

Interviews

Aguirre, Mrs. Manuel, El Paso, Dec. 25, 1953.
Altman, Mrs. Emma, El Paso, May 25, 1943.
Armendariz, Mrs. Elizabeth Fountain, Mesilla, Aug. 17, 1942.
Bentley, L. B., Organ, Nov. 7, 1953.
Blazer, A. N., Mescalero, Aug. 29, 1948.
Brunner, Newcomb, El Paso, Aug. 7, 1954.
Burges, W. H., El Paso, Aug. 10, 1942.
Casad, Humboldt, Canutillo, April 19, 1947.
Elliott, Mrs. Jouett Fall, El Paso, Dec. 22, 1946.
Fairchild, Sam, Alamogordo, Nov. 8, 1942.
Fountain, Jack, El Paso, April 15, 1944.
Fraser, Tom, Alamogordo, Nov. 7. Dec. 29, 1942.
Garcia, Sixto, La Luz, Aug. 14, 1948.

Gilmore, Mr. and Mrs. Wat, Hatch, Aug. 11, 1950.

Given, Joe, Alamogordo, Jan. 1, 1955.

Gonzalez, Sylvestre, Tularosa, Sept. 12, 1947.

Guion, Howard, El Paso, Sept. 16, 1944.

Guion, Margaret Fountain, El Paso, April 10, 1942.

Hughes, Captain John R., Austin, June 26, 1943.

Huss, Ed, Alamogordo, Dec. 30, 1942.

Issacs, Bill, Las Cruces, Sept. 15, 1954.

Jennings, Al, El Paso, July 4, 1948.

John, Father, Three Rivers, Aug. 18, 1957.

Johnson, W. E., El Paso, Sept. 17, 1947.

King, Billy, El Paso, Nov. 21, 1942.

Latham, Miss Rina, Alamogordo, Nov. 8, 1942.

Lee, Mrs. Mary, El Paso, Sept. 25, 1954.

Lee, Mr. and Mrs. O. M., Jr., Alamogordo, Sept. 14, 1954.

McCall, Bill, Radium Springs, March 26, 1948.

McDonald, Tom, Tularosa, Dec. 20, 1942.

McNatt, Mr. and Mrs. A. A., Alamogordo, Dec. 27, 1946.

Mauldin, W. H., La Luz, Dec. 28, 1946.

Mayhill, Frank, White Sands, April 10, 1948.

Morgan, C. W., Alamogordo, Sept. 14, 1948.

Orme-Johnson, W. H., El Paso, April 6, 1947.

Orndorff, Lee, El Paso, Sept. 25, 1955.

Ritch, Mr. and Mrs. Watson L., Tularosa, Sept. 14, 1948.

Ryan, T. F., Three Rivers, Sept. 12, 1947, Sept. 29, 1954, Aug. 18, 1957.

Thompson, Mrs. Emma Blazer, Mescalero, Aug. 29, 1948.

Voorhees, Mrs. Bessie, Orogrande, Dec. 26, 1948.

Additions, 1980

Important work has been done on the Tularosa area since the last printing of this book. Robert N. Mullin's essay "Here lies John Kinney," *Journal of Arizona History*, Vol. 14 (Autumn, 1973), pp. 223–242, throws new light on the outlaw gangs. Leon C. Metz's *Pat Garrett: The Story of a Western Lawman* (Norman: University of Oklahoma Press, 1974) is full of information, much of it new. Julio Betancourt's "Dog Canyon, New Mexico: A Historical Synopsis, 1849–1940," was written as a Report Submitted to the Human Systems Research, Inc., and to the State of New Mexico Parks and Recreation Commission, Oliver Lee State Memorial Park (1979). It digs deep into local history. Hiram M. Dow's "Commentary" on page 96 of this book gives authentic information about his father, Les Dow. J. R. Lovelady, Assistant Public Relations Officer at White Sands Missile Range in a letter to C. L. S. dated August 14, 1979, helped to update the chapter on the missiles, and Joanna White of Silver City, N.M., provided facts about her grandmother, who was, briefly, Mrs. Walter Good.

Notes

With Plow and Rifle

[1] John P. Meadows, "The Round Mountain Fight." Father John of the Tularosa church says he has heard stories of an attempted settlement in 1858 (Three Rivers, Aug. 18, 1957).

[2] Jane Clayton, *Tularosa*, MS.

[3] The original settlers kept no records, and what we know of these early days has been recovered from the memories of the pioneers a good many years after the events took place. On the rear wall of the Catholic church at Tularosa, for instance, hangs a framed list of fifty-three names "obtained from Dionysia López Bruzuelas, who dictated it from memory." This is the only roll we have of the first comers.

[4] "Tularosa," *Rio Grande Republican*, Nov. 6, 1889.

[5] Jane Clayton, *Tularosa*.

[6] *Ibid.*

[7] Parish Records, St. Patrick's Cathedral, El Paso, Texas, unsigned letter dated July 25, 1916, on the history of the Tularosa church.

[8] Sixto García, Aug. 14, 1948.

[9] The *Rio Grande Republican*, Nov. 16, 1889, says Duran was the leader.

[10] John P. Meadows, "The Round Mountain Fight." For the Indian story, see C. L. Sonnichsen, *The Mescalero Apaches*, 129-130.

[11] The first entry in the church book, by Father Boucard, is dated May, 1869. The first resident priest was Father Peter Lassaigne, who lived at Tularosa from January 1870 to May 1876, building, planting, and establishing the first school. Later he was parish priest at Las Cruces (Parish Records, St. Patrick's Cathedral, El Paso, Texas).

[12] *Rio Grande Republican*, Nov. 16, 1889.

[13] Jane Clayton, *Tularosa*. John P. Meadows (Alamogordo *News*, Jan. 30, 1936) says that Perfecto Armijo was the one who obtained the original grant. Laura Hannah Pace (Mrs. Walter Vanderpool) in her MS *History of Tularosa, New Mexico*, names Melendres.

[14] Laura Hannah Pace, *History of Tularosa*, MS.

[15] *Ibid.*

[16] Eugene Manlove Rhodes, "Consider the Lizard," in *Best Novels and Stories*, p. 414.

Texas Cattle

[1] Austin *Weekly Statesman*, June 14, 1877.

[2] *Ibid.*, Feb. 17, 1876: "Last Monday night a man by the name of Herman Gilhardt was shot and killed by one Bill Hooper, on the ranch of Mr. John Good, some twelve miles above this place [Blanco City]. . . . The murderer left immediately, but was captured next day in Hays county by Messrs. John Good and James N. Pace."

[3] Regarding a jail delivery at Brownwood in 1877, J. R. Fleming wrote from Stephenville to Major Jones on May 19: "I sent to you from Comanche last night by Special Messenger a warrant for John Good and his crowd for being accessories" (AGF, State Library, Austin, Texas).

[4] AGF, Frank Jones to Major John B. Jones, Dec. 17, 1877.

[5] Austin *Weekly Statesman*, Oct. 4, 1877.

[6] Billy King, El Paso, Texas, Nov. 21, 1942.

[7] Austin *Weekly Statesman*, Sept. 28, 1876: "The country is becoming so fenced up in Hill County as to force large stock men to take their herds to the frontier."

[8] John Ernest Gregg, *The History of Presidio County*, p. 71.

[9] Giles Bradford, *A History of Mitchell County*, p. 82.

[10] *Ibid.*, p. 83: "My outfit branded four thousand cattle the year before. The next year, after the drift, we branded five hundred."

[11] Interview, Alamogordo, Texas, Nov. 7, 1942.

[12] Eugene Manlove Rhodes, "Beyond the Desert," *Best Novels and Stories*, pp. 458-459.

[13] Eugene Manlove Rhodes, *Stepsons of Light*, p. 10.

[14] Eugene Manlove Rhodes, "West Is West," in *Best Novels and Stories*, pp. 151-152.

[15] *Ibid.*, "Beyond the Desert," p. 458.

[16] Frank Mayhill, White Sands, April 10, 1948.

[17] Mrs. A. A. McNatt, *Memoirs*, MS.

[18] Mrs. K. D. Stoes' MS notes say that Sue wrote to Mrs. Good and told her not to come, whereupon Mrs. Good came right away. Then Sue took up with Charley Dawson and set up housekeeping next door to the Goods. The unpleasant situation that followed was terminated when John Good killed Dawson on Dec. 8, 1885. The trial at Las Cruces, March 24-30, 1886, brought out many interesting facts about Sue. She had killed Robert Black at Socorro in August 1884 and was suspected of other deeds of violence (*Rio Grande Republican*, Dec. 12, 19, 1885; March 20, April 3, May 15, 1886).

[19] Ed Huss, Alamogordo, Dec. 30, 1942.

[20] *Rio Grande Republican*, Dec. 4, 1886.

[21] *Ibid.*, Nov. 27, 1886: "A brother of John Good, Isham Good from Texas, has moved with his family to La Luz, this county."

[22] Tom McDonald, Tularosa, Dec. 30, 1942.

[23] *Rio Grande Republican*, dates cited.

Blood on the Sand

[1] Keleher, p. 212.

[2] Mrs. Emma Altman, May 25, 1943.

[3] Keleher, p. 212. This was on July 4, 1884, shortly after his arrival, according to Keleher.

[4] Sam Fairchild, Alamogordo, Nov. 8, 1942.

[5] Mr. and Mrs. A. A. McNatt, Alamogordo, Nov. 6, 1942.

[6] Tom Fraser told me that China Scott came to Good's rescue when he and Dawson were shooting at each other and missing. Good took the blame anyway and was turned loose (see chapter "Texas Cattle," note 18).

[7] Wat Gilmore, Hatch, New Mexico, Aug. 11, 1950.

[8] Emma Altman recalled this part of the story.

[9] The Fort Griffin *Frontier Echo* noted on Jan. 4, 1879, that Ira Cooper and a party of friends had passed through. "They say farmers are crowding them out of Jack County and they are compelled

to move." Dr. Cooper had a hog ranch on the Double Mountain Fork of the Brazos by 1880.

10 Jim Cooper's account books are in possession of his daughter, Bess Cooper Barton, of Carnegie, Oklahoma.

11 Tom Fraser, Alamogordo, Dec. 29, 1942.

12 Tom McDonald was with the party which found him and made these deductions (Tularosa, Dec. 30, 1942).

13 *Rio Grande Republican*, June 16, 1888.

14 Tom Fraser, Nov. 7, 1942.

15 Tom Fraser, Dec. 29, 1942.

16 *Rio Grande Republican,* June 9, 1888; J. White to C.L.S., Jan. 30, 1979.

17 Tom Fraser, Nov. 7, 1942.

18 John P. Meadows, "My Association with Pat Garrett"; Tom McDonald, Tularosa, N. M., Dec. 30, 1942.

19 Tom Fraser, Alamogordo, Dec. 29, 1942.

20 Ed Huss, Alamogordo, Dec. 30, 1942.

21 Tom McDonald.

22 Mrs. Emma Altman.

23 *Ibid.*

Lead and Law

1 *Rio Grande Republican*, Aug. 25, 1888.

2 Mrs. Emma Altman, May 25, 1943. George Curry, *Autobiography*, pp. 101-102, says that John Good and his men cornered Oliver Lee in a La Luz dance hall but he escaped through a window.

3 *Rio Grande Republican*, August 25, 1888.

4 Mrs. Altman.

5 *Rio Grande Republican*, Sept. 18, 1888.

6 *Ibid.*, Sept. 1, 1888; Henry Stoes, Las Cruces, N. M., Oct. 3, 1942.

7 *Rio Grande Republican*, Sept. 15, 1888.

8 *Ibid.*

9 Betty Hawkins Wood, La Luz, N. M., Dec. 28, 1946. The property was acquired by her father, W. A. Hawkins.

10 Mrs. Altman.

11 *Rio Grande Republican*, Sept. 15, 1888.

12 *Ibid.*, Sept. 22, 1888.

13 *Ibid.*, Sept. 15, 1888.

14 *Ibid.*, Sept. 29, 1888.

15 *Ibid.*, Dec. 13, 1888; Tom Fraser, Nov. 7, 1942.

16 *Rio Grande Republican*, Dec. 16, 1888.

[17] *Ibid.*, Dec. 13, 1888.

[18] *Ibid.*, Dec. 22, 1888.

[19] *Ibid.*, June 22, 1888.

[20] *Ibid.*, Sept. 14, 1889; Flavio Romero, District Clerk, Socorro, N. M., to C. L. Sonnichsen, Dec. 29, 1942.

[21] *Rio Grande Republican*, Dec. 22, 29, 1888; Jan. 12, 1889.

[22] Cheyenne (Oklahoma) *Star*, March 25, 1937.

[23] Keleher, p. 215.

[24] Mr. and Mrs. A. A. McNatt, Nov. 6, 1942.

The Lives of Albert Fountain

[1] El Paso *Daily Herald*, May 3, 1899; Twitchell, vol. 2, p. 494.

[2] Al Jennings (grandson of Edward Jennings) and Mrs. Manuel Aguirre (granddaughter of Colonel Fountain), El Paso, July 4, 1948. John Jennings, according to family tradition, was playing in Washington the night of Lincoln's assassination. The President's first intention was to see the Jennings play. At the last minute he changed his mind and went to Ford's Theatre instead. The same tradition says that John Jennings was picked up by the police because he looked very much like Booth, and his friends had a time to get him released.

[3] *Illustrated History of New Mexico*, pp. 656-658. Fountain contributed, and presumably wrote, the article.

[4] W. Halsey Thomas, Curator of Columbiana, to C. L. Sonnichsen, Jan. 8, 1954.

[5] *Illustrated History of New Mexico*, p. 658.

[6] Muster Rolls of Company E, First California Infantry, photocopy.

[7] Illustrated History of New Mexico, p. 657; Mesilla *Independent*, Aug. 11, 1877.

[8] For Cardis see the Austin *Weekly Statesman*, July 20, 1875 (Legislative Directory, Representatives); Galveston *News*, Oct. 16, 1877 (personal description); Mills, *Forty Years at El Paso*, p. 142. The El Paso troubles, which culminated in the "Salt War" of 1877, were the subject of a Congressional investigation. See *El Paso Troubles in Texas*.

[9] *Illustrated History of New Mexico*, p. 658.

[10] For the Fountain-Mills trouble see Mills, *Forty Years at El Paso*, pp. 111-116; *Weekly Austin Republican*, June 16, Sept. 29, Dec. 1, 1869, July 20, 1870; *Flake's Semi-Weekly Bulletin*, Aug. 9, Oct. 11, Dec. 20, 1871; *El Paso. A Glance at Its Men and Contests; Flake's*

Daily Bulletin, March 13, 30, 1872; San Antonio *Express,* Jan. 17, May 30, 1872.

11 When he was a candidate for a seat in the New Mexico Legislature in 1888, Fountain's record in Texas was brought up and the old scandalous charges were repeated. The *Rio Grande Republican* for Oct. 20, 1888, published a sketch of his career, remarking, "How Colonel Fountain was regarded by the leading men of all parties in Texas . . . is best shown by a large number of newspaper articles published at that time by the press of Texas irrespective of party. . . ." The account cites the Austin *State Journal* of June 12, 1873, describing the presentation of a gold watch to Fountain by his constituents.

12 Keleher, Chapter IV, is devoted to such "Frontier Land Problems."

13 Mesilla *Independent,* Aug. 11, Dec. 8, 1877. Keleher, pp. 204-205, quotes from the first of these. Cf. the *Rio Grande Republican,* June 13, 1885.

14 *Las Cruces 34,* May 26, 1880, says that Fountain had been out in the mountains persuading frightened bands of Indians to come in to the agency after Army detachments had attempted to disarm the entire tribe. In the Agency files at Mescalero is a letter, dated Oct. 11, 1879, from Fountain to Agent S. A. Russell arguing for some Indians who had been confined for supposedly joining a hostile band. Fountain contended that these Indians had actually gone out to persuade the hostiles to turn themselves in.

15 See the Mesilla *Independent,* July 14, 1877, and the *Rio Grande Republican,* Aug. 29, 1885, for light on these campaigns.

16 Mrs. K. D. Stoes, MS notes. The story is also told by Edgar Beecher Bronson, *The Red-Blooded Heroes of the Frontier,* pp. 100-103.

17 Pinkerton Reports, March 18, 1896.

18 Robert N. Mullin, "Here Lies John Kinney," *Journal of Arizona History,* Vol. 14 (Autumn, 1973), pp. 223–242.

19 Mrs. K. D. Stoes, MS notes.

20 Twitchell, vol. 2, p. 494; *Rio Grande Republican,* Aug. 29, 1885, Oct. 3, 1888; Mrs. Manuel Aguirre, El Paso, Dec. 25, 1953.

21 *Rio Grande Republican,* Oct. 3, 1888.

22 Copies of both letters are in possession of Fountain's granddaughter, Mrs. Manuel Aguirre, El Paso, Texas.

23 *Rio Grande Republican,* June 21, Aug. 11, 1888.

24 *Ibid.,* Sept. 29, 1888.

The Rise of Albert Fall

[1] Oct. 3, 1888.

[2] El Paso *Times*, Dec. 1, 1944 (obituary notice).

[3] *Ibid.*; Stratton, *Albert Fall*, p. 2. Dr. Stratton refers to two auto-biographical MSS in the Fall family archives.

[4] El Paso *Herald-Post*, Dec. 1, 1944 (obituary notice).

[5] Keleher, p. 181.

[6] *Ibid.*

[7] *Ibid.*; El Paso *Times*, March 26, 1943; Mrs. Mary Lee, El Paso, Sept. 25, 1954.

[8] Mrs. Mary Lee, *Life of Albert Fall*, MS. E. W. Bowers, Clarksville, Texas, notes a record in his grandfather's diary of the sale of Fall's stock of groceries on Jan. 22, 1884 (Bowers to C. L. Sonnichsen, Dec. 29, 1958).

[9] Keleher, p. 182.

[10] *Rio Grande Republican*, Oct. 20, 1888.

[11] *Ibid.*, Oct. 27, 1888.

[12] *Ibid.*, Nov. 12, 1888.

[13] Margaret Fountain Guion, April 10, 1942.

[14] *Rio Grande Republican*, March 2, 1889.

[15] *Ibid.*, April 6, 1889.

[16] *Ibid.*, May 3, 1889.

[17] *Ibid.*, Oct. 18, Nov. 1, Nov. 2, Nov. 15, 1889.

[18] *Ibid.*, Jan. 26, July 21, Aug. 10, Aug. 18, 1889.

[19] *Ibid.*, Oct. 12, 1889.

[20] *Mesilla Valley Democrat*, May 27, 1890.

[21] Florence Finch Kelly, a newspaper woman who lived at Las Cruces for a time during the nineties, wrote a sensational novel titled *With Hoops of Steel*, based on the troubles in the Tularosa country. Her title obviously refers to the Fall-Lee alliance.

[22] Major W. H. H. Llewellyn told a Pinkerton operative in 1896, "These men, To Wit:—Fall, McNew, Lee, Ellis, Morgan, Tucker and many others are banded into an oath bound organized body" (Pinkerton Reports, March 6, 1896).

[23] Mrs. K. D. Stoes, El Paso, Jan. 25, 1954.

[24] Keleher, pp. 186-187.

[25] Fall told his side of the story to a Pinkerton man four years later, recounting how "Major Llewellyn and other Republicans had placed armed men in the street on election day three years ago and how a

man had been brought in from Nebraska to kill him (Fall) and through all this Oliver Lee was the only man whom he could call on and trust in this country" (Pinkerton Reports, March 20, 1896).

26 *Rio Grande Republican*, March 10, 1893.

Cow Trouble

1 *Rio Grande Republican*, June 2, 1888.

2 *Ibid.*, Dec. 15, 1888.

3 *Ibid.*, June 9, 1888.

4 *Ibid.*, Jan. 26, 1889. The Tularosa correspondent looks forward to the future, "When its banks will be lined with mills and store-houses" and "great smelters will be separating the precious metals now secreted within the shelves of the mountains."

5 *Ibid.*, May 10, 1890.

6 W. H. Mauldin, La Luz, N. M., Dec. 28, 1946.

7 Eugene Manlove Rhodes, *The Little World Waddies*, pp. 90-91.

8 Interview, Three Rivers, N. M., Sept. 12, 1947.

9 Eugene Manlove Rhodes, *The Little World Waddies*, p. 12.

10 Eugene Manlove Rhodes, *West Is West*, pp. 166-167.

11 Interview, El Paso, April 6, 1947.

12 Tom Fraser, Alamogordo, N. M., Nov. 7, 1942.

13 Mrs. A. A. McNatt, Alamogordo, Dec. 27, 1946.

14 O. M. Lee, Jr., Alamogordo, Sept. 14, 1954.

15 Maury Kemp, El Paso, Sept. 25, 1953.

16 *Rio Grande Republican*, Feb. 17, 1893. Mrs. Lucy Raley, Jim Gililland's sister, says the cattle did not belong to Lee at all, and that there was only one stray in the bunch—a steer belonging to a rancher named McDougal. She thinks there was more behind this trouble than livestock (interview, Aug. 10, 1954).

17 Maury Kemp.

18 *Rio Grande Republican*, May 22, 1886: "Tom Williams is in from the Sacramentos. With neighbors Moore and Hilton he has constructed an acequia to water land to be put in alfalfa."

19 El Paso *Times*, Feb. 21, 1894.

20 Alamogordo *News*, April 19, 1936.

21 Lee Orndorff, El Paso, Sept. 1, 1942.

The Temperature Rises

1 This was the second attempt to organize. Four years previously a similar group had started the Southern New Mexico Livestock Asso-

ciation (*Rio Grande Republican*, March 15, 1890). The membership included J. H. Riley, Mariano Barela, Lynch Brothers, Thomas Ingles, and others well known in the region; also Pat Coghlan and Oliver Lee.

2 *Illustrated History of New Mexico*, p. 658.

3 Mrs. K. D. Stoes, MS notes.

4 Keleher, p. 188.

5 *Ibid.*, p. 187.

6 El Paso *Daily Herald*, Jan. 16, 1896; June 12, 1899. When he was on trial Lee was asked, "You were appointed especially to take care of Williams?" Lee replied, "I believe there was some talk about it. I wouldn't tell him that."

7 Pinkerton Reports. Miller's statement was enclosed in a letter from Governor Thornton to Operative J. C. Fraser at Las Cruces, dated March 6, 1896. The prosecution during the trial at Hillsboro in 1899 tried to introduce Miller's story during the examination of George Curry. The defense objected and the objection was sustained (El Paso *Daily Herald*, June 8, 1899).

8 El Paso *Daily Herald*, Jan. 9, 1896.

9 Sam Fairchild, Alamogordo, Nov. 8, 1942, tells a different story.

10 Hiram M. Dow, "Commentary," Ms. November 9, 1960.

The Bravest Man in New Mexico

1 Bill McCall, Radium Springs, March 26, 1948.

2 Declaration of H. Clay Phillips, U. S. Consul at Grenoble, France, in Rochas File, Probate Records, Doña Ana County Court House, Las Cruces, N. M.

3 Mrs. Tom Charles, "Historic Dog Canyon," El Paso *Times*, March 2, 1952, Julio Betancourt, "Dog Canyon," Ms.

4 Rochas to "Cher Frère," Dec. 23, 1894, Rochas File.

5 *Rio Grande Republican*, July 3, 10, 1886.

6 This letter, addressed to Mr. Q. Monier, together with another addressed to his brother in France, was taken from Rochas's house after his death and deposited in the Rochas File.

7 Second interview with Slick Miller, State Prison, Santa Fe, April 17, 1896. Report of Pinkerton Operative W. B. Sayers to Governor W. T. Thornton, April 17, 1896.

8 Report of Coroner Faustino Acuña. Rochas File.

9 Report of T. Rouault, administrator of the estate of Frank Rochas, filed April 3, 1900, Rochas File.

[10] Otero County Deed Record, Book 6, p. 179. For the later history of this property see *Ibid.*, Book 6, pp. 507, 572, 581; Book 25, pp. 104, 106, 474; Book 112; pp. 104, 105, 144, 416.

A Gunfight and a Letter

[1] Margaret Fountain Guion, Aug. 10, 1942.

[2] Keleher, p. 188.

[3] Pinkerton Reports, March 18, 1896.

[4] Howard Guion, Sept. 16, 1944; Mrs. Mary Lee, El Paso, Sept. 25, 1954. The Fall historians say that Morgan fired when he thought Williams was reaching for a gun. Fall and Young dashed inside after arms and Albert actually did no shooting. In later years Fall and Williams became friends and did business together.

[5] Pinkerton Reports, Sept. 16, 1896.

[6] Captain John R. Hughes, Austin, Texas, June 26, 1943.

[7] El Paso *Daily Herald*, Jan. 9, 1896.

[8] *Ibid.*, Jan. 16, 1896.

[9] Scott White, El Paso, Feb. 9, 1942.

[10] El Paso *Daily Herald*, Jan. 16, 1896.

[11] *Ibid.*, June 5, 1899 (testimony of Charles Lusk).

The Shadow of Death

[1] Margaret Fountain Guion, Aug. 10, 1942.

[2] El Paso *Times*, Feb. 4, 1896.

[3] Jack Fountain, April 15, 1944.

[4] Margaret Fountain Guion.

[5] *El Paso Times*, April 6, 1898 (Blazer testified at the preliminary trial but was not called at the later hearings).

[6] Erna Fergusson, *Murder and Mystery in New Mexico*, p. 78.

[7] At the trial in 1899 Humphrey Hill tried to tell about this conversation but the Defense objected and the objection was sustained because the testimony was "third hand." Later Hill was allowed to say that "Fountain had been up there getting indictments against certain parties, and he was afraid of those parties" (El Paso *Daily Herald*, June 3, 5, 1899).

[8] El Paso *Daily Herald*, June 2, 1899.

[9] *Ibid.*, May 31, 1899.

[10] *Ibid.*

[11] Pinkerton Reports, March 6, 1896 (statement of Saturnino Barela).
[12] Margaret Fountain Guion.

Vanished Without Trace

[1] Barela told his story on the witness stand in 1899; in 1896 he told it to a Pinkerton man in greater detail (Reports, March 6, 1896). He said that Santos Alvarado, who made the mail run from Tularosa at night, mentioned to him that two or three men whom he could not identify had patrolled the road for several nights after the disappearance. Pat Garrett scoffed at the idea that these men were out to keep searchers from finding the bodies. Pat had met Dan Fitchett, a man named McDougal, and an unidentified boy, all unarmed, hunting McDougal's cattle. Van Patten contradicted this (Pinkerton Reports, March 7, 1896), asserting that these men rushed on him with drawn pistols but backed off when Garrett and the rest of the posse came over the hill.

[2] Howard Guion, Sept. 16, 1944.

[3] El Paso *Daily Herald*, May 31, 1899 (testimony of Antonio Garcia).

[4] *Ibid.*, May 31, 1899 (testimony of Eugene Van Patten).

[5] John P. Meadows of Tularosa took credit for finding the blood stains. Van Patten said that Nicolas Armijo found them when the two of them were trailing on Feb. 10. Manuel Parra and Abran Gamboa were also written up as finders, and Van Patten felt obligated to deny the story publicly (*Rio Grande Republican*, Feb. 21, 1896).

[6] *Rio Grande Republican*, June 1, 1899.

[7] Pinkerton Reports, March 7, 1896; *Murder and Mystery in New Mexico*, p. 84.

[8] El Paso *Daily Herald*, May 3, 31, 1899 (redirect examination of Albert Fountain, Jr.).

[9] *Ibid.*, June 3, 5, 1899 (testimony of Thomas Brannigan); June 6 (testimony of W. H. H. Llewellyn).

[10] *Ibid.*, June 1, 1899. At the Hillsboro trial, Fall asked Van Patten if he had noticed a dead rabbit near the turn-off point which might account for the blood and for what he thought were the brains of the child. Van Patten denied noticing any such thing. Recently an old man at Alamogordo has been quoted as saying that he saw what happened—that Fountain told Henry to run before he himself died —that Henry tried to do as he was told but was caught and killed.

[11] Mrs. K. D. Stoes, MS notes.

[12] El Paso *Daily Herald*, June 7, 1899 (testimony of Carl Clausen).

[13] *Rio Grande Republican*, Extra, Feb. 4, 1896.

Footprints on the Desert

[1] The first news of a gold strike on the eastern side of the San Andres was heard in 1882. The district revived in 1892 (*Rio Grande Republican*, Oct. 7, 1882; Feb. 8, 1892). Fountain was one of those interested and had a claim in the Organs which he was developing at the time of his death (*ibid.*, March 10, 1894).

[2] El Paso *Times*, Feb. 22, 1894.

[3] *Ibid.*

[4] *Ibid.*, March 27, 1896.

[5] *Ibid.*, May 21, 1896.

[6] L. B. Bentley, Organ, Nov. 7, 1953.

[7] *Pinkerton Reports*, March 19, 1896.

[8] Miguel A. Otero, *My Nine Years*, p. 93, tells of accompanying Pat Garret to the Arizona State Penitentiary to follow up a lead. A prisoner named Johnson told of being at Sunol the day of the murder and seeing where the bodies were buried. He demanded a full pardon before he would say any more and Otero dropped the matter.

[9] *Pinkerton Reports*, March 18, 1896. Operative J. C. Fraser followed the leads on Fall very carefully. He got a statement from W. W. Cox, who met Fall at the San Augustin Pass. According to Cox, there was nothing unusual in Fall's behavior at the time.

[10] *Ibid.*, March 22, 1896.

[11] *Ibid.*

[12] *Ibid.*, March 11, 1896.

[13] *Ibid.*, March 10, 1896.

[14] *Ibid.*, March 12, 1896.

[15] *Ibid.*, April 20, 1896.

[16] El Paso *Times*, April 13, 1898 (Clausen's statement at the preliminary trial); El Paso *Daily Herald*, June 16, 1899 (Catron's summary at the end of the Hillsboro trial).

[17] *Rio Grande Republican*, Feb. 14, 1896.

[18] El Paso *Times*, June 9, 1899 (testimony of Oliver Lee); El Paso *Daily Herald*, June 12, 1899 (testimony of P. S. Fall).

[19] El Paso *Daily Herald*, June 12, 13, 1899. By the time he was called to the witness stand, Rhode had become Lee's brother-in-law.

[20] *Ibid.*, June 8, 1899; El Paso *Times*, June 10, 1899.

Pat Garrett Plays It Cautious

[1] Elizabeth Fountain Armendariz, Mesilla, Aug. 17, 1942.

[2] El Paso *Times*, Feb. 18, 1896.

[3] Editor of the *Independent Democrat*.

[4] El Paso *Times*, Feb. 20, 1896.

[5] Jack Fountain, El Paso, April 15, 1944. Fountain's story is partially confirmed by an item in the El Paso *Times*, Feb. 22, 1896: Oliver Lee, Tom Tucker, Joe Morgan and Jim Baird, "all of Doña Ana County, N. M., have been deprived of their commissions as deputy U. S. marshals." Les Dow was assassinated when he rode into Carlsbad, N. M., three months later. In April 1898 David L. Kemp and W. A. Kennon, on trial for the murder, were acquitted at Roswell (El Paso *Times*, April 5, 1898). O. M. Lee, Jr. (Alamogordo, September 14, 1954), told me about the Santa Fe meeting.

[6] *Rio Grande Republican*, Feb. 21, 1896.

[7] El Paso *Times*, Feb. 27, 1896; El Paso *Daily Herald*, June 2, 1899.

[8] El Paso *Times*, March 20, 1896.

[9] Pinkerton Reports, March 10, 1896.

[10] *Ibid.*, March 12, 1896.

[11] *Ibid.*, March 18, 1896.

[12] *Ibid.*, April 20, 1896.

[13] *Ibid.*, May 3, 4, 5, 6, 9, 1896. George Curry (*Autobiography*, pp. 115-116) says he obtained an admission from Ed Brown that he knew all the participants in the Fountain murder but was sworn to secrecy.

[14] El Paso *Times*, April 24, 1896.

New Days—Old Ways

[1] El Paso *Times*, Nov. 27, 1894.

[2] *Ibid.*, Feb. 27, 1896.

[3] Keleher, p. 246.

[4] *Ibid.* Keleher's chapters on Charles Bishop Eddy and William Ashton Hawkins give an excellent picture of these activities.

[5] El Paso *Times*, March 22, 1898.

[6] *Ibid.*

[7] Keleher, p. 247. Compare the El Paso *Times*, April 1, 1898: "More than 20 persons have located south of La Luz within the last month." The issue of April 8 noted that Beard and Bryan "have put in a large

sawmill near La Luz and have already begun the manufacture of lumber. . . . A great many farmers and orchardists are coming into the country every week . . . and there is plenty of room for more. . . .

8 Interview, La Luz, N. M., Dec. 28, 1946.

9 Miguel A. Otero, *My Nine Years*, p. 12.

10 *Ibid.*, p. 14.

11 At the time of the Hillsboro trial the El Paso *Daily Herald* (May 27, 1899) remarked that the story "concerning the finding of Colonel Fountain in Hawaii caused deep disgust when read here."

12 Keleher, pp. 209-210.

13 *Ibid.*, pp. 218-219. R. N. Mullin, writing to C. L. Sonnichsen, Feb. 16, 1951, gives W. D. Tipton's version of the poker game as he told it to Mr. Mullin. George Curry in his *Autobiography*, pp. 106-107, says the conference over the manner of arresting Lee was actually held in Curry's Tularosa office after the 70-hour game broke up.

14 Keleher, p. 217.

15 *Ibid.*

16 El Paso *Daily Herald*, June 7, 1899.

17 Keleher, p. 220.

18 El Paso *Daily Herald*, June 7, 1899; El Paso *Times*, April 12, 1897. Garrett and Lee told entirely different stories about this first attempt to arrest Lee. Compare George Curry, *Autobiography*, pp. 104-105.

19 El Paso *Times*, April 10, 1898.

20 *Ibid.*

21 *Ibid.*, April 16, 1898.

22 *Ibid.*, April 17, 1898.

23 *Ibid.*, April 9, 1898: Governor Otero orders Major Van Patten to hold his three companies of National Guard in readiness to report to the Sheriff to keep the peace.

The Fight at the Wildy Well

1 Interview, Radium Springs, N. M., March 26, 1948.

2 Lee apparently told William L. Keleher that Espalin had warned him, saying, "There are strangers in the country" (*Fabulous Frontier,* p. 220). On the witness stand, Espalin denied this but admitted that he had gone to Garrett after seeing Lee and Gililland leave Cox's ranch (El Paso *Daily Herald*, June 11, 1899).

3 El Paso *Daily Herald*, June 7, 1899 (Garrett's testimony).

[4] *Ibid.*

[5] *Ibid.*, June 7, 1899; El Paso *Times*, July 12, 13, 14, 16, 1898; Keleher, pp. 221-222; Dick Gililland, Alamogordo, Dec. 25, 1954.

[6] Interview, Alamogordo, N. M., Nov. 6, 1942.

[7] El Paso *Times*, July 14, 1898.

[8] At the trial in 1899 Garrett said he went back to the ranch "to water my horse and saw Tom Tucker. I told him that I was looking for Lee (El Paso *Daily Herald*, June 7, 1899, testimony of Pat Garrett).

On the Dodge

[1] El Paso *Times*, March 29, 1898.

[2] *Ibid.*, April 21, 1898.

[3] *Ibid.*, April 19, 1898. The regulars at Fort Bliss entrained for New Orleans on April 19.

[4] Keleher, p. 189.

[5] Otero, *My Nine Years*, p. 48.

[6] The signers were Numa Reymond, F. H. Bascom, J. R. McFie, Jacinto Armijo, John Riley, Pat Garrett, and Martin Lohman.

[7] Otero, p. 48.

[8] "Aunt Rin" Latham came out from Texas to be with the Yost brothers at Aleman when Ed Yost, her fiancé, died in Burnet County.

[9] Miss Rina Latham, Alamogordo, N. M., Nov. 8, 1942.

[10] Mr. and Mrs. A. A. McNatt, Nov. 6, 1942.

[11] Gene called it Moongate Pass in his stories.

[12] Keleher, p. 223.

[13] *Ibid.* Keleher says the indictment "slumbered" until Oct. 10, 1899, when Albert Fall filed a motion to dismiss which Judge Leland approved on the grounds that there was no such thing in New Mexico as a criminal libel law.

[14] Keleher, p. 225; El Paso *Daily Herald*, March 9, 1889: officer "George Curry has been appointed by Gov. Otero as special officer to arrest Oliver Lee. . . . He will be taken to jail at Socorro."

[15] El Paso *Daily Herald*, March 13, 1899.

[16] *Ibid.*, March 16, 1899.

The Defense Rests

[1] El Paso *Daily Herald*, April 28, 1899.

[2] Jack Fountain, El Paso, April 15, 1944.

[3] Keleher, p. 231.

[4] El Paso *Daily Herald*, May 29, 1899.

[5] *Ibid.*, May 31, June 2, 1899. George Curry (*Autobiography*, p. 115) tells more about Maxwell's history and about his later comments on his own story.

[6] El Paso *Daily Herald*, May 31, 1899.

[7] *Ibid.*, June 2, 1899.

[8] *Ibid.*, June 7, 1899.

[9] *Ibid.*, June 2, 1899.

[10] *Ibid.*, May 31, 1899.

[11] *Ibid.*, June 3, 1899.

[12] *Ibid.*, June 7, 1899.

[13] *Ibid.*, June 6, 1899.

[14] El Paso *Times*, June 10, 1899.

[15] *Ibid.*

[16] El Paso *Daily Herald*, June 14, 1899.

[17] *Ibid.*, June 15, 1899.

[18] *Keleher*, p. 238.

[19] El Paso *Daily Herald*, June 15, 1899.

[20] *Ibid.*, June 16, 1899.

[21] *Ibid.*

[22] El Paso *Times*, June 13, 1899.

[23] Keleher, p. 239.

Aftermath

[1] El Paso *Times*, May 25, 1949. George Curry (*Autobiography*, p. 116) adds another name—José Chavez y Chavez—an earnest Fountain hater who was in the vicinity when the colonel disappeared.

[2] Mrs. Bessie Voorhees, Orogrande, N. M., Dec. 26, 1946.

[3] El Paso *Daily Herald*, Oct. 16, 19, 1900.

[4] El Paso *Times*, Nov. 27, 28, 1950; El Paso *Herald-Post*, Nov. 26, 1950.

[5] El Paso *Daily Herald*, Sept. 24, 1915; April 13, 14, 15, 16, 1916.

[6] Mrs. Lucy Raley, El Paso, Jan. 26, 1947.

[7] Elizabeth Fountain Armendariz, Mesilla, Aug. 17, 1942.

[8] William H. Burges, El Paso, Aug. 10, 1942.

[9] Newcomb Brunner, El Paso, Aug. 7, 1954.

[10] Lee Orndorff, El Paso, Sept. 25, 1955.

[11] El Paso *Times*, Nov. 3, 4, 1919 (Hutchings' death); Oct. 24, 1920 (the murder of Scanland).

[12] *Ibid.*, March 20, 23, 1907.

[13] Joe Given, Alamogordo, Jan. 1, 1955.

[14] Mrs. C. J. Parker, El Paso, March 12, 1943.

[15] A. M. Tenney, El Paso, July 21, 1953.

[16] Sixto García, Tularosa, Aug. 14, 1948

[17] James G. McNary, letter to C. L. Sonnichsen, Sept. 25, 1954.

[18] Maury Kemp, El Paso, April 16, 1954.

[19] O. M. Lee, Jr., Alamogordo, Sept. 14, 1954.

[20] Lee Orndorff.

[21] *Ibid.*

[22] El Paso *Times*, Dec. 16, 1941; O. M. Lee, Jr.

The Bard of the Tularosa

[1] Eddy Orcutt, "Passed by Here," *Saturday Evening Post*, vol. 211, Aug. 20, 1938.

[2] W. H. Hutchinson, *A Bar Cross Man*, p. xii.

[3] Readers object especially to Gene's overly pure and beautiful young women and to the self-conscious talk and mannerisms of his cultured young Easterners. Charles Fletcher Lummis once said to him in a letter, "I never saw any work of yours I didn't admire. I never saw any of it that I didn't want to kick you for not doing it better as you are perfectly competent to do" (May Davison Rhodes, *The Hired Man on Horseback*, p. 151).

[4] E. M. Rhodes, *Stepsons of Light*, p. 62.

[5] *Ibid.*, p. 10.

[6] E. M. Rhodes, *The Trusty Knaves*, pp. 85-86.

[7] Hutchinson (*A Bar Cross Man*, p. 13 ff.) gives an account of both sides of the family.

[8] May Davison Rhodes says the colonel came down when he was appointed Mescalero Indian agent. Actually his service as Mescalero agent extended from January 1891 to the summer of 1892 (E. H. Pubols, Chief, Federal Records Center, Denver, to C. L. Sonnichsen, Dec. 13, 1954). Hutchinson is not sure what brought Col. Rhodes to New Mexico but discusses his work at Mescalero, pp. 36-45.

[9] *Stepsons of Light*, p. 121.

[10] *The Hired Man on Horseback*, p. 23.

[11] Mrs. K. D. Stoes, MS notes.

[12] E. M. Rhodes, *Best Novels and Stories*, p. 142.

[13] W. E. Johnson, El Paso, Sept. 17, 1947. Hutchinson got a more

elaborate version of the story from W. A. Sutherland (*A Bar Cross Man*, pp. 10-11).

[14] Bill McCall, Radium Springs, March 26, 1948.

[15] Mr. and Mrs. Watson L. Ritch, Tularosa, Sept. 14, 1948.

[16] *The Hired Man on Horseback*, p. 36.

[17] Jouett Fall Elliott, El Paso, Dec. 22, 1946.

[18] Mrs. K. D. Stoes, Las Cruces, April 7, 1947.

[19] Humboldt Casad, Canutillo, Texas, April 19, 1947.

[20] *A Bar Cross Man*, pp. 24, 46-48.

[21] *Stepsons of Light*, p. 31.

[22] *Ibid.*, p. 40.

[23] *The Trusty Knaves.*

[24] *The Hired Man on Horseback*, pp. 49-50, 190.

[25] *Stepsons of Light*, pp. 54-55.

[26] *A Bar Cross Man*, p. 31.

[27] *Ibid.*, p. 294.

[28] *Ibid.*, p. 12.

[29] *Best Novels and Stories*, p. 458.

[30] *A Bar Cross Man*, p. 49, tells what happened to the 61 cattle.

[31] Mr. and Mrs. Watson L. Ritch.

[32] E. M. Rhodes, *West Is West*, p. 61.

[33] *Best Novels and Stories*, p. 11.

[34] Humboldt Casad. Hutchinson (*A Bar Cross Man*, p. 43) has a different version of this story too.

[35] *A Bar Cross Man*, pp. 43-44.

[36] District Court Minutes, Doña Ana County, Docket B, 406, no. 2017, 2018, May 26, 1892. *A Bar Cross Man*, pp. 43-44.

[37] *The Hired Man on Horseback*, pp. 190-191.

[38] *Ibid.*, pp. 8-9. Gene's mother had become acquainted with May's sister in California (*A Bar Cross Man*, pp. 67-68).

[39] He was in trouble when he got back. A man he had befriended had turned him in for eating Tom Catron's beef (*A Bar Cross Man*, pp. 70-71).

[40] *The Hired Man on Horseback*, pp. 8-9.

[41] *A Bar Cross Man*, pp. 3-6, tells the story in detail.

[42] It is usually supposed that Gene stayed away until the statute of limitations ran out. Hutchinson, *A Bar Cross Man*, p. 6, shows that the statute did not apply.

[43] *Best Novels and Stories*, p. 4.

[44] *West Is West*, pp. 124-125.

[45] *Best Novels and Stories*, p. 17.

[46] *West Is West*, p. 147.

[47] *The Little World Waddies*, p. 129.

[48] *Ibid.*, p. 13.

[49] *Best Novels and Stories*, p. 326.

[50] *The Little World Waddies*, p. 130.

[51] He was in Los Angeles 1919-1922 but did not revisit New Mexico (*A Bar Cross Man*, p. 142 ff.).

[52] *The Little World Waddies*, p. 130.

[53] Mrs. Lansing Bloom, Albuquerque, Nov. 29, 1947.

[54] Bill McCall.

[55] *Copper Streak Trail*, pp. 26-27. See Hutchinson, *The Rhodes Reader*, pp. 3-13, for an early story called "Loved I Not Honor More," which may be a transcript from Rhodes's life. Bill McNew, Pat Garrett, and a number of others appear under their right names.

[56] *The Proud Sheriff*, p. 74.

[57] *Stepsons of Light*, p. 96.

[58] *Ibid.*

[59] *Best Novels and Stories*, p. 166.

[60] *West Is West*, p. 189.

[61] The novel of that title. There is also a short story so named.

[62] Rhodes moves the Wildy Well from its actual location east of Orogrande to a point west of Chalk Hill, but that is about the only departure from geographical truth.

[63] *A Bar Cross Man*, pp. 132-133.

[64] *Best Novels and Stories*, pp. 308-309.

[65] *West Is West*, pp. 80-81.

[66] *Best Novels and Stories*, p. 462.

[67] *Stepsons of Light*, p. 230.

[68] *The Little World Waddies*, pp. 105-106.

[69] J. Frank Dobie, "My Salute to Gene Rhodes," p. xxi.

[70] *The Little World Waddies*, pp. xxiv-xxv.

Pat Garrett's Last Ride

[1] The letter reached Pat when he was in El Paso (El Paso *Daily Herald*, Feb. 29, 1908).

[2] Bill Isaacs, Las Cruces, Sept. 15, 1954. Bill says that Garrett had not paid taxes for years—finally borrowed $3,500 from his neighbor W. W. Cox. He put some of his cattle and horses in Cox's pasture and branded them in Cox's brand in order to keep them out of the

way. When Cox did not get his money, he refused to give up the stock. Garrett had refused to sell him the ranch, so he called in Oliver Lee for advice on how to get Garrett off. Lee suggested that they "goat him off."

3 El Paso *Daily Herald*, Aug. 24, 1905.

4 John P. Meadows, Alamogordo *News*, March 8, 1936. Meadows mistakenly has Glenn killed instead of Briscoe.

5 Mrs. R. E. White of Portales, N. M., El Paso, April 12, 1952.

6 Max Coleman, "Frontier Sheriff Played Important Role," *Frontier Times*, Nov. 1935. Coleman says Garrett "worked for John Causey and spent one year at Causey's Hill, some nine miles northeast of where the city of Lubbock now stands."

7 Emerson Hough, *The Story of the Outlaw*, p. 296.

8 Miguel Antonio Otero, *The Real Billy the Kid*, p. 92.

9 *Ibid.*

10 Keleher, p. 58.

11 *Ibid.*, p. 58. Keleher has dug up the marriage record at Anton Chico.

12 Personal letter, Patrick J. Hurley to Oscar L. Garrett, Dec. 9, 1950.

13 John P. Meadows, Alamogordo *News*, March 12, 1936.

14 El Paso *Daily Herald*, "Sketch of Garrett," Dec. 13, 1901.

15 The campaign got Pat into considerable personal difficulty. He gave a beating to a man named Roberts, whom he accused of writing an article unfavorable to him, and thereby came in for much unpleasant publicity (*Rio Grande Republican*, Sept. 2, 16, 23, 30; Nov. 4, 1882).

16 El Paso *Daily Herald*, Dec. 21, 1901.

17 Maury Kemp, Aug. 13, 1954.

18 L. B. Bentley, Organ, Nov. 7, 1953.

19 Keleher, p. 72, says he attempted to beat Jim Baird, a neighbor, with a six-shooter, "an incident that did him no good out in the range country."

20 L. B. Bentley.

21 El Paso *Daily Herald*, March 5, 1908.

22 Capitan (New Mexico) *News*, March 6, 1908.

23 Garrett's crippled son Dudley Poe Garrett received a letter postmarked El Paso shortly after the murder. It warned him to be on his guard or he might be killed too, and added that Brazel shot his father from the front while somebody else shot him from the back. It was signed "One Who Knows" (El Paso *Daily Herald*, Feb. 29, 1908). Dr. W. C. Field, who went out with the sheriff after the body, told an interviewer about the disarray of Pat's clothes, the

gloved right hand, the wound in the back of the head (*New Mexico Sentinel*, April 23, 1939).

24 Bill Isaacs, Las Cruces, Sept. 15, 1954.

25 Dee Harkey, *Mean as Hell*, p. 180. For more on Miller see Sonnichsen, *Ten Texas Feuds*, pp. 200-209.

26 Mrs. K. D. Stoes, MS notes.

27 Inez Richmond, assistant librarian, Ada Public Library, to C. L. Sonnichsen, June 5, 1953.

28 Moss Wimbish, Ada, Oklahoma, to C. L. Sonnichsen, Dec. 4, 1953.

29 Harris Walthall, El Paso, Dec. 4, 1953.

30 El Paso *Daily Herald*, March 3, 1908.

31 *Ibid.*, March 5, 1908.

32 Keleher, p. 77, believes that the barbecue "was turned into an occasion of rejoicing over the passing of Pat Garrett."

33 El Paso *Daily Herald*, Dec. 1, 1908.

Three Rivers: A Fabulous History

1 Eugene Manlove Rhodes, *West Is West*, p. 79.

2 Mrs. James A. Baird, obituary notice of Pat Coghlan, *Tularosa Valley Tribune*, Jan. 28, 1911.

3 C. W. Morgan, Alamogordo, Sept. 14, 1948, told me that Coghlan's nephew Fred Crosby of Del Rio, Texas, reported to him that when Coghlan came west he drove a herd that he stole from his father-in-law.

4 John P. Meadows, "The Round Mountain Fight," Alamogordo *News*, Jan. 30, 1936.

5 On Aug. 5, 1883, he got a large block from Nicolas and Lucinda Duran (Otero County Deed Record, Doña Ana Transcript, vol. 17, p. 11 ff.).

6 Keleher, p. 190, note.

7 Otero County Deed Record, Doña Ana Transcript, vol. 17, p. 11 ff.

8 A. N. Blazer, "Blazer's Mill," p. 20 ff.; interview with Mrs. Emma Blazer Thompson and A. N. Blazer, Mescalero, N. M., Aug. 29, 1948.

9 Charles A. Siringo, *A Texas Cowboy*, p. 168.

10 Mrs. K. D. Stoes, MS notes.

11 Sylvestre Gonzalez, Tularosa, Sept. 12, 1947; Morris Wohlgemuth, El Paso, Oct. 13, 1954. The *Rio Grande Republican*, April 24, 1886, notes that Coghlan is planning a trip to Ireland in May, expecting to be gone four months.

[12] *A Texas Cowboy*, pp. 168-170.

[13] *Ibid.*, pp. 171-174.

[14] Sophie A. Poe, *Buckboard Days*, pp. 100-101.

[15] *Ibid.*, pp. 117-118.

[16] *Ibid.*, pp. 215-216.

[17] District Court Minutes, Doña Ana County, Book H, 266, 267, Cases 630, 635.

[18] *Rio Grande Republican*, Sept. 9, 1882.

[19] Mrs. Emma B. Thompson, A. N. Blazer.

[20] *Buckboard Days*, p. 118.

[21] Stoes, MS notes. Philip Rasch, "The Nesmith Murder Mystery," Denver Westerners *Roundup*, vol. XVII (May, 1961), pp. 16-20.

[22] John P. Meadows in the Alamogordo *News*, Aug. 15, 1936.

[23] *A Bar Cross Man*, pp. 374-375.

[24] Otero County Deed Record, Book 17, Doña Ana County Transcripts, p. 11 ff.

[25] The Supreme Court reversed the order to sell, but according to the records no stock was given back. It had been sold or butchered.

[26] Otero County Deed Record, Miscellaneous Record, vol. 60, pp. 128-131, 133-137; vol. 25, p. 50.

[27] Jouett Fall Elliott, Dec. 22, 1946.

[28] Otero County Probate Records, Court House, Alamogordo.

[29] *Tularosa Valley Tribune*, Jan. 28, 1911.

[30] Jouett Fall Elliott; Stratton, *Albert B. Fall*, p. 33.

[31] Otero County Deed Record, vol. 5, pp. 126 (March 28, 1883), 138; vol. 85, p. 630.

[32] Thomas Fortune Ryan, Three Rivers, Sept. 12, 1947.

[33] Fall got his authorization from the Interior Department in 1910 to construct a cement ditch to bring water from the Reservation (*Publications of the Indian Rights Association*, Second Series, 91, 1914, pp. 32-33).

[34] Keleher, p. 189.

[35] *Ibid.*, p. 190n.

[36] Matthew Sniffen, "Conditions among the Indians of the Southwest," *Quarterly Journal of the Society of American Indians*, March, 1914, vol. II, pp. 51-55.

[37] Richard H. Harper, "The Mescaleros in Danger," *Ibid.*, vol. III, pp. 270-282.

[38] John Collier, *The Indians of the Americas*, pp. 246-257, traces Fall's later moves.

[39] David H. Stratton, *Albert B. Fall and the Teapot Dome Affair*, p. 99.

[40] *Ibid.*, pp. 349-365.

[41] *Ibid.*, pp. 509-515.

[42] El Paso *Herald-Post*, Aug. 15, 1935.

[43] El Paso *Times*, Aug. 16, 1935. The Otero County Deed Record, vol. 79, p. 402, records the transfer to Doheny on May 25, 1929, "in consideration of the sum of $10 and other good and valuable considerations."

[44] El Paso *Herald-Post*, Aug. 15, 1935.

[45] Mrs. Tom Charles, "Thomas F. Ryan Rebuilds Tres Ritos Ranch," El Paso *Times*, Dec. 30, 1951.

[46] T. F. Ryan, Three Rivers, Sept. 12, 1947.

[47] T. F. Ryan, Three Rivers, Sept. 30, 1948. With the help of engineers from Holloman Air Force Missile Development Center, Ryan is working on a project to trap the mountain water behind dams high up on the slope of Sierra Blanca. If his project succeeds, the ranch will have plenty of water again (interview, Three Rivers Ranch, Aug. 18, 1957).

[48] T. F. Ryan, letter to C. L. Sonnichsen, Sept. 29, 1954.

Frontiers in Space

[1] Chester Chope and H. A. Michael, El Paso, Aug. 4, 1954.

[2] El Paso *Times*, Dec. 7, 1947.

[3] *Life*, Sept. 2, 1946.

[4] El Paso *Herald-Post*, May 5, Oct. 18, 1957; El Paso *Times*, Sept. 1, 1957.

[5] In 1947 administration was shifted from the Strategic Air Command to the Air Materiel Command for guided-missile work. The first "Gapa" missile was fired on July 23, 1947 (El Paso *Times*, March 17, July 24, 1947, Sept. 1, 1957).

[6] Lt. Col. Harold R. Turner and Maj. Herbert Karsch, White Sands Proving Ground, Oct. 8, 1946; El Paso *Times*, March 24, Sept. 1, 1957.

[7] *Time*, Feb. 17, 1958, pp. 22-23.

[8] El Paso *Times*, Nov. 3, 1957.

[9] *Ibid.*, March 31, 1957.

[10] *Ibid.*, March 31, May 12, Sept. 1, Nov. 3, 1957, Feb. 4, 1958; El Paso *Herald-Post*, Sept. 5, Nov. 14, 19, 1958; *Time*, June 8, 1959, p. 14.

[11] El Paso *Times*, Sept. 1, 1957, Nov. 27, 1958; El Paso *Herald-Post*, May 24, Nov. 3, 4, Dec. 22, 29, 1958.

[12] El Paso *Times*, April 7, Sept. 1, 1957.

[13] *Ibid.*, Sept. 1, 1957.

[14] *Time*, Feb. 10, 1947, p. 55.

[15] El Paso *Times*, Dec. 19, 1946, March 27, 1947, Feb. 7, 1948, Feb. 26, 1949.

[16] *Ibid.*, May 30, 1947, March 10, 1957; El Paso *Herald-Post*, May 16, 30, 1947, Feb. 21, 1957.

[17] El Paso *Herald-Post*, Feb. 21, 22, 1957; El Paso *Times*, March 10, Sept. 1, 1957, June 30, Nov. 3, 1958.

[18] El Paso *Times*, July 13, 1947; El Paso *Herald-Post*, May 24, 1954.

[19] El Paso *Times*, May 1, 1957.

[20] El Paso *Herald-Post*, Aug. 2, 1948.

[21] El Paso *Times*, Aug. 4, 1948.

[22] El Paso *Herald-Post*, June 19, 1951.

[23] *Ibid.*, June 27, 1956; El Paso *Times*, Jan. 30, 1957.

[24] El Paso *Herald-Post*, June 26, 27, 28, 1954.

[25] Hanson W. Baldwin in the New York *Times* Magazine, Aug. 29, 1954; El Paso *Times*, Sept. 5, 1954.

[26] El Paso *Times*, Jan. 30, 1957.

[27] *Ibid.*, June 23, 24, 1955.

[28] *Ibid.*, Oct. 8, 1956, July 18, 1957.

[29] *Ibid.*, Oct. 8, 1956.

[30] El Paso *Herald-Post*, March 20, 1957.

[31] El Paso *Times*, Oct. 8, 1956, March 24, 1957.

[32] El Paso *Herald-Post*, March 29, 1957.

[33] *Ibid.*, Jan. 31, 1957.

[34] El Paso *Times*, March 15, 16, 1957.

[35] *Ibid.*, June 24, 1955.

[36] El Paso *Herald-Post*, April 24, May 11, 1957; El Paso *Times*, April 27, May 1, 2, June 12, Aug. 22, 1957.

[37] El Paso *Times*, July 19, 24, 1957.

[38] *Ibid.*, Aug. 7, 1957.

[39] El Paso *Herald-Post*, Aug. 7, 1957.

[40] *Ibid.*, Aug. 9, 1957.

[41] Briefing officers, McGregor Range, Aug. 24, 1957.

[42] El Paso *Times*, Dec. 20, 1956.

[43] *Ibid.*, Jan. 27, 1957.

[44] *Ibid.*, Oct. 16, 1957, June 30, Oct. 16, 1958; El Paso *Herald-Post*,

May 10, Nov. 20, 1957; Jan. 17, April 29, Oct. 9, 1958; June 23, Sept. 1, 1959.

45 El Paso *Herald-Post*, Aug. 7, 1957; El Paso *Times*, July 19, 1957. Prather appeared in Federal District Court in Santa Fe as defendant in condemnation proceedings on June 22, 1959. He was awarded $106,985.00 for his confiscated land. He said he didn't want the money (El Paso *Herald-Post*, June 24, 1959). He was in the news again in February 1960, when the military authorities barred his housekeeper from her house. John won this round too (El Paso papers, Feb. 21-24, 1960). He died in February, 1965.

46 El Paso *Herald-Post*, Dec. 4, 1946; Lecture, Community Center, Oct. 13, 1948.

47 *White Sands Missile Range: Birthplace of America's Missile and Space Activity*. Mimeographed historical sketch issued at WSMR June, 1971.

48 El Paso *Times*, August 26, September 19, 1971; Owen J. Remington, "Army Contributions to the Space Age." *Army Digest*, Vol. 24 (November, 1969).

Index

Index